Broken

Samuel P. King & Randall W. Roth

Trust

Greed, Mismanagement,
& Political Manipulation
at America's Largest
Charitable Trust

A Latitude 20 Book

University of Hawai'i Press

Honolulu

Printed in the United States of America
11 10 09 08   6 5
Library of Congress Cataloging-in-Publication Data
King, Samuel P.
    Broken trust : greed, mismanagement & political
manipulation at America's largest charitable trust /
Samuel P. King & Randall W. Roth.
        p. cm.
    "A Latitude 20 Book."
    Includes index.
    ISBN-13: 978-0-8248-3014-4 (hardcover : alk. paper)
    ISBN-13: 978-0-8248-3044-1 (pbk. : alk. paper)
    1. Kamehameha Schools/Bernice Pauahi Bishop Estate—
Trials, litigation, etc. 2. Charitable uses, trusts, and foundations
—Hawaii. 3. Hawaiians—Legal status, laws, etc. 4. Chari-
ties—Corrupt practices—Hawaii. I. Roth, Randall W. II. Title.
    KF228.K36K56 2006
    345.969'028—dc22
                        2005032815

University of Hawai'i Press books are printed on acid-free
paper and meet the guidelines for permanence and durability
of the Council on Library Resources.

Designed by Julie Allred, BW&A Books, Inc.
Printed by the Maple-Vail Book Manufacturing Group

To Gladys Kamakakūokalani Brandt
and Monsignor Charles A. Kekumano,
whose wisdom, unfailing humor, and guidance
helped to restore a legacy.

Pau ka ʻoe hana, pio ka ʻoe ahi.
Lele ka haka, ʻēheu o na manu.
Your work is done; your fire is extinguished.
The spirit has flown away, borne on the wings of birds.

# Contents

Acknowledgments

This book describes events in the political, economic, and educational life of Hawai'i that were precipitated by the turmoil at Kamehameha Schools/Bishop Estate between 1997 and 1999. A defining moment occurred on May 15, 1997, when a large group of Kamehameha *'ohana* (close-knit supporters) marched to the offices of the Bishop Estate trustees to protest aspects of the school's management. The marchers then formed Na Pua a Ke Ali'i Pauahi (the Children of Princess Pauahi), whose membership quickly grew to about four thousand.

Na Pua kept the public informed as it pursued meaningful information from the trustees and appropriate action from the attorney general and the state judiciary. Na Pua's leaders included Leroy Akamine, Charles and Bobbie Arnold, Roy Benham, Fred Cachola, Tomi Chong, Beadie Dawson, Donne Dawson, Jan Dill, Irene Dupont, Karen Farias, Rod Ferreira, Chris Hong, Patrick Iona, Albert Joy, Marion Joy, Peter Kama, Carol Kapu, Dutchie Kapu-Saffery, Guy Kaulukukui, Toni Lee, Dudley Makahanaloa, Robin Makapagal, Lopaka Mansfield, Bob and Paulette Moore, Dutchy Mossman, Norman and Bonnie Nam, Julie Nurre, Victor Punua, Leona Seto-Mook, Rocky Tokuhara, Mervyn Thompson, and Noe Noe Wong-Wilson.

Kamehameha teachers also formed a voluntary association, Na Kumu O Kamehameha (The Teachers of Kamehameha), whose leaders, including Kēhau Abad, David Eyre, Charlene Hoe, and Gary Obrecht, mobilized the campus community, at significant personal risk.

Colbert Matsumoto, Robert Richards, Patrick Yim, and Margery Bronster—the first two as court-appointed masters, and the last two as fact-finder and attorney general, respectively—documented trust abuse and sought accountability. The attorney general's dedicated team of deputies, paralegals, and investigators included Fawn Ching, Richard Gabatino, Lawrence Goya, Patricia Greene, Hugh Jones, Daniel Morris, James Paige, Terry Pennington, Dorothy Sellers, Bill Shea, Dawn Shigezawa, Rod Tam, John Tsukayama, Kevin Wakayama, Randy Young, and Pam Zenefsky. Steven Sakamaki and the Arthur Andersen accounting firm supported master Matsumoto's inquiry.

Gladys Brandt, Rick Daysog, Jan Dill, Walter Heen, Pearl Iboshi, John Kawamoto, Pauline King, David Shapiro, Robert Watada, and Barbara Wong provided invaluable assistance at various stages of the book's creation. Hardy Spoehr lent essential organizational support, and James Bickerton performed an independent legal review. Several other individuals who made major contributions have requested anonymity; we are honoring that request, but it does not diminish the key roles they played.

Lavonne Leong was an absolutely superb editor. The entire staff at the University of Hawai'i Press, especially Bill Hamilton, Ann Ludeman, JoAnn Tenorio, Brad Barrett, and Carol Abe, consistently met or exceeded our high expectations. We also want to thank Barbara Norton for copyediting, Jean Kaplan for proofreading, and Jan Williams for indexing this book.

Our wives, Anne King and Susie Roth, gave us needed criticism and loving support.

Several private charitable foundations provided funding for assistance with research, writing, editing, and production: the Atherton Family Foundation, the Harold K. L. Castle Foundation, the Samuel N. and Mary Castle Foundation, the Cooke Foundation, the Mary D. and Walter F. Frear Eleemosynary Trust, the Wallace Alexander Gerbode Foundation, the McInerny Foundation, the Strong Foundation, and the G. N. Wilcox Trust. All book royalties will go to early childhood education in Hawai'i.

The *Honolulu Star-Bulletin* allowed us to use photographs from its archives, free of charge, and the newspaper's photography editor, George Lee, spent many hours searching for exactly the right shots. KHON TV-2 News and Melvin Ah Ching Productions also provided photographs, free of charge. Dick Adair, Daryl Cagle, Clay Jones, and Corky Trinidad generously allowed us to reproduce a cross-section of the nearly three hundred editorial cartoons they created between 1997 and 1999.

More than 250 people were interviewed extensively and/or provided access to key documents. Media coverage helped fill in gaps. Reporters whose coverage of the controversy warrants special acknowledgment include Sally Apgar, Greg Barrett, Rick Daysog, and Jim Dooley.

Links to newspaper coverage, selected source documents, and other background materials can be found at BrokenTrustBook.com.

The authors alone are responsible for the book's contents.

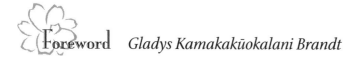 **Foreword** *Gladys Kamakakūokalani Brandt*

I am blessed to have been part of the Kamehameha Schools ʻohana as far back as the early years of the twentieth century, when my father was the first, and for many years the only, Hawaiian member of the faculty of the Kamehameha School for Boys. As a little girl, I lived on campus with my *hānai* mother—Ida May Pope, the girls' school principal. My early schooling was at the Kamehameha Preparatory School for Boys, because the girls' school did not extend to the elementary grades at that time. Many years later, I was privileged to serve as the girls' school principal and then director of secondary education of the combined schools.

My interest in and sense of responsibility toward the Schools did not end with my retirement in 1970. I continued to support Kamehameha Schools to the best of my ability. My efforts included chairing the ill-fated "blue-ribbon" panel for trustee selection and co-authoring the "Broken Trust" essay. I did not enjoy my role as a critic, but I felt I had little choice. The resulting turmoil was painful but necessary.

The media did well in covering daily news items during the controversy but were not able to place the issues and events into a historically and culturally meaningful context. During my own life, and during the life of Hawaiʻi in my time, there have been great changes in what it has meant to be Hawaiian. This book will show this long view.

Renewal at Bishop Estate was possible only because good and industrious men and women articulated common goals and then worked tirelessly and honorably to accomplish those goals. They did not seek leadership positions out of ego or a desire for self-gain, and they did not wilt in the face of adversity or threats to their personal interests. Such acts of moral courage and civic responsibility should be held up as sources of pride and as models for the *keiki o ka ʻāina* (children of Hawaiʻi).

I am pleased that this book's royalties will go toward early childhood education. That, for me, is a particularly worthy cause.

2002

Introduction   *David Shapiro*

When Randall Roth came to the *Honolulu Star-Bulletin* late on the afternoon of August 7, 1997, and asked editorial page editor Diane Chang and me to publish the essay that would become known as "Broken Trust," I sensed I was looking at something of monumental importance. This essay was a bare-knuckled attack on the trustees of Kamehameha Schools/Bishop Estate, a charitable trust of unprecedented power, with lines tracing back to Hawai'i's monarchy as the century-old bequest of a Hawaiian princess who desired to improve the lives of Hawaiian children.

A 1995 *Wall Street Journal* article described Bishop Estate as "the nation's wealthiest charity," with an endowment estimated at $10 billion —greater than the combined endowments of Harvard and Yale universities. With vast land holdings in a small island state, Bishop Estate wasn't bashful about flexing its muscles, and its influence reached deep into Hawai'i's government, judiciary, and business communities in incestuous relationships that increasingly reeked of corruption.

The opening of "Broken Trust" was blunt: "The community has lost faith in Bishop Estate trustees, in how they are chosen, how much they are paid, how they govern. The time has come to say 'no more.'" Strong words, but the essay was more than just rhetoric. It went on to document the misdealings surrounding Bishop Estate—and their devastating impact on beneficiaries of the trust—as never before. It detailed how trustee appointments, which paid nearly $1 million a year, were rigged by politicians and judges; how trustees lined their pockets at the expense of the institution's bottom line; how the supposed protectors of the trust, the attorney general and courts, looked the other way; how investment results were manipulated to mislead, with no accountability; and how Kamehameha Schools, the core of the trust's mission, was being scandalously shortchanged at every step. The essay concluded, "The princess intended a sacred trust. What we ended up with is a political plum." Many of these violations had long been suspected, but they had never been publicly spelled out in a community where even honorable people were reluctant to tangle with the immensely powerful trustees and their legion of loyal supporters among native Hawaiians.

As important as what "Broken Trust" said was who was saying it. Roth was a respected professor of trust law at the University of Hawai'i, but it was his four co-authors—importantly, all of native Hawaiian ancestry—who carried the weight: Samuel King, a Senior U.S. District Court judge; Monsignor Charles Kekumano, a Catholic priest, chairman of the Queen Lili'uokalani Trust, and former chairman of the Honolulu Police Commission; Walter Heen, a retired state appeals court judge and former Democratic state legislator and Honolulu city councilman; and Gladys Brandt, a retired principal of Kamehameha School for Girls and a former chair of the University of Hawai'i board of regents. These were not bomb-throwers, but the most solid of citizens, venerable community leaders who enjoyed wide respect among Hawaiians and non-Hawaiians alike.

Roth brought the essay to the *Star-Bulletin* after first offering it to our larger competitor, *The Honolulu Advertiser*, where the authors had been unable to reach agreement with editors on either a form or a time frame for publication. At the time, there was a major controversy swirling in the Hawaiian community over a trustee's micromanagement of Kamehameha Schools, and the authors of "Broken Trust" wanted to get their essay into print before the trustees moved to purge the school of its popular president, Michael Chun, and of four Kamehameha teachers who had dared to question the trustees publicly.

I could understand why the essay had caused the *Advertiser*'s editors concern. At more than 6,400 words, it was far longer than anything a mid-sized daily newspaper would normally publish, and it was structured as an unusual hybrid of factual reporting and opinion. But I thought *Advertiser* editors had failed to take into account the stature of the authors. It didn't matter whether "Broken Trust" was reporting or opinion; the weighty concerns of these pillars of the community constituted big news that we needed to bring to the attention of our readers. Significantly, no key point of "Broken Trust" has ever been shown to be false.

I had a clear sense of what was the right thing to do in my position as managing editor of the *Star-Bulletin*, but I had to swallow hard when I approved the immediate publication of "Broken Trust" at its full length. I had crossed the powerful trustees before and knew them to be vindictive and relentless. I told my wife that night that if this blew up in my face, I'd probably have to look for work on the Mainland. And I took little comfort from Roth's assurances.

"I'll bet the farm that one or more trustees will be removed," he predicted.

"That would be like moving a mountain," I replied. "I'd save a few acres of the farm for your old age."

What motivated Roth more than anything else was that the manipulations by the trustees—in what he called "a world record for breaches of trust"—had occurred in plain view of people with the power and the legal obligation to do something about it. I had to admit that my own newspaper was aware of many of these questionable dealings but seldom investigated the stories aggressively. But we weren't alone. Historically, all of Hawai'i had generally maintained a hands-off attitude when it came to Bishop Estate. Some feared invoking the wrath of the trustees and their loyal native Hawaiian supporters. But mostly, the reluctance to get involved sprang from the view that Kamehameha Schools was a sacred Hawaiian institution, and even honest citizens and public officials were disinclined to interfere in its affairs if Hawaiians weren't complaining.

And Hawaiians hardly ever complained. To the contrary, they were fiercely protective of the Bishop Estate and its trustees, having been persuaded that attacks on the trustees were really attacks on the legacy of Princess Pauahi, who had created the trust, and on all Hawaiians. Whenever legislative efforts were afoot to rein in trustee pay, reform residential leasing policies, or more closely monitor investment and educational performance, trustees could turn out Hawaiians by the busload to protest. A newspaper that reported critically on Bishop Estate or Kamehameha Schools could expect to be bombarded with angry calls and letters from Hawaiians.

By 1997, however, this was changing. Supreme Court justices increasingly were filling trustee vacancies with elective politicians who lacked humility in dealing with the Kamehameha community, an attitude that created widespread resentment. Bishop Estate appointments had always been political, and the high compensation, speculative deals, and self-serving manipulation of information about the trust had existed to some extent before the group of trustees who were finally held to account came along.

But the earlier generations of trustees were a different breed of political cat—top government executives, well-connected businessmen, and wealthy patricians from prominent local families who knew their way around a boardroom and could comport themselves with some finesse in the diverse circles in which trustees traveled. These trustees took pains to cultivate support from the Kamehameha Schools community and to present themselves as humble servants of the princess.

But a 1978 constitutional convention changed the way trustees were appointed by creating a Judicial Selection Commission to play a leading role in the appointment of Hawaiʻi's judges. The bar elected two members of the Judicial Selection Commission, and the remaining seven were appointed by the speaker of the house of representatives, the president of the senate, the chief justice of the Supreme Court, and the governor. It seemed no coincidence that subsequent appointments to Bishop Estate included a house speaker, a senate president, a chief justice, and a chairman of the Judicial Selection Commission. There was even an aborted attempt to appoint Governor John Waiheʻe. Grounded in politics, these new trustees knew little of the collegiality of a boardroom or the fiduciary duties owed by trustees. They were about gaining power by lining up voting majorities and divvying up personal fiefdoms. The lead trustees, as they were called, were given unprecedented individual authority over investments, education, and trust administration. They operated much like legislative committee chairs and had unbridled control of their domains. Most important was the different way these trustees viewed themselves—not as servants of the princess, but as feudal lords, accountable to nobody. In their own minds, they could do no wrong, and their word could not be questioned. The beneficiaries of the trust were there to serve them.

In a 1995 legal brief, attorneys for the trustees in a dispute over water rights on Bishop Estate land argued that the trustees had inherited the absolute power of Hawaiian *aliʻi* (royalty) going back to the beginning of the Kamehameha dynasty. The trustees contended, "Kamehameha I, by right of conquest, became lord paramount of these islands. He was an absolute monarch. His will was law. He was the lord of life and death. . . . Then logically to the same extent, if not more, the trust of Bernice Pauahi, the legacy of the Kamehamehas, must be entitled to those traditional and customary prerogatives enjoyed by the Kamehameha *aliʻi*." With such a heady view of themselves, it was no surprise that the trustees fell prey to Lord Acton's observation that absolute power corrupts absolutely.

A turning point came in 1993, when the trustee board included two political heavyweights, former house Speaker Henry Peters and former senate President Richard "Dickie" Wong, and two old-school trustees, Myron "Pinky" Thompson and Oswald "Oz" Stender. The swing trustee was Lokelani Lindsey, a career bureaucrat in the Department of Education who had recently run unsuccessfully as the Democratic candidate for mayor of Maui. Justices appointed Lindsey shortly after appointing Wong in the apparent hope that as an educator and the first woman ever named to the board, she would deflect criticism of the perceived political payoffs in Bishop Estate appointments. Peters and Wong wanted to control the estate and its billions without the interference of Thompson and Stender. They needed Lindsey's vote to solidify their power, and to get it they named her lead trustee for education, which gave her absolute authority over Kamehameha Schools.

Unfortunately, neither the justices nor Peters and Wong had done their homework on Lindsey, who would soon become the public embodiment of everything that was broken about the trust. She was crude, imperious, and unpleasant, with controversial notions about education. Her own background was in physical education, and she distinguished herself in the DOE more as a political opportunist than an education theorist as she rose through the bureaucracy. She held a low opinion of the Kamehameha Schools administration and staff and had little interest in what alumni had to say. Her capricious dictates were not open to discussion, and her power tool of choice was intimidation.

At first the Kamehameha 'ohana—teachers, students, alumni, and parents—tried to heal the unpleasantness with respectful requests to the trustees to talk things out, as is the Hawaiian way. But when the trustees stubbornly refused to "talk story," the 'ohana banded together in a group that called itself Na Pua a Ke Ali'i Pauahi—the Children of Princess Pauahi—and staged an emotional and unprecedented march on Bishop Estate headquarters at Kawaiaha'o Plaza in May 1997. The fight was on.

Around the same time, Roth was lining up co-authors for a hardhitting exposé that would support Na Pua's efforts. Each co-author also had broader issues with the management of Bishop Estate and the tainted involvement of the judiciary. King was a leading critic of the Judicial Selection Commission and believed that instead of removing politics from judgeship appointments, as it was intended to do, it had only moved the politics out of public view at the expense of accountability. Brandt and Kekumano were deeply concerned about the impact Lindsey was having on campus and had felt betrayed when the blue-ribbon panel for trustee selection on which they served was manipulated and deceived by Supreme Court justices. Heen, a onetime candidate for the Supreme Court, had been taken aback when asked during the selection process whom he would appoint to Bishop Estate, a question he considered inappropriate.

Until the "Broken Trust" authors weighed in, the trustees faced a limited battlefront—Lindsey's micromanagement of Kamehameha Schools. The trustees could have ended the dispute at any time by simply reining in Lindsey and restoring respectful communications with the 'ohana. In those early days, the possibility of a trustee's being removed from office was barely imaginable, and Na Pua's lawyer said this was not their goal. "Broken Trust" changed everything by demanding that the trustees be held accountable for the breaches of trust that had occurred throughout Bishop Estate operations, moving the conflict beyond Lindsey and Kamehameha Schools. It was devastating in its indictment, not only of the trustees, but also of the judiciary and Hawai'i's political establishment. The authors pressed the attorney general to investigate the obvious wrongdoing and then to seek the trustees' removal, if it was warranted. The authors also called upon the justices to remove themselves from trustee selection and to support the development of objective procedures for selecting future trustees on merit.

"Broken Trust" brought the controversy to critical mass. In short order, the governor asked the attorney general to investigate, Supreme Court justices reluctantly agreed to stop appointing trustees, a court-appointed master confirmed the charges about trustee misconduct, and a retired judge hired at the request of the trustees to whitewash problems at Kamehameha Schools instead indicted Lindsey for everything she had been accused of and more.

It took nearly two years of often chaotic legal wrangling, but in May 1999 the Internal Revenue Service forced the hand of local courts by threatening to revoke Bishop Estate's tax-exempt status if the current trustees stayed on the job. Brandt, Kekumano, Heen, King, Roth, and all of the Kamehameha 'ohana, who had risked everything in pursuit of justice and respect, had moved their mountain.

Change came fast at Kamehameha Schools. The probate court imposed term limits on trustees and drastically reduced their compensation. A court order forced trustees to appoint a chief executive officer and to nominally step away from daily operations to fulfill the more traditional oversight role expected of the boards of charitable trusts. Investment policies were cleaned up, and spending on the core mission of educating Hawaiian children increased dramatically. New campuses opened on Maui and the Big Island, and trustees restored innovative outreach programs and cooperative efforts with public schools—policies that had been eliminated by the previous board.

Still, elements of the resolution were ominous for the future. Once the trustees were removed, their replacements pressed for "closure and healing," with no apparent concern for accountability. Judges and other public officials, who felt they had aired enough of their dirty laundry and wanted nothing more than for it to be over, gladly embraced the call for "healing." Legal proceedings were concluded quickly, and no attempt was made to assess damages or collect restitution from the trustees—or from their lawyers and contractors—for the millions of dollars in losses attributable to the breaches of trust. Nor was there any organized inquiry by the new trustees or the judiciary to get to the bottom of what went wrong and determine how to prevent it from happening again.

Trustee compensation, though reduced, remained high for part-time overseers of a charitable trust. The chairman was paid $120,000 and other members $97,500, compared to a national average of $6,500 for trustees of charities with assets of more than $500 million. But even then a court-appointed salary panel subsequently recommended that Bishop Estate trustee pay be nearly doubled. Another public outcry led the new trustees to reject the raises, but compensation clearly seemed headed back up.

Trustee selection was shifted from the Supreme Court to the probate court; critics, however, saw potential for continued political favoritism, with an unchanged judicial selection process, compensation still temptingly high, and an absence of transparent criteria for choosing trustees. The new trustees remained secretive in their actions, and the attorney general and probate court reverted to their pre-scandal reluctance to provide close oversight of trustees.

The impact of the Bishop Estate scandal in the broad community was far-reaching and profound. It exposed Hawai'i's political rot and helped set the stage for putting a new party in the governor's office for the first time in forty years. It showed Hawaiians what they could accomplish when they worked together, raising hopes of forward movement on other important issues. It demonstrated the wisdom and value of the federal intermediate sanctions law that Bishop Estate trustees had so opposed, which allowed the IRS to deal with serious irregularities by going after the trustees responsible for the mismanagement instead of punishing the trust's beneficiaries.

"Broken Trust" proved the value of having two competing newspapers in a city and was recognized as a major reason for the public outrage and landmark litigation that forced owners who tried to shut down the *Star-Bulletin* in 1999 to instead sell to a new owner, who kept it publishing. Trustee Henry Peters told CBS's *60 Minutes* that his biggest regret was not buying the *Star-Bulletin* when it was first offered for sale in 1992, so that trustees could have stopped "Broken Trust" and controlled the coverage of the scandal.

The Bishop Estate scandal shined a harsh spotlight on Hawai'i's legal profession, revealing conniving justices, in-house attorneys who provided legal cover for the trustees' breaches, and outside counsel who collected millions from the charitable trust to defend the trustees' personal interests. All of these lawyers had a professional obligation under Hawai'i law to report serious breaches of trust, not to enable them; but no sanctions were ever sought. The saving grace for the profession was that attorneys also were prominent among the heroes who stepped up to protect the Pauahi legacy—Heen, King, and Roth from "Broken Trust"; Attorney General Margery Bronster; court master Colbert Matsumoto; the court-appointed fact-finder Patrick Yim; and Na Pua attorney Beadie Dawson, among others.

By far the most important effect of the fall of the Bishop Estate trustees was to energize the community spirit and elevate public expectations, ending the pervasive and demoralizing perception that official corruption was an inescapable fact of life in Hawai'i—the price of living in paradise. As Matsumoto put it, "This story is really about the democratic process—people standing up to do the right thing despite odds and intimidation."

The Bishop Estate scandal inspired a chorus of "no mores" that reverberated through other power centers in Hawai'i. Two members of the Honolulu City Council and four state legislators were sentenced to prison for corruption—two of them for offenses directly related to Bishop Estate—as federal and state prosecutors became newly aggressive in weeding out public corruption. Airport employees and city liquor inspectors were prosecuted in kickback schemes. Gary Rodrigues, one of the state's most politically powerful labor leaders and a member of both the Judicial Selection Commission and the Supreme Court's blue-ribbon panel to screen Bishop Estate candidates, was convicted of multiple counts of fraud and sentenced to federal prison. A five-year investigation by the state Campaign Spending Commission and the Honolulu prosecutor broke up a corrupt system of political money laundering in which local businesses donated large sums to leading elected officials in the hope of being rewarded with lucrative government contracts. Dozens of prominent contractors were convicted for making illegal contributions. A lawyer was sentenced to jail for his role in hiding the true source of a political contribution, an activity one witness described as "a business tradition" in Hawai'i.

Before the Bishop Estate trustees fell, corrupt officials felt confident they could act with impunity; after, they had to seriously fear being caught and punished.

The era of the Bishop Estate scandal will be remembered as one of the most exciting and pivotal times in Hawai'i's short history as a state, and nobody is better qualified than two of the authors of the "Broken Trust" essay to place these watershed events in their sharpest focus yet, capturing all of the human drama along the way. This book should serve as a reminder of the positive things that can happen when good and industrious people stand up to do the right thing. Appropriately, the story begins with a respectful remembrance of the Hawaiian princess who left her people the blessed gift that inspired such courage in her name.

*Her dress could be from London, Paris, or New York, but her look is
from somewhere else. She is neither European nor American,
neither Asian nor African. The background is blank, saying nothing
about the world she lives in or who she is in that world.*

Her name is Pauahi. She is a Hawaiian princess.

chapter 1

Princess for a New Hawai'i

The Hawaiian Islands are remote specks of land in the largest ocean on Earth. Europeans had been exploring the Pacific for two and a half centuries before Captain James Cook happened upon the Islands in 1778. Although Hawaiians had navigated to the archipelago more than a thousand years before Europeans found it and had continued their voyages for hundreds of years, the Hawaiians Cook encountered had long since lost contact with other cultures. From their Polynesian roots they had evolved their own version of the creation and workings of the cosmos, the origins of life, and the nature of the gods.

The Hawaiian gods were the givers of life. Their power was everywhere—in the rush of the winds, in the crashing of the waves, and, above all, in the land, the *'āina*. The gods guided every aspect of life. Hawaiians lived secure in the faith that if they observed the *kapu*—the gods' strict prohibitions—and if they obeyed the high chiefs as gods on Earth and made proper offerings and sacrifices, then they would prosper.

Their language was filled with layers of subtle meaning. A single line of a chant could be about nature, human beings, the gods, or all three at once. The Hawaiian vocabulary was capable of great precision in naming and classifying things in nature. There were more than thirty descriptive names for clouds, forty for land, more than eighty for rain and mist, two hundred for wind, and more than two hundred for the plant *taro*, the Hawaiian staff of life.

But Hawaiians did not have ways to alter their world on a large scale. That was the province of the natural world: a volcano erupted at the will of a goddess, a hurricane roared in at the bidding of a god. Hawaiians had no metals with which to make engines, no fossil fuels to drive them. They had no wheels, winches, pulleys, or gears. Nor did they have beasts of burden; they themselves hauled the stones to build *heiau*, temples for the gods. They moved across the land on foot and rode over the water at the speed of the wind and the waves. What they made, they made by hand from the materials around them: wood and stone, coral and shell, bone and hair, bark, foliage, fiber, and feathers.

Then the first Western ships sailed over the horizon, bringing with them awe-inspiring goods and technologies and stories of faraway places and different ways. It was the end of Hawaiian solitude. Over the next forty years, fewer than a hundred ships touched the Islands, their landfalls random. The number of white foreigners, *haole*, was limited, at the most only hundreds a year. Few went ashore for any significant length of time, and only a handful stayed permanently. Those few visitors, however, brought with them disease and disrespect for the established way of life: they allowed women to join them in eating and engaged in other activities strictly prohibited by the *kapu* system. Despite such behavior, the gods did not strike down the newcomers. Meanwhile, natives who continued to honor the *kapu* system were dying in increasing numbers from strange new ailments.

In 1819 the ruling chief gave up on the gods, ordering the destruction of every *heiau* and the burning of every idol, cutting loose the close web of beliefs and understandings that gave structure and meaning to life. One year later the first of many Christian missionaries arrived on ships and spread word of a single, all-powerful God. These stories came in four versions, two—New England Protestantism and French Catholicism—before Pauahi was born, and two—Mormonism and Anglicanism—during her lifetime.

Pauahi was born in 1831, twelve years after the rejection of the old gods. By then, the place where she was born, Honolulu, on the island of Oʻahu, had become a busy port town. During her lifetime the harbor acquired tide tables and a customhouse, whalers, and Yankee clippers. Ninety-gun vessels of war and steamships dropped anchor there, and merchants from the other side of the world discharged their cargoes for sale: boots and shoes, shirts, broadcloth suits, hammers and nails, frame houses in pieces, knives, forks, china plates, tin mugs, eyeglasses, fishing rods, pocket watches, chamber pots, and compasses—and, of course, muskets and powder, playing cards, tobacco, and alcohol.

Honolulu grew from a town into a city. There were buildings of bricks, mortar, and concrete, paved sidewalks, parks, public clocks, a post office, and a fort. There were also general stores, bowling alleys, grog shops, dance halls, brothels, fire hydrants, drinking fountains, gas lighting, a police force, brass bands, and an opera house. Commerce flourished. Businessmen did their buying and selling with coins of copper, silver, and gold, with bank drafts, and with promissory notes. There were doctors, vaccinations, and anesthesia—and lawyers and lawsuits, too. There were newspapers, first weekly and then daily, and magazines, bookstores, and libraries.

As the kingdom's capital city, Honolulu was also the place where new laws were made that dictated change everywhere in the Islands. Before long there were a census, taxation, and public education, along with divorce petitions, probate proceedings, fines for drunkenness, prison terms for adultery, and, every so often, a sentence of death by hanging for murder. There were a parliament with an upper and a lower house, elections by ballot, a privy council, treaties with foreign nations, a land survey, a private property system, and the beginnings of plantation agriculture and contract labor.

Three generations before Pauahi was photographed looking like a modern, city-dwelling lady, her great-grandfather saw the first Western ships drop anchor, heard the guns, and took the measure of the first *haole* sailors. He was a giant of a man: tall, heavily muscled, athletic. Born a high chief, *ali'i nui*, and directly descended from the gods, he took part in ceremonies of human sacrifice and carried within him the sacred power of the gods, *mana*. For a commoner to step into the shadow of such an *ali'i nui* meant death.

Pauahi's great-grandfather was also a great warrior. He fought his way to becoming *ali'i 'ai moku*, ruler of an island, and went on to unify all the islands into a single kingdom. He controlled these lands by brutal conquest and founded a dynasty that carried his name: Kamehameha. Disaffected *ali'i* who tried to leave the Kamehameha hegemony were ruthlessly eliminated. Outsiders, however, were dealt with differently. Hawaiians never fought back against the aggressions of foreigners the way other Polynesians did. Instead, Hawaiians relied upon diplomatic means—treaties and negotiations with foreign powers—in their effort to maintain independence.

At the overthrow of the Hawaiian monarchy in 1893, there was no armed resistance, by the chiefs or by their people, against the takeover by a handful of *haole* civilians and militiamen with only token military support from the U.S. government. The kingdom was brought down in a matter of hours. The only shot fired was a single round from a revolver. It hit a Hawaiian policeman in the shoulder, the only Hawaiian to shed blood for the life of his land. There might have been organized resistance, but Liliʻuokalani, the reigning monarch, ordered otherwise.

Nineteenth-century aliʻi nui died deaths of the Western world. Kamehameha II died of measles, which had been unknown in Hawaiʻi before Western contact. He was also fond of alcohol, another Western introduction. Alcohol in excess figured in the deaths of three other kings: Kamehameha III, Kamehameha IV, and Lunalilo, from a related Kamehameha line. Lunalilo's successor, David Kalākaua, died of Addison's disease.

Commoners, *makaʻainana*, were also being cut down by the sicknesses that came ashore with *haole* sailors. Syphilis and gonorrhea took hold, then tuberculosis. In 1804 there was an epidemic, probably of cholera. Hawaiians had no resistance to this kind of invasion. In their centuries of isolation, they had never been exposed to the common diseases of continental civilization. In 1848 and 1849 epidemics of measles and whooping cough, followed by dysentery and influenza, killed ten thousand Hawaiians; a few years later, in 1853, smallpox killed another ten to fifteen thousand.

Nobody knows how many Hawaiians there were in 1778; the chiefs ruled without exact head counts. Population estimates made by early Westerners averaged about 300,000. But whatever the number had been at the beginning of Western contact, it declined rapidly over the next century. A census taken in the year Pauahi was born, 1831, counted 124,000 natives. Five years later the count was 108,000. The census of 1849 counted 87,000. In 1855 the number was down to 71,000. Cartload after horse-drawn cartload of stacked corpses rolled down the streets during Pauahi's lifetime, pulling the Hawaiian people closer to extinction. By the 1870s, when she posed for her portrait, the number of Hawaiians was down to about 50,000.

Pauahi was born into this era of great change on December 19, 1831, a great-granddaughter of Kamehameha the Great. Coming into the world as a high chief, Pauahi was welcomed as she would have been a hundred or two hundred years earlier, exalted with birth chants, *mele hānau:* "The royal one is born, the drums are sounding, the thunder resounds and the lightning is flashing, the blood rain is falling and is moving along with the floating clouds, the wondrous rainbow pillar stands alone in the ocean." By sacred custom, after Pauahi was born, the afterbirth was buried under a tree. A sapling was planted for Pauahi, but it was not a native species; it was a tamarind from India.

The naming of a firstborn, *hiapo*, was a serious business among *ali'i*. Often the child was given the name of an older relative. Pauahi was named after an aunt, one of Kamehameha II's wives. Both of her birth parents, Laura Konia and Abner Pākī, were converts of the Protestant missionaries. Pauahi was given a Christian name, Bernice, to go with her Hawaiian name, as was by then required by law. She was called Bernice Pauahi.

According to custom, any Hawaiian child, whether chief or commoner, could be spoken for and brought up by relatives or close friends of the birth parents. This practice was called *hānai*. Pauahi was carried to the home of her uncle and aunt, both chiefs, and as her *hānai* parents, they raised her. Pauahi, living in an *ali'i* household, was surrounded by retainers whose job was to take care of her the way chiefs' children had always been cared for, teaching her what it was to be an *ali'i* and attending to her every wish.

In April 1839 Pauahi's *hānai* mother, Kīna'u, died at age thirty-five of mumps. Two months later Pauahi, age seven, began a different education. It was at a new school run by Protestant missionaries, initially called the Chiefs' Children's School, later renamed the Royal School.

The chiefs saw value in having the future rulers of a modern kingdom educated to Western ways of thinking. They recruited teachers for the school from the Protestant mission, whose workers had converted many of them. Pauahi's teachers were Amos Starr Cooke and his wife, Juliette, New Englanders in their twenties. They had been in Hawai'i for only two years.

For the Cookes, civilization and proper education meant Christian living. And Christian living meant quarantining the young chiefs against Hawaiian living. Over the first eleven years of the school's existence, there were sixteen *ali'i* scholars, eight boys and eight girls, most of them *hānai*, and most related to each other. They lived on the premises, and their comings and goings were strictly supervised. To teach them the value of time, their days were regulated from 5:00 A.M., when they were roused, until 8 P.M., when they were sent to bed. The students at the Royal School came to class at the ringing of a bell. If they hung back and were late, or if they whispered when they should have been listening, or if they dozed off in the heat of the day, they got a black mark in order to teach them habits of industry. They were not to overeat or eat between meals, and they were to learn Western ways of understanding, from electricity to astronomy. When an eclipse of the sun occurred, the phenomenon was not taken as an omen of the inevitable death of a chief—it was explained scientifically, using a model planetarium.

The Cookes kept school five and a half days a week, Monday to Saturday, teaching history, geography, and arithmetic, and progressing to trigonometry, chemistry, and botany. On Sundays they marched the children to church, two by two. The students prayed each morning and evening and studied scripture. They memorized one Bible verse each day —in Hawaiian in the morning, then in English in the evening. That was all the Hawaiian language that was tolerated, with the exception of Sunday church service.

Classes were in English, and outside of class the scholars were instructed to have English always in mind and always on their tongues. It was considered good when they showed a better command of English than Hawaiian, and even better when they came to the school so young that English could be made their first language.

The students kept journals in English that were reviewed and corrected by the Cookes. Lot and Alexander, princes of the kingdom, wrote down things that the Cookes demanded of them, habits and rules to be practiced and followed. "1st Seek God & do that which will please him." "Use no deception." "Be always pleasant and cheerfull." "Have a place for everything & every thing in its place." "Improve in English get four new words & correct four errors every day." "Speak not without Sir or some title of respect which is due to him to whom you speak." "Stare not at what you see that is unusual whether person or thing." "Quarrel not with one you meet." "Go not singing, whistling or hollaring along the street or Road."

If the students misbehaved or were inattentive, indifferent, or impudent, they were punished. The boys, in particular, often misbehaved. They were the children of high chiefs, indulged from infancy. "Troublesome fellows," Juliette Cooke called them in a letter home to New England: a set of little tyrants. Lot swore and was forbidden to play outside for a week. When the future King David Kalākaua made noise in church, Cooke hit him across the face in front of everyone. In Kamehameha the Great's time, Cooke would have been clubbed to death on the spot.

As these boys grew older and bigger, they grew more and more prone to Christian sinning. They drank wine smuggled across the fence. Lot and his brother Moses were caught in bed with girls, which was a torment to the Cookes—they were certain that such behavior put their own children in peril. A separate fenced yard inside the schoolyard was built to separate them from the students at the Royal School.

Bernice Pauahi, a student from the school's first day of instruction in 1839 to its last days in 1850, was different. She was the one the Cookes wrote about most often in their letters and journals, and almost always approvingly. They rarely called her Pauahi. To them she was Bernice, Miss Bernice, Miss B, or just plain B. She was intelligent and willing, dutiful, "extremely prudent, seldom giving cause for any reproof." She was less trouble over a period of years than most of the others were in a week, hardly ever needing to be punished.

Bernice was quick to learn to read and write English. Her penmanship improved until it looked like Mrs. Cooke's. She loved books and served as the school librarian. Western music was encouraged at the school as a civilizing influence that prevented idleness and nurtured a taste for rational pleasures. Bernice had a beautiful contralto singing voice. Visitors often asked her to perform, and she led the scholars in four-part harmony. Bernice took piano lessons, could sight-read, and practiced diligently. Her playing was accomplished and impressed visiting dignitaries.

Bernice was also happy to be useful to the hard-working Cookes. Mr. Cooke was busy with classes and discipline, and Mrs. Cooke, in addition to teaching and caring for her sixteen students, had five children of her own to care for while she and her husband were running the school. Bernice helped with housework, child care, washing clothes, and scrubbing floors. She was properly grateful for the chance to assist. "All I am and hope to be," she said, "I owe to Mrs. Cooke."

A *haole* woman from a missionary family described Pauahi as "a slender, graceful child, with an exquisite figure. Her hands, always small and remarkable for their beauty, were perfectly formed, the fingers delicate and tapered, having been partially shaped by the manipulations of her nurses in babyhood, a custom that prevailed amongst all Hawaiians of high rank. She had beautiful dark hair that fell in a cloud of lustrous, silken ringlets to her waist, and her skin, as in infancy, was fair."

Bernice had known the "troublesome" Prince Lot all her life. They grew up in the same house and had gone to the Royal School at the same time. When on Sundays the students marched to church two by two, Lot walked with Bernice. When Bernice was seventeen, Kekūanaōʻa, her *hānai* father and Lot's biological father, put it to her that she should marry Lot. Bernice was horrified. Amos Cooke, in whom she confided, wrote that "it made her quite unhappy all day & she went to bed early with a headache."

There was more pressure from her *hānai* family and from her biological parents, Konia and Pākī, to marry Lot, whose *aliʻi* status made him an appropriate match even if his temperament did not. Bernice continued to resist. In the fall of 1849 the pressure was stepped up. Lot and his brother Alexander were accompanying the *haole* minister of foreign affairs on a diplomatic mission to Europe via the United States to get an education in the big world. Her parents wanted Bernice married to Lot before he went—in fact, immediately.

Bernice told Lot that she would consent to her parents' commands, but she knew it would always make her unhappy because he did not love her, and she did not love him. Konia came to see the Cookes: "Konia took tea with us; she has been blaming Bernice because she talked so plainly to Lot."

Bernice wrote to her *hānai* father, Kekūanaōʻa, using stronger words. Amos Cooke noted that Bernice said, "If they wished her buried in a coffin, she would submit to their authority, & she would as soon have them do so to her, as to promise to marry Lot." Lot saw what Bernice had written to Kekūanaōʻa and wrote to her that he did not want to be "the means of murdering her or rendering her unhappy." He told Bernice that he was unworthy of her, absolved her from any promises, and then sailed for San Francisco, leaving her lighthearted. In his letter Lot mentioned that someone else might be worthy of Bernice and might possibly even be the one she loved. He did not need to name the someone. It was Charles Reed Bishop.

Bishop had taken to calling at the school in the evening. Very few single *haole* men at Honolulu would have been allowed inside the fence—a handful at most out of the fifteen hundred or so then in town. Charles Bishop was one of the few respectables.

Bishop had a responsible job as collector of customs. He had been in the Islands for several years and had become a citizen of the Hawaiian kingdom, all signs that he was not just one more scrap of *haole* flotsam, washed up on the shores of Oʻahu and apt to drift away with the next tide.

Bishop was of good Yankee stock. He called himself a "liberal Protestant," meaning that he was not as strict as a missionary, but he was sober and discreet, a man of uprightness. He was also almost ten years older than Pauahi, but that did not matter to Cooke: "We much prefer she would take up with such a man as he, than with either of the Princes."

The Cookes considered Bernice a suitable wife for a respectable *haole*. Her coloration was often remarked upon favorably by *haole*—light, bright, approaching the Grecian. Her fairness could have been inherited from her father, Pākī, who was noticeably light-skinned; some Hawaiians were. Considering Bernice from another angle—from outside the Royal School fence—some Hawaiians said her skin color was the result of eating so much white bread in there. However it was phrased, it was certainly true that, more than anyone else at the Royal School, Bernice had become a part of the Western world.

The Cookes were looking forward to Bernice's marriage to Charles for more than one reason. When Bernice left the school, they could leave too. Most of the young chiefs for whom the school had been started were gone, and there were no more coming. Two little *ali'i* girls had been in line, but they had died in the epidemic of 1848. The school was quiet; some of the rooms were empty. All that was keeping the Cookes there was Bernice. "She is very anxious to have us remain until she can have a home of her own," wrote Amos, "and as we have brought her along so far, we cannot bear to leave her until she is lodged in safer hands than her own parents, who are kind enough, but they are ignorant of what civilization consists in, and wish their daughter to be great in *their* way, and not in *our* way."

Reverend Richard Armstrong performed the marriage ceremony in the parlor of the Royal School at 8:00 P.M. on June 4, 1850. Although the bride was beautiful in white muslin, with a wreath of jasmine, it was a sober occasion. Her parents, disappointed that she was not marrying an *ali'i*, refused to attend. There were no bridesmaids or groomsmen, no chiefs, no respectable people from the town, no Hawaiian feast, no cake or lemonade. "After the ceremony," wrote Amos Cooke, "we sat down to tea, & at 9 o'clock they went in a wagon to Judge Andrews', where they are to board." Bernice's decision to marry Charles Bishop meant defying her parents, who as high chiefs were looking to a marriage of state. There was a brief disruption in family relationships and communications, but within a year there were good feelings again, helped by the fact that the marriage turned out to be a good one.

Bishop had resigned as collector of customs to embark on what

Princess Pauahi defied her parents in 1850 by marrying Charles Reed Bishop. Pauahi's parents, disappointed that she was not marrying an aliʻi, *refused to attend the wedding. © Bishop Museum, Honolulu, Hawaiʻi*

was to become a long and highly successful business career. Pākī, Bernice's biological father, died in 1855. Long since reconciled with his daughter, he had written his will in Bernice's favor. He bequeathed his lands on Oʻahu, 5,780 acres, and Haleakalā, his big house, to her. The Bishops lived at Haleakalā with Konia, Bernice's widowed biological mother. When Konia died in 1857, she bequeathed another 10,231 acres to Bernice.

Now only in her mid-twenties, Bernice Pauahi Bishop had become a landed chief with a large estate. At the same time, her inheritance had come with serious obligations to her hundreds of tenants. Commoners with traditional expectations made claims on their *ali'i*, and such Hawaiian relationships had survived the high chiefs' dismissal of the old gods. These responsibilities were Bernice's, as Ke Ali'i Pauahi, or Princess Pauahi.

Pauahi spoke in Hawaiian with her people who came in from the country, sitting among them under her tamarind tree in the gardens that she had cultivated. She always had time for them; if a matter took hours, then it took hours. She supported dozens of servants, feeding them from her lands in rural O'ahu: mullet from fishponds, *poi* from the irrigated *taro* patches—a ton of it a month.

Under her roof at Haleakalā she cared for Lydia Kamaka'eha, Lili'uokalani, who had been adopted by Konia and Pākī. Lili'uokalani was seven years younger than Pauahi and had been at the Royal School. After the school closed, Lili'uokalani lived with her *hānai* parents at Haleakalā, and when Pauahi and Bishop moved in, she stayed. When Lili'uokalani married, the wedding was at Haleakalā.

Pauahi and Bishop had no children of their own. Although the *hānai* custom survived, no babies suitable for Pauahi were being born: for *ali'i*, those years were almost completely childless. Then, in the summer of 1862, Pauahi's cousin Ruth Ke'elikōlani became pregnant. Like Pauahi, Ruth was descended from Kamehameha. A *hānai* arrangement between Bernice and Ruth was made. Born in February 1863, the baby was given the name Keolaokalani—the Life of the Heavenly One. He brought joy and great expectations, but like many other Hawaiian babies, he died before reaching his first birthday.

Pauahi surrounded herself with other children. She taught music to some at Haleakalā, and they often stayed for lunch. Out riding in her carriage, she would pick up a child passing in the street, enjoyable company for both of them. She taught Sunday school classes at Kawaiaha'o Church, which she had attended as a student. Pauahi kept up her music too, serving on the committee of the Amateur Musical Society, singing in the chorus of works by Haydn and Verdi, oratorios and operas.

The Bishops were generally recognized as the social leaders of Honolulu, according to Sanford Dole, son of a Protestant missionary. Dole wrote approvingly that "their leadership was largely of a nature that covered more of life than the gaieties: music, reading, conversations, as well as dancing." Pauahi was hostess to every notable who visited from around the world—admirals, ambassadors, British aristocrats—organizing croquet and tennis on the lawns at Haleakalā, evenings of music and dancing, formal dinners with silver tableware and attendants holding *kāhili*, the ceremonial feathered standards of the *aliʻi*. For the Duke of Edinburgh Pauahi arranged a *lūʻau*, the traditional Hawaiian feast. Bernice, Mrs. Bishop, Ke Aliʻi Pauahi—she was all three in one. She made her way through the complications of Hawaiian and *haole* life as sensibly and graciously as anyone could have done.

Bishop, for his part, was becoming more and more prominent in business and in public life. In 1858 he started a bank that did well for him by doing well for merchants and sugar plantation owners. In 1859 Kamehameha IV made him a member of the Privy Council, and in 1860 he was made a life member of the House of Nobles, sitting among the chiefs. In 1864, under Kamehameha V, he became a member of the foreign relations committee of the House of Nobles, and in 1870 he was made chairman. In 1872 he served as president of the government board of education. Bishop had become a substantial member of the community, not only highly placed by marriage to an *aliʻi nui*, but a useful citizen in his own right, as well regarded as any *haole* in the kingdom.

$\mathcal{L}ot$, in his early forties, had grown obese and suffered from various maladies. He was ill for months toward the end of 1872, and by December 10, the day before his forty-third birthday, he was dying. Pauahi had been at many deathbeds, and on the morning of December 11 she was at Lot's, together with a number of other *aliʻi nui*. A gathering was customary when a chief was dying. But there was more to this assembly: Lot was Kamehameha V, the king, and he had not written a will. He did not have an heir, and he had not named a successor.

Everyone eligible for the throne was in the room. There were David Kalākaua and his sister Lydia Kamakaʻeha, Liliʻuokalani, but they were not in the Kamehameha line. Neither was Emma, queen by marriage to the late Kamehameha IV, Alexander Liholiho. There was William Lunalilo, related to Kamehameha but not in the direct line. And Ruth Keʻelikōlani and Bernice Pauahi were there, both Kamehamehas in direct descent.

When the king managed to rouse himself to speak about the succession, he spoke first in Hawaiian, but incoherently. Then, speaking in English, he named Pauahi: "I wish you to take my place, to be my successor."

Pauahi refused. "No, not me; don't think of me. I do not need it."

The king asked a number of the chiefs and others to leave the room, then spoke again to Pauahi: "I think it best for my people and my nation."

Again Pauahi refused: "Oh, no, do not think of me, there are others; there is your sister, it is hers by right." Ruth was Lot's half-sister and his closest relative. She had been governor of the island of Hawai'i for seventeen years. During this exchange she was sitting on the floor, some distance from the bed.

Lot told Pauahi, "She is not fitted for the position."

"But we will all help her; I, my husband, your ministers," said Pauahi.

No, said Lot, Ruth "would not answer."

Then, said Pauahi, "There is the queen, Emma; she has been a queen once, and is therefore fitted for the position."

Lot replied, "She was merely queen by courtesy, having been the wife of a king."

The husband of Lili'uokalani, John Dominis, governor of O'ahu, took all this down, in English. Then, wrote Dominis, "The King wishing at this time to get out of his bed, we all left the room, and after that he never alluded to the subject of a successor or expressed any further wishes." An hour later the king died.

The throne passed to the enormously popular William Lunalilo by election. In an informal public vote, he found overwhelming favor. The formal vote in the legislature was unanimous.

$\mathcal{P}art\ of\ the\ reason$ Pauahi did not want to be queen had to do with her husband. Charles was, to be sure, a citizen of the kingdom of Hawai'i. But many considered him an American, and the United States was beginning to look like a real threat to Hawai'i's independence.

There had been earlier foreign menaces. A French warship had dropped anchor aggressively in Honolulu harbor in 1839; another arrived in 1849, and its sailors had come ashore to wreck the fort. In between, in 1843, there had been a brief British takeover of the kingdom by an arrogant naval commander, a titled aristocrat acting without authorization, whose action had been reversed by the Foreign Office in London in a matter of months. But from the 1850s onward the main threat was from America.

In the 1860s and 1870s the sugar industry in Hawai'i grew quickly. American plantation owners, whose main market was their home country, mostly controlled the industry. Economically, Hawai'i was becoming more and more dependent on the United States, and American citizens in Hawai'i were becoming more and more assertive. As early as 1854 there was talk of annexation.

As many Americans pointed out, close ties with the United States did not have to mean loss of independence for Hawai'i. A commercial treaty could allow Hawaiian sugar into the American market on favorable terms and American goods into the Hawaiian market on equally favorable terms; a reciprocity treaty like this would give a huge boost to the economy of Hawai'i.

The way Hawaiians saw the picture developing, however, Americans had designs on their country. American plantation owners were buying more and more large tracts of land. The thought was in the air that the entire kingdom might wind up in the hands of the United States, and this stirred up bad feelings.

When Bishop married Bernice in 1850, there had been at least some friendliness between the Hawaiians and the *haole*. Ten years later, during Lot's reign, that relationship was fraying. In the legislature, which was bilingual, English-speaking *haole* members were refusing to speak the Hawaiian language, and Hawaiian members were refusing to speak the English language. In one session a fistfight broke out, with the Hawaiians shouting a warrior chant from the time of Kamehameha the Great.

Relationships did not improve under Lunalilo. Negotiations for a reciprocity treaty had been dragging on, with no favorable outcome for Hawai'i in sight. As an incentive to the United States, the Hawaiian government offered to lease or cede a magnificent harbor on O'ahu that could be used as an American naval base. Its ancient name was Pu'uloa; now it would be known as Pearl Harbor. The proposal brought hundreds of angry Hawaiians onto the streets of Honolulu. Not that all Hawaiians were against reciprocity—but to trade away the lands and waters of Hawai'i for money seemed intolerable.

The negotiator in charge of the government's offer to cede Pearl Harbor was Lunalilo's minister of foreign affairs, Charles Reed Bishop. He saw the economic future of Hawai'i as inevitably tied to the United

States. If Pearl Harbor had to be bargained away to get reciprocity, so be it. Looking past Pearl Harbor, Bishop could see the economic logic of annexation, and he would live to see it happen. Yet in the present, ordinary Hawaiians, *maka'āinana*, were shouting right outside his window that they would not stand for seeing Pearl Harbor—or any Hawaiian soil —under the American flag. Bishop had to withdraw the government's offer.

In 1875 the Bishops took a long trip to celebrate their twenty-fifth wedding anniversary. They had been to the American Mainland together twice before, in 1866 and 1871, but this excursion was much more ambitious. It took months of planning and was to last the better part of a year and a half.

They sailed to San Francisco, then traveled across country to New York for dress fittings and "Herculean" shopping, then across the Atlantic to Europe, and on to more than thirty cities, where they visited dozens of museums filled with Old Masters and saw eight operas in eight months. In Ireland they made a climb of 108 steps to kiss the Blarney Stone; in Scotland there was grouse shooting. There were a cruise down the Rhine, a gondola ride on the Grand Canal in Venice, a day among the ruins of Pompeii, a day at the palace of Versailles, two nights in the casino at Monte Carlo, photographs taken in Vienna, vintage wines drunk in a sophisticated club in Bremen, and the buying of oil paintings and a piano to be shipped to Honolulu. They spent four weeks in Rome, six in Paris, in high society all the way: dinners and parties by introduction, conversations with the titled, an audience with the pope, then London and the monuments of centuries of royal rule—Westminster Abbey, the Tower, Windsor Castle—and, finally, presentation to the queen of England.

The Duke of Edinburgh, who had been guest of honor at a *lū'au* at Haleakalā, did the honors in return. Bishop wore his uniform as an ex-minister of the Hawaiian kingdom; Bernice wore a Paris gown made of two shades of rose silk, with a low bodice and a three-and-a-half-foot train she added in London, decorated with feather plumes and flowers.

While the Bishops were away, the reciprocity treaty with the United States was renegotiated. It passed the Senate in Washington, was ratified in Honolulu, and went into effect three weeks before the Bishops arrived home in September 1876. Anyone could see that the treaty was going to make the sugar planters and landowners rich. Bishop, the money man, would also do extremely well. He was going to need a much bigger bank building, and he started on it right away.

Bernice Pauahi and Ruth Keʻelikōlani, cousins by birth, were bound so closely by ties of blood and *hānai* family that they called each other sister. But they could not have been more different. Pauahi, small and fair-skinned, was a world traveler, at home in *haole* society, in the English language, at the keyboard of the organ in Kawaiahaʻo Church, in Paris gowns, in corsets. Ruth was a Hawaiian great chief in an older sense, darker-skinned, standing six feet tall, weighing by some estimates as much as four hundred pounds. She had a thunderous voice and a temper, and she smoked a pipe. Ruth knew how to speak English but chose not to and in fact had as little as possible to do with *haole*.

As a child, Ruth did not go to the Royal School. She never left the Islands and spent her final days on her lands at Kailua on Hawaiʻi, where she had a favorite grass house. It was close to the spot where Kamehameha died, and the only thing that marred her view was a Protestant missionary church with a tall steeple. She composed her own farewell chant, her *kanikau*. When she died on May 24, 1883, Pauahi was at her deathbed.

"I miss her greatly, as a mother misses a child she has watched over, and cared for during illness," wrote Pauahi, who was five years younger than Ruth. "So have I missed mine, for she was like a child in many ways, so careless and wayward, and she was the last nearest relative I had."

In Ruth's lifetime, which was also Pauahi's lifetime, there were many deaths among the *aliʻi nui*, young as well as old. Ruth's mother died giving birth to her; her first *hānai* mother died when she was six, her second *hānai* mother when she was thirteen, and her first husband when she was twenty-two. Her children and *hānai* son also predeceased her. Each *aliʻi nui* death reduced the number of inheritors and concentrated larger and larger acreages in fewer and fewer hands. Ruth had inherited lands from her first husband and her father's brother and more from her half brothers and sisters. When Lot died without a will, Ruth petitioned for his lands, and they were awarded to her. Eventually, Ruth's lands—Kamehameha lands—amounted to 353,000 acres.

When it came time for Ruth to write her own will, her only close relative still living was Pauahi. Aside from six temporary interests in land and the gift of an express wagon and two horses, Ruth left everything to Pauahi: "I give and bequeath forever to my beloved younger sister Ber-

Princess Ruth Keʻelikōlani was governor of the island of Hawaiʻi for nearly three decades.

nice Pauahi Bishop, all of my property, the real and personal property from Hawaiʻi to Kauaʻi, all of said property to be hers."

Although there had been some debate among Hawaiians about Ruth's and Pauahi's true genealogical descent, Ruth's will was not challenged, and Pauahi's claim was confirmed by the Buke Māhele, from which all land titles had flowed since 1848. At age fifty-one, Bernice, Mrs. Bishop,

Ke Aliʻi Pauahi, was now far and away the largest landowner and the richest woman in the kingdom.

Until now, Pauahi had seen no need to make a will. But she had become the owner of valleys and plains, forests and grasslands, from the mountains to the sea. It was valuable as real estate, especially with the reciprocity treaty in force and demand for sugar plantation land growing rapidly. Beyond that, it was the sacred legacy of Kamehameha, the royal ʻāina. On October 31, 1883, she signed her own will.

Early in 1884 Pauahi began to feel ill. At the beginning of April, on the advice of her doctors, she went to San Francisco for a change of scenery and for medical advice. The doctor diagnosed breast cancer, already advanced. She was operated on before Bishop could get there.

By June, she was well enough to travel home, but at Haleakalā her condition worsened. Late in the summer she went to her villa at Waikīkī for the sea air. Friends called and visited, children came to play with her, but now Pauahi was in great pain. One of her doctors gave her opium, and when the pain intensified, he injected morphine. In early October she added two codicils to her will. On October 9, the date of the second codicil, which was witnessed by her doctors, she was moved to Keōua Hale, the big house she had inherited from Ruth, where she and Bishop had planned to live. She died there on October 16, 1884, at the age of fifty-two.

For fifteen days, Pauahi's coffin lay at Keōua Hale, with the royal court in full mourning. There were black kāhili, symbols of royalty, 150 of them; her name songs and death laments were chanted day and night, and mourners came on foot through the rain to pay their respects. It had started to rain while she was dying, and it was raining on November 2 when her funeral cortege formed, four white horses to carry the casket to Kawaiahaʻo Church, kāhili bearers in yellow capes and tall black hats. The funeral procession after the service had police at the head, cavalry in plumed helmets at the rear. Crowds lined the roadside, and while the Royal Hawaiian Band played "The Pauahi March," aliʻi nui, servants from her household, children from her Sunday school class, stewards of her lands, the consular corps, judges of the Supreme Court, and seventy-five carriages processed toward Nuʻuanu Valley. There, the rain clouds parted.

At Mauna ʻAla, the Hawaiian royal mausoleum, built in the form of a Christian cross, Pauahi joined three generations of the Kamehameha dead, who were laid out in the crypt beside the kāʻai, the sennit caskets, of two ancient chiefs from generations before Kamehameha, whose own bones were buried on the island of Hawaiʻi in a place kept secret to this day. The kings after Kamehameha all lay at Mauna ʻAla: Liholiho, Kauikeaouli, Alexander Liholiho, and Lot. Alexander's son, Albert Edward Kauikeaouli, and the *aliʻi nui* Kaʻahumanu, Kamāmalu, Kalama, Leleiohoku, Keaweaweula, William Pitt Kīnaʻu, David Kamehameha, Moses Kekuaiwa, and Victoria Kamāmalu. Pauahi's mother Konia; her father Pākī; her *hānai* parents, Kekūanaōʻa and Kīnaʻu; her *hānai* child, Keolaokalani, son of Ruth Keʻelikōlani; Ruth herself; and now Pauahi.

chapter 2

A Culture Suppressed

Ruth Keʻelikōlaniʻs will was written in Hawaiian and signed "R. Keeli-kolani." Pauahi chose English for her will, and in flawless Royal School penmanship she signed it "Bernice P. Bishop," her Hawaiian name reduced to an initial.

In her will Pauahi made more than forty individual bequests of money or interests in land to *aliʻi*, friends, servants, retainers, charities, and Charles. Namesakes—five Bernices and two Pauahis—got $200 each. The gifts to married women were for their "sole and separate use free from the control of their husbands."

The bulk of the estate, 325 parcels of land totaling 378,569 acres, went in trust to five named individuals: Charles R. Bishop, Samuel M. Damon, Charles M. Hyde, Charles M. Cooke, and William O. Smith. As trustees, they were subject to strict fiduciary duties that required them to manage the trust estate prudently and to pursue the charitable mission spelled out in article 13 of Pauahi's will: "to erect and maintain in the Hawaiian Islands two schools, each for boarding and day scholars, one for boys and one for girls, to be known as, and called the Kamehameha Schools." Pauahi instructed her trustees to prefer Hawaiians when providing "support and education [to] orphans and others in indigent circumstances," but she did not limit admission to just Hawaiians. Instead, she authorized her trustees to decide who could attend the schools. As legal owners of the trust estate, Pauahi's trustees also had the authority, acting jointly by majority vote, to buy and sell property, hire and fire employees, and expend trust money in pursuit of the charitable mission. In Charles Bishop's written communications, his wife was always "Mrs. Bishop." The custom in Hawaiʻi at the time of her death was to refer to testamentary trusts as "estates." That is why the trust described in Pauahi's will came to be known as Bishop Estate.

Several provisions in the will suggest that Princess Pauahi had in mind two trade schools where moral training and religious instruction would be emphasized. (For a full listing of the provisions of the will relating to the trust, see the appendix.) But she specifically authorized her trustees to make the rules and regulations for the schools, including who and what would be taught. Pauahi's ultimate goal was production of "good and industrious men and women."

From its start in 1884, the trust estate was huge in size. But in absolute monetary terms, there was no hint of the financial colossus it would eventually become. The land had an estimated value of $470,000 and an expected annual income of $36,000. The only other asset was $4,127 in cash.

In Bishop Estate's early years, Charles Bishop's money was vital in getting the schools "up and running." He also deeded back his life interest in the lands Pauahi had left him and added substantial acreage of his own, making the trust even more land-rich: 440,184 acres at its peak.

Charles Bishop's schooling in New York State had ended at the eighth grade, but he never stopped reading, thinking, and learning. In Hawai'i he took a strong interest in education, devoting himself to his cause with true Victorian zeal. Years before the founding of Kamehameha Schools, Bishop had been a trustee at the missionary-founded Punahou School, where he paid for the construction of Charles Reed Bishop Hall, the Bishop Hall of Science, and Pauahi Hall. He provided financial help for kindergartens throughout the state and was one of the founders of the public library and the Hawaiian Historical Society. Bishop was also well read in the current thinking of his time, which emphasized that a good education for all, not just for some, was fundamental to a good society. As he put it, "The masses must work up together gradually, and the character of the masses, not the favored few, will be the character of the nation. In a field of cane there are large hills and towering stalks here and there, but the group depends on the average of the field and the good cultivation of the whole."

Under Bishop's watchful eye, the boys' school opened with great ceremony on November 4, 1887, enrolling thirty-nine pupils; the girls' school followed in 1894, with thirty-five pupils. A preparatory school for younger boys had preceded the girls' school. Bishop personally paid

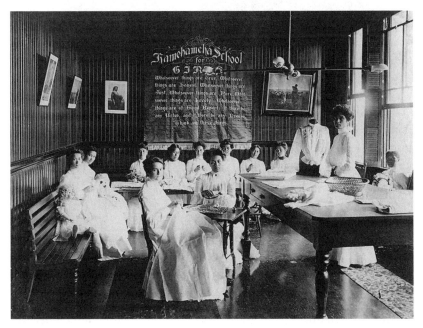

The Kamehameha Schools started out as trade schools.

Charles Reed Bishop was the only trustee named in his wife's will who did not have a strong missionary identification.

for the preparatory buildings and for part of the girls' school, as well as the Bernice P. Bishop Museum. He also had a chapel built as a memorial to his wife.

The original Bishop Estate trustees—Bishop, Damon, Cooke, Hyde, and Smith—were all *haole*, Protestant, and very much in favor of annexation to America as the best thing for Hawai'i. Damon was a banker to his core and, thanks to Pauahi's generosity, also a large landowner; in a codicil to her will, Pauahi gave Damon the *ahupua'a* (district) of Moanalua. Cooke, whom Pauahi had looked after at the Royal School, had become a successful businessman, a major investor in sugar and shipping. Hyde was a strong-minded clergyman who saw little value in Hawaiian culture. And Smith, a lawyer with a specialty in trusts, had been a member of an armed anti-Kalākaua militia and then in 1893 was part of the Committee of Safety, the driving force in the overthrow of the monarchy. Of the five trustees, Bishop was the only one who did not have a strong missionary identification. Cooke and Smith were the sons of missionaries; Damon was the son of the first seamen's chaplain in Honolulu; and Hyde, himself a missionary, had come to Hawai'i to train Hawaiians to be missionaries. The connection of four trustees to Pauahi's chosen religion apparently was intentional. Her will required that all future trustees be "persons of the Protestant religion."

The first trustees hired someone very like themselves as the first principal of the boys' school at Kamehameha: William Brewster Oleson. Oleson, a New Englander, had been pastor of a Congregational church (the denomination of the Protestant mission to the Islands) before he came to Hawai'i to run the Hilo Boarding School. The Reverend Oleson was a fervent American democrat, with no tolerance for monarchies. He had a particularly low opinion of Kalākaua, the monarch who had succeeded Lunalilo. Oleson claimed that Kalākaua ruled by bribery, corruption, lasciviousness, sorcery, and tyranny. In 1887, the year Oleson took charge at Kamehameha Schools, he and other members of an all-*haole* committee forced a re-written constitution on Kalākaua sharply limiting the king's power. The Kamehameha boys under Oleson, however, were instinctive royalists, reverential to their *ali'i nui*. When Kalākaua paid a surprise visit to a Kamehameha classroom, the boys immediately sprang to their feet and sang "Hawai'i Pono'ī," the national anthem, whose lyrics had been written by Kalākaua. When Lili'uokalani visited the schools and drank coffee, her cup became sacred, *kapu*.

Immediately following the overthrow in 1893, students and their parents voted with their feet against a school run by annexationists. So many students left and did not come back that enrollment went down by almost half and remained at that level for several years.

Hawaiians attempted a counterrevolution in 1895 to restore Lili'uokalani to the throne. No Hawaiians had taken up arms in 1893, but this time some did, and two of the leaders came from Kamehameha: John Wise, one of the first graduates, and David Kanuha, who taught tailoring, the only Hawaiian on the faculty. All the other Kamehameha teachers were *haole,* and three picked up guns on the side of the *haole* government. One of them was Uldrick Thompson. He felt torn but made his choice decisively, by skin color: "If I take part in this matter, I must resign and go home. I cannot shoot Hawaiians and then return to teach these boys. But if it comes to a choice between the whites and the Hawaiians I must of course stay with my own race."

At Kamehameha classes were canceled. The principal posted armed patrols of teachers and students to guard the campus. He organized baseball games as a way to occupy the boys, but they could hear gunfire, and their attention to the game wavered. Someone cut the telephone line to the school. A rifle hidden in Dormitory D went off mysteriously but harmlessly.

The counterrevolution did not last long. One *haole* was killed. Uldrick Thompson did not have to shoot any Hawaiians, so he decided not to resign. David Kanuha was dismissed from Kamehameha and charged with treason against the republic. He spent only a few days in jail, however, and was soon back to teaching tailoring, instructing Hawaiian boys in how to make work shirts for themselves and suits for the *haole* teachers.

Military training quickly became part of the program at Kamehameha. Oleson was not only principal, but also commandant and drillmaster. He got the boys up in the morning, standing to attention

For many years, military training was a major part of the curriculum at the Kamehameha School for Boys.

in uniform, and he kept them straight-backed in class. The principals who came after Oleson were also military-minded. They took the boys through the manual of arms, initially with wooden rifles, later with the real thing. There was a demerit system, and there were punishments: rawhide and the classroom ruler, chopping wood, marching outside Bishop Hall. In extreme cases there was solitary confinement on bread and water. The Stars and Stripes flew on campus every day. On Sundays there were dress parades, and the boys were marched to church by teachers on horseback. The boys wore military uniforms much like those of the cadets at West Point.

The first principal of the girls' school, Ida May Pope, put her indelible stamp on the school's early years. She was a strong-minded, energetic Midwesterner who picked her own teachers; the first, like her, were all single women from the Mainland.

Pope set a tone to discipline the Hawaiianness of her girls. "Constant and consistent restraint is the way to control the careless, joyous, happy-go-lucky nature of the Hawaiian," she wrote. Kamehameha girls were to be self-respecting, standing firm for truth and purity and having the moral fiber to resist temptation. As at the Royal School, the students' time was spoken for from 6 A.M. to 9 P.M. They took classes in academic subjects in the morning and in practical subjects in the afternoon, and five days a week they did three hours of manual work, with additional hours to do laundry on Monday, ironing on Thursday, and housecleaning on Saturday. Healthful physical exercise was compulsory. There were prayers and Bible lessons every day, church on the Sabbath, voluntary prayer meetings three times a month on Sunday nights, and on the fourth Sunday, a meeting of the Bernice Pauahi Bishop Missionary Society.

Pope went into the country districts and found beauty in nature, but not in the Hawaiian way of living.

> The glimpses I had of the homes from whence come some of the best girls at Kamehameha has oft times marred the pictures Nature gave of sea and hill and sky. So little of the attractiveness of life comes in the way of these girls socially, mentally or morally. Do you much wonder that the growth is not always upward tending? What books, pleasures, or helpful companionships enter into the lives of most of these girls?

At Kamehameha the girls always had books in their rooms, and they were instructed to keep their rooms neat enough to stand inspection on the spot—which was a real possibility, since their teachers lived in the same building. As for pleasures, Pope was modern enough to countenance social dancing. She got the trustees to agree to the waltz and the two-step, to be learned by the girls under her supervision. Boys from the school could be invited to dance with the girls, though not often, and always at arm's length.

Pope set high standards for everything. Her women teachers were better qualified than the men teachers at the boys' school, and they stayed longer, even though they were paid less. Pope herself started on less than half the salary of the boys' principal.

Pope's girls did better than the boys in every way. Their manners were better, their English was better, and they did better in class, too. Fewer girls dropped out than boys. There were years, sometimes two or even three in a row, when the boys' school had vacancies in sizable numbers. But once Pope got the girls' school going properly, there were always more applicants than spaces.

Pope, referred to by the girls as Mother Pope or Mama Pope, was principal for twenty years, until her death in 1914. During the last few years of her life, she also took on personal responsibility for a young child, a little girl whose life would be linked inextricably with the story of Kamehameha Schools until her own death in 2003. The child's mother, Esther Staines, had been brought to study at Kamehameha by Pope from Kawaiaha'o Seminary, where Pope had been principal before coming to the girls' school. Staines was in Kamehameha's first graduating class. She impressed Pope as a deserving girl, one who should not marry just any nondescript man. Pope and the Kamehameha chaplain arranged a marriage for Staines with David Kanuha, the tailoring teacher. The couple's first five children were all sons. When they were finally blessed with a daughter in 1906, the Kanuhas named her Gladys, telling friends that they chose the name because the child made them "glad." Several years later, Gladys' mother and Pope decided that it would not be good for a young girl to grow up surrounded by boys, so Pope took Gladys to live with her on campus as her *hānai* daughter.

Two years before she died, Pope started what she called the Senior Home Management Cottage. Built partly by shop students from the boys' school, it was to be a place where "gentle speech and manners shall prevail, and respect for property and the rights of others be observed." One of the things the girls were taught at the cottage was responsible

Senior Home Management Cottage at the Kamehameha School for Girls, where students practiced being good mothers by taking care of real babies.

motherhood. In Pope's time they practiced with dolls, but beginning in 1924 the girls cared for real babies. The first Kamehameha baby was Lillian Kamakea, six months old, from the Salvation Army Rescue Mission. Each student at the cottage was baby director for a week, responsible for the baby twenty-four hours a day, feeding it, changing it, writing down its weight and all the other measures of its development, giving it its sunbath, playing with it, waking through the night when it cried, holding it and rocking it and walking the floor with it.

Some of the babies brought to the cottage were as young as six weeks old. By the school's preference they were Hawaiian, and there was never a shortage. Some were rescued from institutions; others were from single mothers. Many were children of Kamehameha graduates who were happy to share. This was Hawaiian. It was a temporary *hānai*, a newborn child given, for a year, to a family of high-school students, an *'ohana*. Among Hawaiians, the notion of family was broader than shared genealogy. *'Ohana* included others for whom one cared. To be part of an *'ohana* meant moving easily back and forth from home to home, a relaxed willingness to welcome and embrace others, to offer and to accept what was offered without calculating. The mothers of the babies visited the cottage regularly, and at the end of the year they carried their babies back to their Hawaiian homes.

In planning for the new girls' campus, a cottage was sited in a beautiful spot, high up, cool enough for a fireplace, close to a fragrant green forest (and to a steep cliff, down which diapers might occasionally be thrown by the baby director of the week as a home management shortcut). Everything went so well that a second cottage was added, then a third. And the number of babies in residence went up from one to two to three to five.

The girls prized the babies, looked after them, gave them special names, and sent them off at the end of the year with clothes they had sewed, scrapbooks of pictures, and letters they had written, to be saved for when the baby was old enough to read them. The girls later had reunions with their babies. The Kamehameha girls would remember the senior cottage all their lives.

Students came to Kamehameha as Hawaiians. That was understood. But the purpose of their time at Kamehameha was to make them into hardworking Christians and, even more fundamentally, into patriotic Americans. During the schools' early years the American plantation owners, businessmen, and professionals spoke openly about how life in Hawai'i should be lived. There were many different levels of loudness and many shadings of tone, but the dominant note was this: in a Hawai'i that was becoming increasingly Americanized, nothing "Hawaiian" had any intrinsic value.

Charles Reed Bishop cared deeply about the Hawaiian people, but even he felt that the only way for Hawaiians to survive the coming changes was to Americanize themselves. A founding principle at Kamehameha had been that the further from Hawaiian ways students could be kept, the better they would be, and the better Hawai'i would be. For decades, Kamehameha looked to the Mainland as the best place to recruit teachers. After them, local *haole* were preferred. If they could not speak or understand Hawaiian, so much the better. The boys and girls of Kamehameha Schools were told repeatedly that to be American meant, above all, to compete; and they could not compete successfully if they lived and thought like Hawaiians. One of the first orders Oleson had given when he signed on as Kamehameha's principal was to ban the

Hawaiian language, not just in the classrooms but on the playground and in all student activities as well.

This was not just the thinking of non-Hawaiians. David Kanuha, the Hawaiian tailoring teacher who had participated in the failed counterrevolution, forbade his children to speak Hawaiian at home or anywhere else, including at Kamehameha, where he worked and they studied. He never explained why they were prohibited from speaking the language of their parents and grandparents; his daughter, Gladys, who moved back home following Pope's death, figured it must have been because anything Hawaiian was "junk."

In the first decades of the schools, the goal of Americanizing every student was never questioned; what was in doubt was whether any Hawaiian could achieve it. Some said that Hawaiians did not have what it took to flourish in modern industrial society—a society that required quick thinking, hard work, and steadfastness of purpose, all qualities valued by the culture of Protestant Americans and perceived by them as lacking in most Hawaiians.

Kamehameha had started out almost exclusively as a trade school, which was what the trustees said Pauahi wanted. In her will, she had specifically empowered them to determine to what extent the schools should be "industrial, mechanical, or agricultural." Each of these three directions added up to vocational education, a fact that was acknowledged in the name that everybody used for the boys' school: "The Manual." Not that this was in itself derogatory; at the time Kamehameha was founded, manual education was considered a new and forward-thinking approach to education. The theory was that the hand and the mind would work together, and both would benefit. At Kamehameha there would be moral benefit as well: manual education shaped character, teaching the need to follow rules, meticulousness, diligence, and honesty of purpose.

The trustees did not see Hawaiians as becoming anything more than workers—certainly not leaders. The thought of Hawaiians being leaders in the community at large appeared nowhere in Pauahi's will, in the policies or expectations of the government schools, or at Kamehameha. Hawaiian boys could work in the mills, tending steam pumps or repairing the rollers that crushed the cane. They could be land surveyors. In town, they could be blacksmiths, linemen, mechanics, carpenters, and printers. The girls could be typists, switchboard operators, nurses, seamstresses, teachers in government schools, and servants. But that was all. None of the trustees ever hired a single Kamehameha graduate or, for that matter, any other Hawaiian to work in a supervisory position. Kamehameha boys and girls were supposed to be content and not to look higher. A generation after their founding, the stated policy of Kamehameha Schools was still "to avoid all work that might arouse their ambitions towards the professions." But some graduates managed to become leaders anyway. The first generation of Kamehameha alumni included architects, engineers, lawyers, physicians, newspaper publishers, judges, elected politicians, heads of government departments, pastors, and, in two cases, generals in the U.S. Army.

Girls at Kamehameha, like most girls around the world at the time, were raised to defer to men. Women in the United States did not even have the right to vote until 1920. But at ten minutes after midnight, at the beginning of the day the woman suffrage law went into effect on August 30, 1920, a Kamehameha graduate had the county clerk roused out of bed to allow her to place her signature on record. The first woman to register to vote in Hawai'i was Johanna Wilcox, Kamehameha class of 1914.

"Where Are All the Hawaiian-Looking Ones?"

Kamehameha's first class—fourteen boys on the verge of becoming men—graduated in 1891. The first class of graduating girls—fifteen of them—followed in 1897. In 1907, the twentieth anniversary year of the founding, there were 163 students at the boys' school, 94 at the girls' school, and 69 at the preparatory school.

In the mid-1920s the trustees, envisioning a total enrollment of a thousand students, announced a plan for a new campus on the heights of Kapālama. This time, the girls would come first: their new school opened in 1931. The new boys' school had to wait out the Great Depression and didn't open until 1940. Total enrollment of the two schools would reach one thousand by 1949.

The new campus was magnificent: six hundred acres, two hundred of them forest, with cool breezes and sweeping views—a rainbow-shrouded world high above the city of Honolulu. There was nothing remotely like it for any other school in Hawai'i, public or private.

Pauahi was to be thanked for all this—and more than thanked, revered. Each year on Pauahi's birthday, December 19, immaculately dressed boys and girls made an annual pilgrimage to the royal mausoleum at Mauna 'Ala to decorate her tomb with flowers and to sing for her:

> Blest type of womanhood,
> So true, so pure, so good
> Thy praise we sing,
> Thy praise we sing.

The Kamehameha Schools' new Kapalāma campus on the island of O'ahu was completed just before the beginning of World War II.

For bounteous gifts and free,
In all around we see,
Of what God gave to thee,
Full hearts we bring.
Pauahi ke Ali'i,
Loyal we bend to thee,
Queen of our hearts,
Queen of our hearts.
Alohas loud resound,
From all these hills around,
Where e'er thy name be found,
Where thou still art.

The remembrance did not take place only on her birthday. Pauahi was ritually exalted throughout the year, held up as the official soul of Kamehameha Schools. At vespers, the lives of both Jesus Christ and Princess Bernice Pauahi Bishop were commemorated.

ᴀＡ𝒜lthough the students revered Pauahi and wanted to honor her wishes, what it meant to be a Hawaiian in Hawai'i was changing during the twentieth century in ways Pauahi could not have foreseen. Most people agreed that Kamehameha should be exclusively for Hawaiians, but in a Hawai'i in which each generation of children had a lower quantum of Hawaiian blood, who was Hawaiian? And what kind of education was appropriate? In a changing world, should Kamehameha continue to focus on vocational instruction, character development, and the Protestant religion, as the will suggested?

There were also questions about which Hawaiians should be benefiting from Pauahi's legacy. Should it be the top tier of potential students, the ones who were likely to do well in any event, or the bottom tier, the children who had little going for themselves? Should there be relatively few students, to whom many resources would thus be devoted, or as many students as possible, with resources spread more thinly among them?

Most perplexing of all for an institution founded upon the sacred will of a revered benefactress: what if the preferred approach in the modern world differed from the one Pauahi described in her will?

Pauahi wrote her will at a time when many believed in the absolute need for Hawaiians to assimilate to Western ways, even if it meant giving up their own language and culture. Could it be that eventually Pauahi's will might stand in the way of what was best for Hawaiians? If so, would it then be right to deviate from her will? And who would decide which way to deviate?

There were many voices, but not much agreement.

𝒻rom the beginning, Bishop Estate trustees personally strove to protect the trust estate and make it productive; they hired others to run the schools. It was appropriate to rely upon professional educators in this way, but the trustees remained ultimately responsible for carrying out the primary charitable mission, which was Kamehameha Schools.

The first serious challenge to Bishop Estate trustees came from a group the trustees had not expected to show leadership: Kamehameha alumni. Charles E. King led the critics. King, one-quarter Hawaiian and a godchild of Queen Emma, had graduated from Kamehameha in 1891 and gone on to attend a good teacher training school on the Mainland, his expenses paid by Charles Bishop personally. He returned to teach at Kamehameha from 1900 to 1902—mathematics, woodworking, and music—then worked in the public schools as a teacher, inspector, and supervising principal. He also was a gifted musician, fully immersed in Hawaiian music. In his middle years King became the leading composer of his generation.

In 1916 King and nine of his fourteen classmates from the class of 1891 issued a devastating criticism of education at Kamehameha. They contended that standards needed to be raised, that most graduates were unprepared for college or for responsible positions in business, and that they would never obtain good jobs at good wages or live in good houses.

All this caught the attention of the sitting probate judge, Clarence Ashford, whose job it was to approve (or not approve) the trustees' annual accounts. This year, in addition to the usual review, Ashford appointed a three-person committee to look into the program of instruction at Kamehameha. Like King's group of alumni, Ashford's committee rejected the notion that the mind of a Hawaiian child was incapable of absorbing education above a relatively low level. They advised raising academic standards and cutting back military hours.

All this was noteworthy, but it grew into debate over more than just academic standards; the first major controversy about choosing trustees was now brewing. Pauahi had named the original set of trustees and requested that Hawai'i Supreme Court justices fill vacancies as they occur. For many years, however, whenever there was a vacancy on the board, the remaining trustees decided who would fill the seat.

When Samuel Mills Damon resigned in 1916 because of poor health, the trustees, as usual, sent a name to the Supreme Court. As usual, they had chosen a *haole* businessman—this time, William Williamson, a Punahou teacher-turned-stockbroker who was about to be named president of a sugar company. The Supreme Court, also as usual, approved and sent Williamson's name to the probate court for official confirmation of their selection. But then Judge Ashford, shocking everyone, rejected Williamson and on his own say-so appointed Charles E. King. Ashford declared that the probate judge, whose court by law oversaw trusts, had the exclusive power to appoint trustees and that Bishop Estate, founded to benefit Hawaiians, should have a Hawaiian trustee. The trustees immediately questioned Ashford's authority to do this, and the dispute eventually ended up in the territorial Supreme Court. The justices of that court, whose power to name Bishop Estate trustees had never before been challenged, ruled that their selection of Bishop Estate trustees was perfectly legal and proper, but only because they had made each selection "unofficially," as mere citizens, not as justices.

King did not become a trustee, but the arguments he made for higher standards drew vocal support from the Hawaiian community. Bishop Estate trustees were for the first time feeling intense pressure to do their job differently—in this case, to raise standards and expectations at Kamehameha Schools.

With the goal of raising academic standards, the trustees hired Frank Midkiff as president in 1923. His view of Hawaiians was considered "progressive":

> We find as wide a range of intelligence in our students as is found at Punahou [a missionary-founded and largely *haole* private school]; in other words, it is likely that whereas we have many who will succeed only in manual vocations, we may have some who would be discontented unless placed where they have more scope and opportunity. Thus many will find satisfaction in trades as journeymen, others will become foremen and superintendents, while some will wish to grow into other types of activity which demand more thought and more administration and leadership. . . . The schools serve the Territory best not by grooving a student into agriculture or into a certain trade . . . but rather by carefully finding out the qualities of the new student and then giving him adequately planned and effective training along the lines of his aptitudes. Any other course will produce a large percentage of discouraged and dissatisfied misfits.

Couched in language about serving the needs of the Territory, Midkiff was suggesting that Hawaiians had as many innate abilities as *haole*—and that they might become "discouraged" in American society, not because they were destined to be so, but because of the low expectations placed upon them and their futures.

To help move Kamehameha in the right direction, Midkiff recruited Homer Barnes in 1934 to serve as principal of the boys' school. Barnes, who had a Ph.D. from New York's Columbia University and had spent a term in England at Oxford, was passionate about the need to raise academic standards. He was not against military training or Kamehameha's highly successful football team, the Warriors, but he did not want them dominating and defining Kamehameha. Barnes took school discipline away from the regular army officer who had been running the military program and started a chapter of the National Honor Society. Contending that Kamehameha had been admitting children whose IQ scores were too low, Barnes split the classes into two tracks based on academic ability so slow learners would not hold back the others. He also flunked students who did not show enough improvement. These were controversial moves, and in his first year on the job a group of alumni took Barnes to task. They said they didn't like him because he didn't like Hawaiians, and they were going to get him fired. That didn't happen. Barnes stayed on and continued to push for higher standards and expectations.

People talked in those days about two kinds of Hawaiian children. One kind was from a good, Westernized home, where parents took a sincere and vital interest in rearing their children. This kind of child needed comparatively little training in manners and morals; higher education was seen as a possibility. The other kind of Hawaiian child had a lower standard of living, often came from a broken home, was raised by people other than parents, spoke pidgin, and had little apparent scholastic aptitude. Many believed that Kamehameha could not function as a school for both kinds of child: let the bad in, and the good would stay away. Midkiff and Barnes were in this camp: They were for educating a few children to the highest level, rather than, as Midkiff put it, schooling many in a "slapdash fashion."

Barnes stressed the connection between small numbers and high standards. He also strongly supported making Kamehameha a boarding school, undiluted by day students. Boarders could be supervised twenty-four hours a day, while day students were subject to outside influences from the time they went home in the afternoon to the time they showed up in school the next morning. Barnes's thinking about the benefits of keeping students on campus was not new. It had been a founding principle at Kamehameha that the further Hawaiian students could be kept from Hawaiian ways, the better their education would be, the better they would be, and the better Hawai'i would be. The same commitment made at the Royal School had taken the form of a high fence.

Under Midkiff and Barnes, the number of applicants and their test scores increased significantly, and the school's academic reputation rose dramatically. There was serious talk about Kamehameha's becoming a school of the very highest quality, as good as any in the country, one that would produce great leaders.

The changes made by Midkiff and Barnes ran into a barrage of criticism in 1943 from two Hawaiian senators in the territorial legislature: William Heen and David Trask. Heen had started his education at Kamehameha but then moved to Punahou. He was a founder and first president of the Hawaiian Civic Club and had developed a keen interest in Bishop Estate when he was hired by the state attorney general in 1939 to review the trustees' accounts. Trask had personal reasons for casting a cold eye on Kamehameha's stringent admissions policies: some of his close relatives had wanted to attend the schools but had not been admitted.

According to Heen and Trask, Hawaiians were in trouble—at home, on the job, with the law—and Kamehameha was not doing nearly enough about it. These senators were in favor of reaching far more Hawaiians, especially the ones most at risk. In public committee hearings, Heen and Trask berated the trustees for what was happening at

The 1943 territorial senate. Senators William Heen (top row, third from the right) and David Trask (top row, far right) criticized Bishop Estate trustees for admitting only high-scoring applicants to Kamehameha Schools.

Kamehameha: using entrance examinations and IQ tests as the filter, the schools were admitting fewer than 2 percent of school-age Hawaiian children—350 out of 26,000. Many of the faces on campus looked more *haole* and Chinese than Hawaiian, complained Trask; "Where are all the Hawaiian-looking ones?"

As part of the same hearings, Heen and Trask invited a University of Hawai'i professor, Stephen Porteus, to testify on the implications of using IQ tests to make admissions decisions. Talking about the fundamental choice at issue, Porteus said, "Either you are going to do 90 percent good to 10 percent of the people or 10 percent good to 90 percent." The crowded room reportedly erupted in cheers when Porteus added that he personally favored doing 10 percent good for 90 percent of the people.

Heen and Trask attributed the problem at Kamehameha to attitudes in the Bishop Estate boardroom. They said the trustees were acting like "landed barons," each getting big fees for part-time work while treating Hawaiians like beggars. The senators could not force new admission policies on the trustees, but they could introduce legislation that would limit the earnings of trustees of charitable trusts, and that's what they did—not specifically Bishop Estate trustees, but the measure was obviously aimed directly at them, and everyone knew it.

The trustees responded that they had heavy responsibilities and could be sued personally if they made a mistake that cost Bishop Estate money. Under the circumstances, they argued, their fees were reasonable, maybe too low; if the job paid any less it might not be worth doing. Each of them had taken fees that year of $10,250.

Heen and Trask were not impressed with the trustees' "sacrifice": $10,250 was six times the average full-time wage in Hawai'i. This was clearly excessive, according to the senators, especially when you considered that some of the trustees had full-time jobs elsewhere and that the five trustees met only twice a week to conduct Bishop Estate business. The senators got a legislative resolution passed that instructed the attorney general, Garner Anthony, to start removal proceedings immediately for all five trustees. Because the resolution failed to cite a specific breach of trust, Anthony ignored it.

Despite strong opposition from the trustees, Heen and Trask managed to pass a law in 1943 that held down trustee fees, but not by as much as the two senators wanted. For the next fifteen years trustee compensation at Bishop Estate averaged about $9,000 per trustee.

$\mathcal{A}$ generation earlier, the fundamental complaint of Charles E. King and other alumni had been that expectations at Kamehameha were too low and that students were not being prepared for college and leadership positions. That set the stage for men like Midkiff and Barnes, who raised the schools' standards significantly. Then Senators Heen and Trask pushed in the opposite direction, accusing the trustees of setting standards that were beyond their reach of the children who needed help the most and of "trying to make *haoles* out of Hawaiians." That set the stage for a new round of major changes: the trustees agreed to increase significantly the number of day students (including children who did not score high on IQ tests), hire more local teachers, expand vocational training, and take steps to build up pride in Hawaiian heritage. Barnes resigned, and the policy of deliberate elitism at Kamehameha ended.

During the rest of the 1940s and through the 1950s, the number of alumni on the faculty increased dramatically. Enrollment doubled and then doubled again. Kamehameha went from being predominantly a boarding school to being predominantly a day school, and from a small school for Hawaiians who tested well on IQ tests to a big school with no formal entrance tests. A geographical basis for enrollments was established, with percentages allotted to each island according to the numbers of Hawaiians.

Meanwhile, equally dramatic changes were brewing on the money side of Bishop Estate. Hawai'i was on its way to becoming the fiftieth U.S. state, ensuring a level of economic prosperity that earlier trustees had probably never imagined possible. Within a generation, Bishop Estate would be described by the *Wall Street Journal* as the wealthiest charity in the United States.

chapter 4

Newfound Wealth, Cultural Rebirth, Seeds of Discontent

In 1959, the year Hawaiʻi became the fiftieth state of the Union, passenger jets began flying from the West Coast to Honolulu. This was the start of mass tourism, which almost overnight became a major economic driver for Hawaiʻi, quickly matching sugar and pineapple and then far outstripping them. These were also the years of the Cold War and then the Vietnam War. Hawaiʻi became the forward base of the United States, and military spending grew rapidly to exceed all sectors of Hawaiʻi's economy other than tourism.

Everything conspired to push land values higher and higher, in some cases by 1,000 percent, then 2,000 percent, a real estate boom that seemed to have no end. Bishop Estate was far and away the biggest private landholder in the state. Its name was on about one in every nine acres, a concentration of private land ownership seldom seen anywhere else in the world. All Bishop Estate had to do was exist, and business would come to it in record dollar amounts. The sky was the limit. To be at the center of one of the hottest real estate markets in the world was an interesting position for a charitable trust.

Bishop Estate trustees recognized that statehood would mean serious money for the trust and that now was the time to re-think every aspect of the trust's charitable mission. They hired a Mainland consulting firm, Booz, Allen and Hamilton, to spend the better part of 1960 gathering statistics, interviewing hundreds of stakeholders, and preparing recommendations. The report, submitted in 1961, filled four volumes and included 526 recommendations. The vision proposed to the trustees was eyebrow-raising: rather than duplicate Hawai'i's other schools, Kamehameha should set a standard. Graduates should be the top leaders, not just in the state, but in the nation as well. To realize this vision, the report recommended that the schools return to a highly selective admissions policy and cap enrollment at levels that would permit scholastic excellence. In this respect, the report essentially shared the vision that had been championed by Midkiff and Barnes many years earlier. But the Booz, Allen and Hamilton report did not stop there. It also recommended that Bishop Estate reach out to other Hawaiian children, the ones who would never gain admission to Kamehameha Schools, and help them in their own communities. As envisioned, these programs, which came to be called "outreach" or "extension" programs, would complement what the public schools were already providing and would also promote Hawaiian culture. They specifically would benefit the kind of Hawaiian children whose cause had been championed by Senators Heen and Trask in 1943.

By the mid-1960s Kamehameha's extension division served six thousand children in thirty-eight communities on six islands, and was growing rapidly. Specific programs included alternative learning centers for both the gifted and the alienated; workshops in Hawaiian culture; large-scale production and dissemination of Hawaiian studies materials for use in public schools; weekend enrichment activities; summer classes and cultural activities; agricultural and environmental initiatives; canoe-making projects; night classes for adults; and pre- and postnatal classes for young, first-pregnancy mothers.

The 1960s brought another major change to the Kamehameha campus: the separate boys' and girls' schools were merged to form a single school called Kamehameha Schools. (Calling it Kamehameha School might have highlighted that the trustees had ceased to honor Pauahi's instruction to maintain "two schools.") Coeducation was in vogue, and the trustees concluded that one large school could operate more efficiently than two smaller ones. They also saw social benefits to having boys and girls interact in the classroom and cited "a material change . . . in this community with respect to the relations between males and females."

ROTC was still big on campus; but during the 1960s, especially when young people everywhere were protesting the Vietnam War, Kamehameha boys started resisting the mandatory military uniforms and short haircuts. There were even sporadic protests. Many people were re-thinking old traditions and considering liberal alternatives. Some of the more progressive teachers persuaded the administration to loosen the rigidity of the school week, offering seniors free time to be used in their own way. It was meant to be unstructured, and it was: Gladys Brandt, who by that time was principal of the combined high school, called it Wandering Wednesday. There were sightings of seniors surfing at Waikīkī during school hours, or on the bus to Chinatown, where the pool halls were, or up in the forest at the high end of the campus on bedding taken out from the dorms and laid under the trees. One Wandering Wednesday Brandt saw smoke rising in the woods, from mattresses accidentally set alight during a session of "contemplation enhanced by inhalation."

By the end of the 1960s the baby cottage was no more. The home management course that had always been compulsory had become an elective, and fewer than one in five senior girls were taking it. Women's liberation was in, and homemaking was out.

Another thing that came back in during the 1960s was *hula.* The New England Protestants had disliked *hula's* intimate connection with ancient Hawaiian religious practices and were offended by its sexual connotations. When the first missionaries saw *hula* spectacles with hundreds of dancers and thousands of spectators, it seemed to them a vision of Sodom and Gomorrah, the incarnation of everything that was evil about Hawaiian living.

Although many members of the royal families converted to Christianity, most of them saved a privileged place in their lives for *hula,* making it part of their royal observances. Pauahi was different. In all her years of entertaining, no *hula* was danced at Haleakalā. In accordance with what would presumably have been Pauahi's wish, early Bishop Estate commercial leases banned *hula* along with liquor. There also was a rule on campus: no standing *hula.*

James Bushong, president of the Kamehameha Schools at that time, had positive thoughts about the *hula:*

> In Italy, Russia and other countries their national ballet has achieved world acclaim for variety, intricacy and expression of movement. In similar fashion, the traditional *hula* epitomizes

the historic culture of Hawai'i. When properly taught and appropriately performed, this courtly *hula* provides a poignant recapitulation of ancient Hawai'i and its humanities.

This was a strong endorsement, but Bushong did not want to be the one to ask the trustees to lift the ban. Such a decision would be made by consensus, not majority vote, and Bushong did not think it possible to get even most of the trustees—let alone all of them—to agree to lift the ban. But when Gladys Brandt insisted that the time was right to try, Bushong did not say no.

The first trustee Brandt approached was Richard Lyman. He was proud of his Hawaiian ancestors, but he was also descended from mis-

Bishop Estate trustees in 1965 (left to right): Atherton Richards (whose father, a Protestant missionary, had been principal of the boys' school from 1893 to 1898), Frank Midkiff (an educator who came to Kamehameha in 1913 to teach and direct athletics and then served as president from 1923 to 1934), Edwin Puahaulani Murray (an alumnus who had expertise in finance), Herbert Kealoha Keppeler (who previously had served as the top staff person in charge of land management at Bishop Estate), and Richard Lyman (a part-Hawaiian whose haole ancestors included the Protestant missionary who founded Hilo Boarding School).

Gladys Kamakakūokalani Brandt's life was intertwined with Kamehameha Schools: her father was the first, and for many years only, Hawaiian on the faculty; she grew up on campus as the hānai *daughter of a* haole *principal; and she herself later served as principal of Kamehameha Schools.*

sionary stock. Brandt had expected Lyman to be on her side, but he told her to forget about it—she would never get the rule changed. Brandt thanked Lyman for his time but added that she had no intention of giving up so easily.

Next on Brandt's list was Atherton Richards, the son of Theodore Richards, who had been a principal at Kamehameha when Brandt's father was on the faculty. Atherton Richards was exceptionally fond of Brandt and wanted her to do well as the first Hawaiian principal at Kamehameha. He used to send his car to take her to parties at his house on the beach at Diamond Head, where there was *hula* dancing on the immaculate lawn; some of the dancers had been Kamehameha girls, a fact Brandt pointed out to Richards. He responded that they were graduates, not students, and they were not on campus. Brandt suggested that those differences were *manini* (small); eventually she brought Richards around to her way of thinking.

Frank Midkiff, the progressive school president from the 1920s, and

Herbert Keppeler, a corporate executive, were next on Brandt's list. Neither was personally opposed to the idea of *hula* at Kamehameha Schools, but they did not like unnecessary controversy. Why make waves now? Brandt responded that it was the right thing to do and should have happened long ago. They were not easy to convince, but Brandt managed to do it.

Brandt then got a call from Lyman. He had just heard that three of the others had given their approval. He expressed surprise that she had gotten this far and said he would not be the one to stop her. But he added that he still did not think much of her chances. "One to go," he said, and he laughed, "you will not pass this one."

"This one" was Edwin Murray, a Hawaiian and a 1909 Kamehameha graduate. Murray did not like the idea of anyone doing the *hula* at Kamehameha, not just girls. He had called a teacher on the carpet several years earlier over a performance by Kamehameha boys.

Brandt already had a *hula* history with Murray, and it was not promising for her cause. Not long before, she had attended a *lū'au* at which the acclaimed 'Iolani Luahine was dancing. In the middle of the performance, Brandt spotted Murray off to the side. She went over to him and, to find out what he was thinking, remarked, "Isn't she lovely?" Murray took his cigar out of his mouth and said, "She dances like she has ants in her pants." Recalling that exchange did not give Brandt confidence, but she had come too far to stop now. She made an appointment to see Murray at Bishop Estate headquarters.

It was a fiasco. Murray told Brandt he had had no idea she had come to Kamehameha to promote indecency. Brandt did not take this well: "I just went haywire. I just thought I got slapped in my face left and right, and so I lost my cool. I was just rocking all over the place. I thought I would use every four-letter word I knew. His chair flew back. I said something about the military, missionary ethic, and all that kind of dumb thing. I should have known better. . . . I went out bawling."

She got back to campus and had started to pack her bags when a message came for her to call Murray. Brandt reported: "I said 'Hello,' and he said, 'Woman'—I would never forget that—'Woman, if those girls wiggle too much, you know where you'll be.' And *bang* went the phone."

Brandt dried her eyes, blew her nose, and went looking for Nona Beamer, a Kamehameha teacher whose legendary family had danced and taught *hula* for generations. They handpicked the girls. Beamer rehearsed them; Brandt encouraged them and told them they looked

Dancers of the hālau *Na Pua Mai Ka Lani perform in front of the Bishop Museum, which was the original site of Kamehameha Schools.*

lovely. The girls performed on campus to a large audience and were a huge success, receiving applause and more applause after each of their dances. Murray sat through it all and said nothing.

The next day newspapers ran the big story, but the news had already spread throughout the Hawaiian community. Seventy-eight years after the school's founding, standing *hula* had finally arrived at Kamehameha.

$\mathcal{S}$ince the end of World War II there had been a pressing need for more housing in Hawai'i, and Bishop Estate was by far Hawai'i's largest private landowner. However, as a tax-exempt charity, Bishop Estate was limited to passive investments. Renting out undeveloped land fell into this category, but developing or systematically selling land did not. Any income from that kind of activity could be taxed. Also, it had long been doctrine at Bishop Estate that Pauahi's land—the *'āina*—should be kept intact, in the trust. So instead of selling or developing land, the trustees made large tracts of undeveloped land available to independent developers on long-term leases ranging from fifty-five to ninety-nine years, typically with fixed rent for the first thirty years so that homeowners (whose homes would be built on the leased land) could qualify for mortgage financing.

When land values spiraled upward in the decades following statehood, the fixed rents on existing leases lagged behind the market. Homeowners continued to pay their fixed monthly rent, but the amounts seemed smaller and smaller when compared to the escalating land values. It was a good deal for the renters in the short term, but there would be a day of reckoning when the fixed-rent period would expire and rents would have to be renegotiated. At best, the renegotiated amounts would be affordable. At worst, Bishop Estate would demand such a large increase that the homeowners would be forced to sell their houses, perhaps for little or nothing. In many cases, all the value was in the land.

As the long-term leases approached their renegotiation dates, homeowners across the state were filled with apprehension and fear, and many blamed Bishop Estate for their predicament. Emotions ran high. The newspapers reported on a husband and wife who had taken their own lives during the renegotiation period on their land lease; the note they left behind was filled with angst over the prospect of losing their home. The trustees' fiduciary duty to make the trust estate productive and to use it solely to pursue the charitable mission in Pauahi's will was clashing with the American postwar ideal of homeownership.

During this time Hawai'i's legislature considered many bills that would force Bishop Estate trustees and other large landowners to sell land to the people who already owned homes on it. Legislative session after session, such measures were introduced. Session after session, Bishop Estate resisted. The conflict stemmed from more than just the trustees' desire to maximize the value of the trust estate. Among Hawaiians, it was an article of faith that Pauahi's legacy of 'āina should not be dismembered. After a century of dispossession, Bishop Estate stood as a kind of Hawaiian fortress, real and symbolic, land and 'āina, a sacred link to the past to be defended at all costs.

At the historic Kawaiaha'o Church, where Pauahi had worshiped and taught Sunday school classes, the pastor, Reverend Abraham Akaka, condemned the proposed leasehold reform legislation as theft: "A century ago it was the overthrow of our beloved *ali'i* Queen Lili'uokalani. Today it is the overthrow of her sister, Princess Bernice Pauahi Bishop and her will. Both overthrows are crimes, however righteous the overthrowers may feel about themselves and their actions."

Hawaiians were generally not public protesters, but in 1963, on the eve of a key legislative vote on a leasehold reform bill, they marched at

The outspoken Reverend Abraham Akaka was kahu *(pastor) for twenty-eight years at Kawaiaha'o Church, Christianity's mother church in Hawai'i.*

night to 'Iolani Palace, home of the vanished monarchy, where the state legislature now sat in session, and ringed the building with burning torches. The measure did not pass.

$\mathcal{D}$uring the 1960s and 1970s the industrialist Henry J. Kaiser developed Hawai'i Kai, a commuter suburb of Honolulu, on Bishop Estate land at the southeast corner of O'ahu. These six thousand acres had previously generated only negligible income for the trust. With a long-term lease in hand, Kaiser used his considerable wealth to correct the area's drainage problems, build a much-needed bridge, and then develop thousands of house lots, square mile upon square mile of modern American suburbia. The first McDonald's in Hawai'i opened in 1968 on the road to Hawai'i Kai, and it did a booming business.

In line to be developed next, as Hawai'i Kai expanded, was Bishop Estate land at Kalama Valley. Life there was primitive. There were pig farms, junked cars, and poor people, by one count sixty-seven families living in broken-down shacks. In 1970 Bishop Estate started to clear Kalama of tenants and squatters. Some left voluntarily; others resisted. Bulldozers started leveling homes.

The resistance was organized. A community group, Kōkua Kalama, put out a newspaper whose logo was a *poi* pounder in a brown fist. The name of the newspaper was Kōkua Kalama's chant: *Huli* (Overthrow).

Everyone knew that Bishop Estate would win in the end. It had the law on its side and many lawyers. Kōkua Kalama used 1960s "people power" tactics: civil disobedience, tours of the "disaster area" for reporters and the public, a protest and sit-in at the Capitol, occupation of the pigpens, and defiance of the bulldozers. Bishop Estate cut the electricity at Kalama, turned off the water, and bent the pipes. Policemen moved in to arrest everyone—for trespassing on Bishop Estate land. Kōkua Kalama's "Minister of Defense" put out mimeographed instructions: "No weapons of any kind, no bricks, no rocks, no sticks. No violence. No provoking the police. If arrested, sit down and let the police carry you. If tear gas is used, run; do not throw the canisters back. If there is gunfire, stay out of range."

The last of the pig farmers was George Santos, whose house still stood. About two dozen protesters climbed onto Santos' roof and pulled the ladder up after them. They sang the Kamehameha Schools song, "Sons of Hawai'i." As the protestors were being arrested, without violence, a *kahuna* placed a curse on the Bishop Estate trustees. George Santos' 185 pigs were trucked away and temporarily housed in a rented pen that cost a dollar per pig per day—"a first-class pigpen," according to Bishop Estate's director of communications. The pigs started dying. Santos loaded two of the carcasses into his old pickup truck and drove to Bishop Estate headquarters. When he got there, he found that the building was locked and the police had been called. Santos said he would come back with all his dead pigs—within a month, forty-three were dead—and dump them on the desks inside. He did not, but Kalama got lots of newspaper space and TV coverage, most of it negative for Bishop Estate.

The Bishop Estate trustee who publicly defended the Kalama development was Richard Lyman. He acknowledged that progress did not always benefit everyone, and that was unfortunate; but the trustees of Bishop Estate were duty bound to pursue just one mission: to educate as many Hawaiian boys and girls as possible. That took money, and lots of it. The rent from one piggery, or two, was nothing compared to the rent that thousands of homeowners would pay. Read the will, said Lyman; Kamehameha Schools was where Bishop Estate's responsibility began and ended.

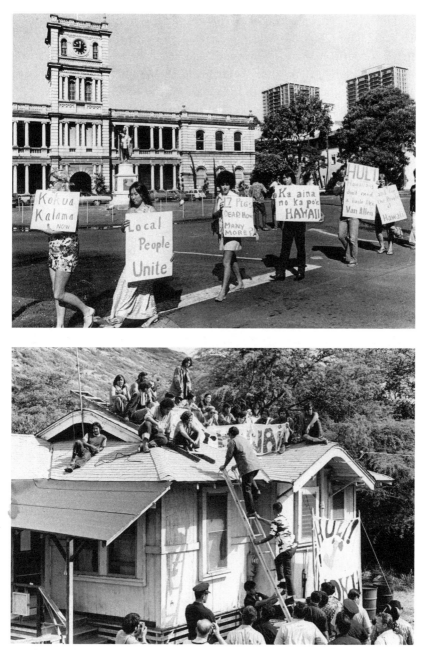

Graduates of Kamehameha Schools led "people power" protests in the early 1970s when Bishop Estate cleared Kalama Valley of tenants and squatters so the land could be developed to its highest income-producing potential.

The Kalama resisters believed that Bishop Estate had greater responsibilities. They took their case to court. Among the plaintiffs they put up was a young nephew of Reverend Akaka who was a student at Kamehameha. The judge, Yasutaka Fukushima, wasted no time in sizing up the situation and announcing his decision: the Kalama attorneys did not know anything about the land laws of Hawai'i. Case dismissed.

Kalama Valley was cleared for development: Bishop Estate had won completely. But the victory did not look good or smell good. It reeked of rich Bishop Estate making yet more money by bulldozing poor Hawaiians off the land, with Kamehameha alumni shouting *"Huli!"* and George Santos hauling his dead pigs to Bishop Estate headquarters. In the minds of many Hawaiians, Bishop Estate was supposed to be looking out for them, and now they believed it wasn't.

Feelings intensified as Bishop Estate's lawyers continued to get land reclassified and rezoned from conservation and agriculture to urban, resulting in more Hawaiians' being uprooted from the *'āina*. Kōkua Kalama turned into Kōkua Hawai'i: "We must save our farm lands to grow food on. We must stop the developers who want to pour concrete over everything. . . . We must get back our land from the few big landholders that have most of it. It was stolen from us in the first place."

In the minds of many, Bishop Estate had turned, within a short time, from the esteemed guardian of Hawaiian lands to the greedy landowner that evicted Hawaiians in the name of the bottom line. In the forests of Nu'uanu Valley, where Pauahi used to go horseback riding, Kamehameha graduates were secretly drilling for paramilitary action, with Brown Power berets and a version of a Black Power salute. Out in the country, signs marking Bishop Estate land as "Private Property," "No Trespassing," and *"Kapu"* were starting to show bullet holes.

The Trust Plays Politics as Activism Grows

The American Benefactor magazine in a 1998 article concluded that politics was at the core of Bishop Estate's many problems: "Princess Pauahi's will, which named the justices of Hawaii's Supreme Court as selectors of the trustees, inadvertently put her estate at the mercy of a political spoils system. . . . Unlike most states, Hawaii has never had a true two-party system, in which each party serves as a brake on the excesses of the other."

In the first half of the twentieth century, the Republicans controlled politics in Hawai'i. In the second half, with the G.I. Bill, the end of the plantation era, and the rise of a generation of immigrants and children of immigrants who had fought for the United States, control shifted overwhelmingly to the Democrats. Their spiritual leader was John A. Burns, governor from 1962 to 1974. Burns' most loyal support came from Japanese Americans, at the time the biggest single ethnic group in Hawai'i. Japanese Americans were strong in the civil service and the public school system, increasingly strong in the professions and in business, and politically very well organized.

In 1971, during Jack Burns' third term as governor, a seat on the Bishop Estate board became vacant. Burns had appointed all five sitting justices of the Supreme Court: Masaji Marumoto, Kazuhisa Abe, Bert Kobayashi, Bernard Levinson, and William Richardson. Now he had someone in mind for the Bishop Estate opening: Matsuo Takabuki.

The chief justice, Richardson, had been Burns' lieutenant governor until the governor moved him to the top seat on the bench. Now, in

65

Governor John Burns (center) celebrates an election victory with Lieutenant Governor William Richardson (right) and others, including Burns's closest political associate, Matsuo Takabuki (left).

1971, Richardson and the other justices did as Burns asked: they chose Takabuki as a trustee. Takabuki, a party insider, had first been elected to the Honolulu board of supervisors in 1952 and then to the city council after statehood, eight terms in all. As the governor's campaign organizer and moneyman, he was Burns' closest confidant.

The selection of Takabuki, announced in the middle of the standoff at Kalama Valley, stirred up a storm of protest. At the time, the only Hawaiian on the Bishop Estate board was Richard Lyman, and there was strong feeling among Hawaiians that there should be more. The bigger concern, however, was the perception that Takabuki was a political appointee, heavily involved in the politics of money. Detractors pronounced Takabuki's name "Take-A-Buck-y." A rally against Takabuki brought a thousand marchers out in Waikīkī along Kalākaua Avenue to Kapiʻolani Park, chanting "*Huli* Takabuki!" The Royal Hawaiian Band played. Speakers gave five non-stop hours of reasons why Takabuki was the worst possible Bishop Estate appointee. Tom Gill, a reform Democrat who had run against Burns for governor the preceding year, called Takabuki a skilled operator in the politics of land and power. According to Gill, "Takabuki could probably move a subdivision around faster than you can see it." Others called Takabuki "the governor's man," meaning that his first loyalty would be to the head of his political party, not to Bishop Estate or to the people it was there to serve.

During this time there was a perceptible split in the Hawaiian community itself. Activist Hawaiians of the 1960s had lost patience with "establishment Hawaiians," including churches with predominantly Hawaiian memberships. Where had Kawaiaha'o Church been, the activists wanted to know, at Kalama and other places where Hawaiians were being pushed off the land onto the streets? At the rally in Kapi'olani Park, a Kōkua Hawai'i man took the microphone: "Stop singing, start swinging." One Sunday morning in 1971, worshippers arrived at Kawaiaha'o Church to find, spray-painted on a doorpost in large green letters, *"Huli."*

Responding to these calls for action, Reverend Akaka called special meetings at Kawaiaha'o Church that overflowed, attracting six or seven hundred people, including many from Kōkua Hawai'i. At one meeting, when Lyman spoke in support of Takabuki, he was laughed at and then booed.

Out of these meetings came the Ad Hoc Committee for a Hawaiian Trustee, a coalition of twenty-two organizations, mostly Hawaiian. The committee organized a lawsuit. They wanted Takabuki's appointment rescinded, and they also sought changes in the way trustees were being selected. On the day of the hearing the courtroom was packed, with a number of people standing outside the room and even more outside the building. The plaintiffs argued that the probate court had the right to name the new trustee and did not have to rubber-stamp the justices' nominee—who everyone knew had actually been chosen by Burns.

Judge Fukushima, the same Burns appointee who had so hastily dismissed the Kalama Valley lawsuit, called the plaintiffs' arguments in this case "a lot of garbage." He ruled that the plaintiffs had no legal standing; the naming of trustees was up to the justices of the Hawai'i Supreme Court. It was just that simple: "The plaintiffs have labored hard and have not even brought forward a mouse." Within minutes, Takabuki was vested with the title of Bishop Estate trustee. A hundred yards from Fukushima's courtroom, the bells of Kawaiaha'o Church tolled in mourning for nearly an hour. Reverend Akaka called it a dark day for Hawaiians: "We are now a nobody as far as the government is concerned."

The Ad Hoc Committee appealed Fukushima's decision to the state Supreme Court. Chief Justice Richardson stated that he and the other justices could personally decide the appeal if they wanted to do so, even though they were the ones who selected Takabuki and each of them was a named party in the lawsuit. Without conceding this position, however, Richardson and his fellow justices eventually agreed to let substitute justices handle the appeal.

On behalf of the plaintiffs, Samuel P. King argued that the substitute justices should be chosen by lottery from among circuit court judges, which he said would promote public confidence in the final decision. Richardson countered that the law clearly allowed the chief justice to select the substitute justices. King responded that the issue was not what was legal, but what was right.

Richardson chose the five substitutes, and in 1973 they ruled unanimously against the Ad Hoc Committee. Takabuki remained a trustee, and the justices maintained their control over the selection of future Bishop Estate trustees.

The 1971 Bishop Estate board of trustees (left to right): Matsuo Takabuki, Frank Midkiff, Richard Lyman, Hung Wo Ching, and Atherton Richards. There were many clashes between Takabuki, a strong-minded, highly intelligent lawyer and politician, and Ching, a strong-minded, highly intelligent businessman.

Takabuki's controversial path to the Bishop Estate board of trustees stood out in the trust's history. His appointment, questioned publicly by an increasingly active Hawaiian community, cemented the sentiment that it was time for Bishop Estate to be run by Hawaiians—and in that sense, it closed a door on the past. But Takabuki's presence in the boardroom also marked a new direction for the trust. He was the first of what would prove to be an almost unbroken string of political insiders who would be put on the Bishop Estate board.

No one was surprised when the next three vacancies at Bishop Estate went to individuals who were both Hawaiian and political insiders: Myron "Pinky" Thompson had headed Burns' administrative staff and served in his cabinet; William Richardson had been Burns' lieutenant governor and chief justice; and Henry Peters was in the legislature for ten terms, serving as speaker of the house when he was appointed a trustee.

Takabuki's appointment also marked a turning point in how the trustees did business. Before Takabuki the trustees had made decisions jointly, as is required by Pauahi's will and trust law. After Takabuki became a trustee, he increasingly functioned as a "lead trustee" for asset management. With the blessing of three other trustees, Takabuki effectively took control of investing for the trust—which meant control over the flow of increasingly large sums of money. The lone dissenter in those years, Hung Wo Ching, sometimes tried to stop Takabuki's recommendations from passing, but he never managed to succeed. One of the many battles between Takabuki and Ching ended up in court. Takabuki wanted Bishop Estate to buy into a project being promoted by Kawaiahaʻo Plaza Associates (KPA), a limited partnership whose managing partner, James Trask, had political and family connections with the Burns administration. KPA had been plagued by financial problems, and its Kawaiahaʻo Plaza project was publicly reported to be, in the words of the Supreme Court decision, "on the brink of disaster." To Ching, it looked as though Takabuki's primary goal was to bail out KPA rather than to do what was best for the trust. An independent consultant told the trustees that the proposed transaction was "questionable as a sound fiduciary investment." Despite these warning signs, the other three trustees sided with Takabuki against Ching. Believing this to be a serious breach of trust, Ching sued Takabuki. He did not prevail: The probate judge and a unanimous Supreme Court declined to intercede in this matter of "business judgment."

Part of Takabuki's deal with KPA was that Bishop Estate would

The new headquarters of Bishop Estate, Kawaiaha'o Plaza, was the subject of a boardroom battle in which Ching accused Takabuki of using trust funds to help out a developer because of the developer's political connections.

move its headquarters to the new, modern-looking building next to Kawaiaha'o Church, which was called Kawaiaha'o Plaza.

Real estate development in those years was booming. A growing demand for more hotels, condos, retail stores, and housing, and not nearly enough land available to satisfy this demand, meant that developers virtually begged to do business with Bishop Estate. There was no way the trustees could deal with all of them. Exactly how the few winners were chosen was never made clear. The attorney general attempted to find out, but got nowhere. According to his report, "Neither the trustees nor the staff could explain why they chose certain developers or how they arrived at the terms of development agreements." This led some people to believe that Ching had been right—that decisions were not always made with the trust's charitable mission first and foremost in mind.

The selection of a new trustee in 1989 could have been the most politically controversial of all, had it not been for a stalemate among the justices. The new governor, John David Waihe'e III, had ideas about who he wanted in the Bishop Estate boardroom, but he didn't yet have "his guys" on the Supreme Court, and some holdover justices had a low opinion of him. Under the circumstances, no one knew what to expect.

The justices started with more than a hundred names and eventually got down to three, but then they could not narrow the choice to one. Two of the candidates each had two of the five justices solidly in his camp. After more than a year arguing among themselves, none of these four justices would budge, and the fifth justice refused to vote for either of the two top candidates: Tony Ramos, principal of Kamehameha Secondary Schools, and Larry Mehau, a Big Island businessman. Both of these top candidates were graduates of Kamehameha—Ramos in 1958, Mehau in 1948. It was Mehau who was controversial. After Kamehameha he had gone into police work, running a vice squad. He was physically formidable; stories were told about how he had lain on his back with a three-hundred-pound rock on his stomach and had a man pound it with a sledgehammer until it broke in two. When Mehau left the police force in the 1960s he became active in politics, went into ranching on Hawaiian homestead land, and started a security company called Hawai'i Protective Association, which quickly grew to be the largest security business in the state, with contracts at Aloha Stadium, Honolulu International Airport, and other major government facilities.

In 1970 Governor Burns appointed Mehau to the Board of Land and Natural Resources, one of the major intersections of land and power in Hawai'i. When Mehau's term ended, house Speaker Henry Peters introduced a resolution of thanks in the legislature, which passed fifty to one, commending Mehau for his untiring service; his devotion, dedication, sincerity, patience, thoroughness, decisiveness, and fearlessness; his concern with the welfare of the state and of its people and culture; his balancing of the interests of conflicting groups; his fairness and reasonableness with the public; his work with drug and other problems among the young; and his championing of the cause of the needy, the poor, and the neglected.

In 1977 another view of Mehau appeared in a Maui newspaper, the *Valley Isle*. An article implicated Mehau in the deaths of several people and called him the "godfather" of organized crime in Hawai'i. The word was picked up and published elsewhere. Mehau sued for defamation of character, naming TV stations, newspapers, and a radio news station. According to newspaper reports, the case was first assigned to Judge James Burns, Governor Burns' son, but Judge Burns said he could not take the case because he was a personal friend of Mehau's. Burns

For many years Larry Mehau (right) was considered Hawai'i's most influential political insider. In 1989 he was one vote shy of becoming a Bishop Estate trustee.

was not alone; nine of the thirteen circuit court judges also refused to hear the case. The remaining four were not asked because they were about to retire or were otherwise unavailable. The case was settled out of court.

The author of the *Valley Isle* article, Rick Reed, later went to work in the Honolulu city prosecutor's office, where, he said, he saw additional documents that led him to repeat the word "godfather," this time in a luncheon talk. He also quoted from a report on "Operation Firebird," which involved the U.S. Drug Enforcement Agency, the Federal Bureau of Investigation, the U.S. Customs Office, the Internal Revenue Service, and the Treasury Department's Division of Alcohol, Tobacco and Firearms. Reed added his own opinion, which was that Mehau's influence "permeated [Hawai'i's] government, [its] criminal justice system, and even [the] business community." Reed associated Mehau with the murders of a union leader and a government informant who had once worked for Mehau, and quoted the testimony of two former Mehau associates who already had been convicted of murder. Mehau sued again. This lawsuit, too, was settled out of court.

Ironically, the deadlock among justices over Larry Mehau ultimately led to the only non-political appointment of the era—Oswald Kofoad "Oz" Stender, a non-candidate who emerged as the compromise choice. Because of the circumstances of his selection, many people referred to Stender as the "accidental trustee."

Stender was only the second Kamehameha alumnus in 106 years of Bishop Estate to join the Bishop Estate board, and his personal story brought to mind the words of Pauahi's will as no other trustee selection had done before. Stender had grown up an orphan, and his family had been indigent. His mother had died when he was two years old, and Stender and his five siblings were parceled out. He said that being a boarder on a scholarship at Kamehameha gave him a new life: "To sleep in a bed by yourself with two sheets . . . a blanket and a pillow! . . . And then in the dining hall, to have a knife, a fork, a spoon, a napkin, and to eat three meals a day!"

Stender was not among the best students, nor was he much of an athlete—he was usually the last to be picked for sports teams—but he found ways to pull himself up. He had a newspaper route and ran a little concession selling candy and soda in a closet-sized space on campus and at sporting events. He managed the track and baseball teams and taught Sunday school classes. He graduated in 1950, and so did his future wife, Ku'ulei, who as a senior experienced the baby cottage. After Kamehameha, Stender served in the Marines and then earned a business degree from the University of Hawai'i. In 1958 he started work in property management at Campbell Estate, a private trust second only to Bishop Estate in size of Hawai'i landholdings, and rose through the ranks to become chief executive officer. By the time he was selected as a Bishop Estate trustee, Stender had acquired decades of experience in large-scale land management and development.

Stender had not applied to be a Bishop Estate trustee. One day he got word that Chief Justice Herman Lum wanted him to come to the Supreme Court building right away. Stender was amazed by what happened next: "I walk into the room and Lum sits me down and calls all the other justices. They come in. On the table is a piece of paper, $8\frac{1}{2}$ by 11, and Lum announces that that piece of paper just appointed me a trustee of the Bishop Estate."

Stender could not find the words to respond. When he finally could speak, he asked for time to think things over. He wanted to get the advice of his mentor at Campbell Estate, Herb Cornuelle. Stender also wanted, if he decided to take the job, to be able to talk to the Campbell

Oz Stender was not even a candidate for Bishop Estate trustee until the justices reached a stalemate. For that reason, and because at the time Stender was the only trustee who was not a political insider, some people referred to him the "accidental trustee."

trustees and to tell his staff before they heard about it from others. No, said the chief justice. If Stender wanted the job, he had to say so immediately, on the spot.

"You know, it's appalling," Stender said later of the way he had been chosen. "It's such a responsible job. No interview. Nothing. It was totally irresponsible."

From the moment Stender joined the Bishop Estate board in January 1990, the way trustees did business made little sense to him. At Campbell Estate there were clear policies, internal controls, annual reviews, regular appraisals. Campbell Estate staff knew what was expected of them and the extent of their authority. Fiduciary responsibility and responsiveness to the needs and concerns of beneficiaries were constantly emphasized. Herb Cornuelle had regularly talked about this as well as the importance of strategic planning, of having a map. At Bishop Estate, Stender could not see any map at all. After spending three months sizing up the situation, he wrote a memo to the other trustees that gave a broad overview of the entire operation. He noted the need for strategic planning and organizational accountability at Bishop Estate. The entire board should take a systematic look at production of income, preservation of assets, enhancement of values, and minimization of investment risks. Investments should be quantified and an investment strategy articulated, with due diligence up front, annual reviews against benchmarks, and exit strategies. It also would be good to have better expense planning, with systematic review and updating. None of these suggestions was radical or even novel. Stender was simply describing what the Bishop Estate trustees were supposed to be doing already to satisfy their fiduciary duties.

Stender put a lot of time into this memo, which ran to more than four single-spaced typed pages. "I would be pleased," it concluded, "to spend some time with the trustees to review this memorandum—perhaps after one of our regular trustees' meetings." It was a polite way, a Hawaiian way, of saying that the contents of the memo needed special attention.

A special meeting was called. Chairman Takabuki thanked Stender for his memo, explained to the group that Stender had not yet been around long enough to understand how things were done at Bishop Estate, and adjourned the meeting. It had lasted thirty seconds.

The other trustees said nothing. They recognized that Stender had experience managing a large land-based trust, but they did not appreciate being told that their way of doing things was not up to his standards. Nor did they appreciate an interview Stender had given shortly after his appointment to the board. A reporter had asked whether Stender thought the trustee selection process was "rigged." Trying to be diplomatic, Stender said that seemed to be the perception of some people. The reporter persisted, asking if Stender agreed with that perception. Stender, taught at Kamehameha always to be truthful, said yes, he thought it was "rigged."

Stender wanted to get along with his fellow trustees, but he also wanted to fulfill his fiduciary duties. He continued to probe, trying to understand why things at Bishop Estate were as they were. The more he understood, the less he liked, but he could not see how he alone would be able to turn things around. The other trustees seemed content with the status quo. They were sitting on assets believed to be worth at least $10 billion. Each trustee was taking nearly $1 million in annual trustee fees and enjoying the perks of a Bishop Estate trustee, such as the offer of free membership at exclusive golf courses located on trust land.

Stender became disillusioned. He started talking about going back to Campbell Estate. Cornuelle was about to step down from that board, and Stender believed he might be in line for the opening. He discussed it with Cornuelle and other close friends and associates, whom he called his "focus group" and who he said helped keep him grounded in reality. They suggested that he stay at Bishop Estate. If things were as bad as he described, then something obviously needed to be done. If he quit, things would never get better.

One member of Stender's focus group, William "Doc" Stryker, was a public-relations man who had been around local politics for decades. He saw another reason for Stender to keep this high-profile position. Hawaiians, said Stryker, "desperately need a symbol of goodness, generosity, unselfish dedication, and simplicity." Stryker said Stender was someone who could be that symbol.

Stender decided to stay.

As politicians tightened their grip on the Bishop Estate boardroom, a different kind of political activism was growing in the Hawaiian community, ignited by the Kalama Valley and Takabuki fights and further nurtured by a burgeoning sense of cultural identity. Although it was not obvious at the time, these parallel developments put the politicized trustees on an inevitable collision course with large segments of the Hawaiian community.

In the 1960s Hawaiians had used new tactics, namely organization, rallies, and resistance, to consolidate a strong political voice that was being heard all over the newest American state. In the 1970s the renewed energies of Hawaiianism—political, social, cultural, and spiritual —coalesced under one name: the "Hawaiian Renaissance." *Hula*, restored to the Kamehameha campus in 1965, was central to the Hawaiian Renaissance. *Hula* schools, *hālau*, were everywhere. Men as well as women were dancing ancient *hula, kahiko,* as well as the modern version, *'auana.* A festival named for Kalākaua, known as the Merrie Monarch, had begun in Hilo in 1963. By the 1980s the festival was drawing *hālau* by the dozens and crowds in the thousands, and it was watched by tens of thousands on TV.

Hawaiian music was experiencing a renaissance of its own. It was being sung and played in nightclubs and on radio: both the old songs, from the time of Kalākaua and Lili'uokalani, and new ones. Among the star performers were dozens of Kamehameha alumni.

At Kamehameha itself, song and dance flourished. Singers and dancers went to Europe and Japan, to arts festivals in Australia, and to other Polynesian island groups, including the Marquesas and Tahiti. Some of their visits were linked with voyages of the Hōkūle'a, a traditional double-hulled oceangoing canoe built to help rediscover one of the great Hawaiian accomplishments, the lost art of long-distance navigation.

This cultural renewal was accompanied by political recognition. In 1978 a state constitutional convention met. At the prior constitutional convention in 1968, Hawaiians and Hawaiian issues had been underrepresented. By 1978, however, Hawaiian interests were everywhere. The Hawaiian Affairs Committee was energetically staffed, with Kamehameha graduates prominent among its workers. The convention proposed five constitutional amendments of major concern to Hawaiians. An Office of Hawaiian Affairs (OHA) would be established as a semiautonomous statewide political entity, its leaders elected by Hawaiian voters only. Traditional Hawaiian rights of access to land and water and religious sites would be protected. The taking of land by adverse possession, something to which small Hawaiian landholdings were particularly vulnerable, would be limited. Hawaiian was to be an official state language along with English, and the teaching of Hawaiian language, history, and culture would be compulsory in public schools. All five propositions were later adopted by a statewide vote of the electorate.

On the federal level, Hawaiians persuaded Congress in 1980 to form a commission to consider reparations for native Hawaiians for lands lost in the United States' annexation of Hawai'i, similar to the restitution package already granted to Alaskan natives. The exercise, which did not bear financial fruit, energized Hawaiians' emerging political activism.

Political consciousness among Hawaiians gathered momentum through the 1980s and into the early 1990s. The social statistics about Hawaiians were dismal, and Hawaiian protest became a powerful mix of historical insult and modern-day grievance. As the one-hundredth anniversary of the 1893 overthrow of the Hawaiian monarchy approached, the list of Hawaiian claims and causes began to include the ultimate demand: the return of political control over Hawai'i to Hawaiians. In different ways, in different forums—local, national, and international—Hawaiians were making a case that the overthrow of the monarchy had been an illegal act and that justice demanded restitution and restoration of Hawaiian independence.

To mark the centennial, five days of public observances commenced under the name of 'Onipa'a, which had been the motto of Lili'uokalani and meant steadfast, resolute, determined, firm. 'Onipa'a events were expressions of grief as well as resolve. 'Iolani Palace was draped in black cloth. The Hawaiian flag was flown at half-staff. No American flag was flown. There were gatherings at Mauna 'Ala, the royal mausoleum, chants and prayers to the ancestors, processions to the sound of traditional drums and conch shells, and a hundred-torchlight vigil at the statue of Kamehameha the Great, a torch for each of the last hundred hours of the monarchy. There were careful re-enactments of the events of the five fateful days; speeches in the very words of 1893 delivered in the coronation pavilion of Kalākaua on the palace grounds, along with Lili'uokalani's last utterance as queen—and the declaration by the hated, all-*haole* Committee of Safety of the inauguration of the provisional government.

Later in the centennial year, the U.S. Congress passed an "apology resolution" that included many "whereas" clauses:

> whereas the indigenous Hawaiian people never directly relinquished their claims to their inherent sovereignty as a people or over their national lands to the United States, either through their monarchy or through a plebiscite or referendum;
>
> whereas the health and well-being of the Native Hawaiian people is intrinsically tied to their deep feelings and attachment to the land;
>
> whereas the long-range economic and social changes in Hawai'i over the nineteenth and early twentieth centuries have been devastating to the population and to the health and well-being of the Hawaiian people; and
>
> whereas the Native Hawaiian people are determined to preserve, develop and transmit to future generations their ancestral territory, and their cultural identity in accordance with their

own spiritual and traditional beliefs, customs, practices, language, and social institutions.

For these and a number of other reasons cited, Congress went on to formally apologize "for the overthrow of the Kingdom of Hawai'i on January 17, 1893 . . . and the deprivation of the rights of Native Hawaiians to self-determination."

Back in Hawai'i, a sense of militancy was growing. At one gathering, a chanting procession—sixteen thousand strong—was led through the streets of downtown Honolulu to 'Iolani Palace by the Trask sisters: Haunani-Kay, a University of Hawai'i professor, Kamehameha class of 1967, and Mililani, an attorney, class of 1969. The two sisters marched now under the banner of Ka Lāhui, one of many militant Hawaiian organizations, and one that had already declared that Hawai'i was still an independent, sovereign nation. On the steps of 'Iolani Palace, Haunani-Kay Trask shouted to the assembled masses: "We are not Americans! We will die Hawaiians!"

chapter 6

Shell-Shocked Lottery Winners

During Bishop Estate's first century, most of its cash came from long-term leases of land, which produced a steady flow of income while preserving ownership of the *ʻāina*. That eventually changed because of a law passed by the Hawaiʻi legislature in 1967. The new law, called "mandatory leasehold conversion," gave homeowners on leased land a way to buy the land under their single-family dwellings, even if owners of that land did not want to sell.

Bishop Estate trustees argued that this law was not just unconstitutional, but un-American. Being forced to sell their property was bad enough, but what made this the equivalent of theft, in the trustees' eyes, was the requirement that they sell each lot to a specific buyer, the homeowner. They argued that if they had to sell land, it should be at auction, to the highest bidder. Only that would ensure the trust received full compensation. In 1984, however, the U.S. Supreme Court upheld the law, noting that forced land sales served a valid public purpose in Hawaiʻi because landownership was so concentrated.

Under the new law, homeowners who did not want to pay Bishop Estate's asking price could go to court, where a jury would decide what the selling price should be. The trustees complained that jurors probably would themselves be homeowners, who would naturally sympathize with the homeowners in front of them. Homeowners viewed the situation differently. They complained of the trustees' hardball tactics, pointing out that although other landowners negotiated with individual homeowners, Bishop Estate just set a price—a high price—and basically told prospective buyers to take it or leave it. Because court proceed-

Growth problem

ings tended to be slow, expensive, and uncertain, most homeowners just paid Bishop Estate's asking price.

The trustees' aggressive pricing and refusal to negotiate alienated many homeowners, but it paid off for the trust. Within just a few years, Bishop Estate's land sales brought in nearly $2 billion for the trust. Better yet, the gains were all tax free. Although profit from the sale of developed real estate is generally taxable even when the seller is a charitable trust, the forced nature of these sales made them exempt from taxation. The question on everyone's mind was, how would the trustees invest all that money?

Bishop Estate's principal financial consultant at the time, Cambridge Associates, proposed a plan based on the concept of financial equilibrium: invest and spend to provide the same level of services to future generations as to the current generation. Cambridge's approach to investing gave high priority to a well-diversified portfolio of marketable securities that was professionally managed and took full advantage of Bishop Estate's tax-exempt status.

The trustees, however, took a different route. With the proceeds from land sales during the 1980s and 1990s the trustees set up tax-paying companies, wholly owned by Bishop Estate, that actively pursued "special-situation investments." These were private business deals that offered the potential of large gains somewhere down the road, with the likelihood of little or no income in the meantime. They tended to be risky, illiquid, and not easily managed: oil-drilling deals spread across six states; a Bermuda-based reinsurance company; urban real estate development in Las Vegas; a luxury golf course just outside Washington, D.C.; developable forest land in Michigan; a research park in North Carolina; a savings and loan company in California; an Internet start-up; a bank in China.

Trustees could make investments that were complicated and risky without breaching their fiduciary duties only if they understood each investment and made sure that it fit into an overall investment plan. Bishop Estate trustees at the time lacked an overall plan and in many instances the necessary expertise. As described by a court-appointed master years later, the investing was "ad hoc," often based primarily on Takabuki's connections with other investors—what the master called "relationship investing."

A 1995 *Wall Street Journal* article described the cash-flush trustees as having the look of "shell-shocked lottery winners" and reported that people close to these deals "were a bit puzzled by Bishop Estate's apparent willingness to bank on Mr. Takabuki's intuition about potentially risky ventures."

One prominent example of the trustees' special-situation investments was McKenzie Methane, a family-owned company that had leases and drilling rights to 150 coal-bed methane gas wells. The trustees had agreed in 1988 to invest as much as $12 million in McKenzie. Individual trustees also invested millions of their own money in the same deal, even though trustees are not supposed to invest personally in private deals in which they invest trust funds. One reason for this prohibition is the concern that trustees might be tempted to consider their own interests when making subsequent decisions about the trust's interest in the deal. That is what happened to Bishop Estate in this deal. There came a time when more money was needed to prevent a total loss, and then more still. Within a year of their initial investments, the trustees had pumped in additional trust funds totaling $85 million. Eventually the deal was declared a complete loss, and lawsuits followed. It turned out that the person who got them into the deal had not invested any of his own money as the trustees had been led to believe, and that he secretly had been paid a large fee for his role in getting the trustees to invest trust funds. The trustees ended up spending another $10 million from trust funds on McKenzie-related litigation.

Had it not been for the litigation, Oz Stender might never have known that trustees had taken interests for themselves. When he joined the board, no one at Bishop Estate had bothered to tell him that they had done that. He found out only when lawyers for the opposing party in the litigation started asking him questions about such irregularities while taking his deposition.

Stender was not the only one in the dark. The court-appointed masters who reviewed Bishop Estate accounts for those years and who were responsible for monitoring the estate's accounts were also unaware of the "co-investing." So were the attorney general and the probate judge, two others who were supposed to provide oversight for the trust: the names of the individual investors had been hidden behind the name HAK, which was short for *hū 'āina koa,* an effervescent bubbling up from the ground.

Bishop Estate also had a major stake in the elite Robert Trent Jones Golf Club in northern Virginia. Presidents of the United States played there, as did U.S. Supreme Court justices, other Washington movers and shakers, and Fortune 500 CEOs. Bishop Estate was a development partner and, beginning in 1991, the sole guarantor of a $40 million construction loan. When this deal ran into financial trouble a few years later, the partners decided to sell the golf course and the surrounding residential property to club members. Henry Peters had an interest on both sides of the pending transaction: he was on the board of the club, which was buying, and he was a trustee of Bishop Estate, which was selling. Despite the obvious conflict of interest, Peters insisted upon representing the club in negotiating the purchase price. He later explained that he had "recused" himself as a trustee of the Estate during the negotiation. The deal Peters struck resulted in a lawsuit, which the trustees did not report to their insurance carrier and which they settled out of court on confidential terms that were never disclosed. Critics complained that the secrecy made it impossible to hold Peters properly accountable for whatever harm his actions might have caused the trust.

The public found out about McKenzie Methane and Robert Trent Jones only because those particular deals ended up in litigation. Otherwise, Bishop Estate's financial activities were a sealed book. The trustees treated all information about their investments, including their very existence, as top secret, attorney-client privileged, strictly confidential. They insisted that any unwanted scrutiny would harm the trust's proprietary interests, which would harm Hawaiians. The language of Pauahi's will, however, indicated she had wanted the public to know specific information about Bishop Estate.

For decades, no party who had legal responsibilities or power to monitor charitable trusts—namely, attorneys general, masters, probate judges, and Supreme Court justices—seriously questioned any Bishop Estate investments. Nor did they question the process by which the decisions to invest were made, even when publications such as the *Wall Street Journal* expressed incredulity over the way Bishop Estate operated. When one trustee, Hung Wo Ching, tried to keep his fellow trustees in check by suing Matsuo Takabuki over the Kawaiahaʻo Plaza deal, he ran into a brick wall at the state Supreme Court.

Elected officials and newspaper editors in Hawaiʻi lauded the trustees' unique investment program as visionary and credited Takabuki for making it happen. At Takabuki's retirement *lūʻau* in 1992, Judge James Burns saluted Takabuki as a financial wizard.

Toward the end of 1992, when three trusteeships were due to turn over within a fourteen-month period, Oz Stender talked with Henry Peters about what it would be like when the two of them had three new co-trustees. Stender suggested that Peters become the new chairman; after all, Peters had been a trustee the longest. Stender offered to take Tak-

*Henry Haalilio Peters had been speaker of the state house of
representatives for three years when he was tapped by the justices
in 1984 to be a Bishop Estate trustee. Peters continued to serve
as house speaker for another three years and did not leave the
legislature until 1994.*

abuki's place, heading up asset management. Peters responded that he
wanted asset management. Stender could be chair.

Stender was unsure of Peters' financial acumen, but as board chair
Stender would be in a position to steer Bishop Estate in another direction. If he was to be chair, however, he wanted two top priorities: an
overall plan, from which investment and spending decisions would follow, and a CEO-based governance structure. Peters said that was fine
with him. But then, said Stender, when two of the new trustees, Dickie
Wong and Lokelani Lindsey, joined the board at the beginning of 1993,

Richard Sung Hong "Dickie" Wong had been president of the state senate for a record thirteen years before being named a Bishop Estate trustee near the end of 1992.

"I was making this speech, how we're gonna reorganize, I'm gonna be the chair, and we gotta do the strategic plan first, and Peters said, 'I changed my mind'"—Wong should chair the board. And that was that.

Richard Sung Hong "Dickie" Wong, fifty-nine years old at the time of his appointment, was a union business agent turned career politician. Successful in state politics for twenty-six years, he had been president of the state senate for the last thirteen of those years, longer than anyone else in history. Wong was known for his political shrewdness and for letting key senators operate their respective committees like fiefdoms, making their own rules and wielding their power freely. He also managed to always be on good terms with the sitting governor. In 1987, when Governor John Waiheʻe wanted a close associate, Gerard Jervis, added to the Judicial Selection Commission without putting his own fingerprints on the appointment, Wong offered to "trade picks."

The culture of the Bishop Estate board changed as much under Wong as its investment approach had changed under Takabuki. Had there been verbatim records of the twice-weekly meetings, they would have reported late starts, with trustees appearing anywhere up to an hour after the scheduled time, wandering in and out. Wong, the chairman, would joke, "Next guy comes in, you lock the door now, OK?" Eventually the meeting would begin, with trustees continuing to walk in and out, talking across and over each other, asking questions that had been covered in the written materials already circulated, and arguing, often with Peters banging the table, Lindsey laughing loudly, and Wong saying and doing next to nothing to move the meeting forward. Staff members could be left cooling their heels for an hour or two, maybe three. Even Michael Chun, the president of Kamehameha Schools, was treated in this way. Once inside, anyone could become the victim of a vicious attack. A senior staffer described what it was like to make a presentation to these trustees: "One dog barks and all the others start barking." Another staffer said, "We dreaded going in there. No one wanted to give them bad news. We knew we'd get hammered."

Stender considered such meetings a waste of time and an insult to Pauahi, and for a while he stopped attending. Wong, on the other hand, bragged about the environment he had created. Years later, while being questioned about his tenure as chairman, he described the boardroom as a place where trustees should be able to "wash their laundry" and "yell and scream" without having to air their dirty laundry in public.

Under Wong, the doors to the trustees' offices, which used to be open as a matter of policy, were always closed. There was a new set of locks on the boardroom level of Kawaiahaʻo Plaza. When activated, the centralized automatic locking system made a steel-to-steel noise. It sounded like lockdown.

chapter 7

The "Black and Blue" Panel

$\mathcal{B}y$ 1994 Governor John Waihe'e had appointed all five justices to Hawai'i's Supreme Court. In February of that year, trustee Myron Thompson would be seventy years old, the mandatory retirement age that had earlier been set by the state Supreme Court justices. It was no secret that Waihe'e was looking down the road to the end of his second and final term, which would be later that year. A Bishop Estate trusteeship would be a crowning achievement for the soon-to-be-former governor—and would bring with it a tenfold increase in his pay.

Normally the justices began their search for a successor well before a scheduled vacancy, but this time they did not. They never explained why. Many people speculated that the justices wanted to appoint Waihe'e. For justices to appoint to the board of Bishop Estate the man who had personally appointed all of them to the Supreme Court might strike the public as overly political, but then, what did not operate politically in Hawai'i? A president of the senate, Dickie Wong, had made it to the boardroom, as had William Richardson, a chief justice. Henry Peters had kept on being speaker of the house after his appointment to the supposedly non-political trusteeship. All three had appointed people to the Judicial Selection Commission, which played a key role in the selection of the justices. This struck many as a bit too cozy, yet it had happened, and without adverse political consequences to anyone.

Even so, the justices appeared skittish about appointing the governor. Waihe'e's popularity was at an all-time low. During his two terms as governor, he had managed to turn a large budget surplus into a huge

George Ariyoshi (left) became governor in 1974 after serving as John Burns'
lieutenant governor; John Waihe'e (center) became governor in 1986 after serving
as Ariyoshi's lieutenant governor; Ben Cayetano (right) became governor in 1994
after serving as Waihe'e's lieutenant governor.

deficit, and, because of a series of procurement and land-use scandals, a
growing segment of the public perceived his administration as corrupt.

It would assuredly look bad for a sitting governor to be moonlight-
ing as a Bishop Estate trustee. On the other hand, if the selection could
be delayed until later in the year, and if his name could be put on a
short list by a supposedly independent panel of people who were prominent in the community, then maybe the same result could be achieved:
Waihe'e might be made a Bishop Estate trustee without its provoking
the public too much.

Shortly before Thompson's scheduled retirement date, Chief Justice Ronald Moon announced that the justices had decided to appoint a
panel of community leaders to assist in filling the vacancy. This would
be the first time in the trust's history that anyone other than the justices
would have an official role in selecting a Bishop Estate trustee. It would
slow down the process, but Thompson would be allowed to serve beyond the end of his term, which would be another first. This approach,
as described by Moon, would instill public trust in a process that critics
had taken to calling "political."

The justices appointed eleven community leaders to what came to be called the "blue-ribbon panel." Two were former Bishop Estate trustees: Takabuki and Richardson. Three others were experienced in business: Henry Walker Jr., a former chairman and CEO of Amfac, one of the largest corporations in Hawai'i; Robert Pfeiffer, chairman of Alexander & Baldwin, another large Hawai'i corporation; and Herbert Cornuelle, chairman of the board at Campbell Estate. There were also Kenneth Mortimer, president of the University of Hawai'i; Gary Rodrigues, state director of the United Public Workers, a powerful union; Alvin Shim, an attorney with a long involvement in politics; Melody MacKenzie, a founding member of the Native Hawaiian Bar Association; Monsignor Charles Kekumano, a retired Catholic priest who served on the board of the Queen Lili'uokalani Trust; and Gladys Kamakakūokalani Brandt, who had retired as the principal of Kamehameha Schools and was the current chair of the University of Hawai'i board of regents.

Mortimer had been at the University of Hawai'i for less than a year. Advisers told him to turn down Moon's invitation because service on the panel would be too political. When Mortimer relayed that message to Moon, the chief justice responded, "That's why you have to serve, Mr. President. We need to have a group that is not enmeshed in local politics and whose integrity is beyond question."

A few days later Mortimer and the other panel members gathered at the Supreme Court building, where Moon assured them that they could determine their own process; the justices would not interfere. Some of the panel members had doubts. They were concerned that the panel's list would be honored only if it had "the right name" on it. Pfeiffer looked squarely at Moon and asked, "Would the justices select from our list even if there were only one name on it?" For Pfeiffer and at least four others on the panel, getting the right answer to this question was a make-or-break condition of serving. Moon did not hesitate. He said he would rather have a longer list, but, yes, the panel's list would be honored, regardless of the number of names on it.

At its first working session the group named Brandt chairperson. She suggested a rule: that each name on the panel's list of finalists must have broad support, that a name not be there simply to accommodate a determined minority. She wanted to avoid the horse trading that was known to occur in sessions of the Judicial Selection Commission, where Waihe'e insiders like Gerard Jervis and Gary Rodrigues were adept at getting "the right name" added to each judicial selection list. A majority of Brandt's panel members agreed to her suggestion.

Gary Rodrigues ran the powerful United Public Workers union from 1981 until 2002, when a federal jury convicted him of mail fraud, money laundering, and embezzlement. He also stepped down from the Judicial Selection Commission at that time.

Brandt set an ambitious schedule for the panel and stuck to it. Within two months, members had received and considered more than a hundred applications. Deliberations went smoothly until Waiheʻe came up for discussion. Richardson, Shim, and Rodrigues wanted Waiheʻe's name added to the list of finalists; the others did not. The discussion dragged on and on, even after the panel cast formal votes and Waiheʻe fell well short of the required majority, eight to three. Rodrigues refused to move on. He eventually shouted at the others, ripped up the papers in front of him, and threw the shreds across the table. Brandt, now eighty-seven years old, told Rodrigues to behave himself. He responded that he was tired of being treated like a child. "Gary," said Brandt, "when you act like a child, you must expect to be treated like a child." Rodrigues stormed out of the room, reportedly straight to a telephone. According to Henry Walker, within minutes Rodrigues had reached Waiheʻe.

The next day Brandt took the list (which contained the names of five candidates and had been signed by everyone on the panel but Rodrigues) to the Supreme Court building. There were five copies for the justices, each one sealed in a separate envelope. Brandt intended to drop them off and leave, but a secretary asked her to step into a side room, where the justices had gathered. Following a brief exchange of pleasantries Brandt handed them the envelopes, then stood by silently as the justices each took out the list and looked at it. Brandt later recalled, "They didn't say anything; they just looked at the paper. Finally, one of them said, 'Where's his name?'" Brandt responded that the panel had considered adding the governor's name to the list but a motion to do so did not pass. She added that some panel members were of the opinion that there already were enough politicians serving on the board.

Brandt could tell that the justices were not pleased with the list, but she just assumed that in a matter of days the justices would announce which one of the five individuals on the list would be the next Bishop Estate trustee. But days passed without a word from the justices, and then more days. After a week without uttering a public word, the justices announced that they had decided to postpone the choosing of the new trustee. They said they first would seek an opinion from the Commission on Judicial Conduct, an unofficial group whose members they had chosen. Five months later, that commission announced that the justices were not legally obligated to use a trustee-screening panel. Moon wrote to the blue-ribbon panel: "Based on the advisory opinion and based on our individual consciences, we believe it only fair to reopen the application process."

When Pfeiffer heard what the justices had done, he swore that he would never again serve on a government panel in Hawai'i. Others from the blue-ribbon group agreed, telling Brandt that they felt "used and abused." From then on, she referred to the group as the "black and blue" panel.

The justices eventually wrote that although they had "set no parameters on the search and [given] no directions," they had wanted "a list of finalists who were the most eminently qualified individuals." According to the justices, "for reasons known only to the panelists, their list did not include the names of all 'eminently qualified' applicants."

On November 25, 1994, more than nine months after a retirement date that had been known for years, the justices filled the vacancy with someone whose name had not appeared on the blue ribbon panel's list. In the opinion of Hawai'i's five Supreme Court justices, the most "eminently qualified applicant" was none other than Waihe'e's closest associate, Gerard Jervis.

"Wait and see," said Supreme Court Justice Steven Levinson. "Gerry Jervis will be a great trustee."

Many suspected that Jervis was just a seat warmer who would resign when a politically safe opportunity arose to appoint Waihe'e, but the trustees encountered bigger troubles before this scenario had any chance to play out.

Gerard Jervis, a close political associate of Governor Waiheʻe, became a Bishop Estate trustee in 1994 despite not making it to the short list of candidates provided by the independent blue-ribbon panel.

*A*fter *leaving office,* Waiheʻe joined a Washington, D.C., law firm that the trustees immediately hired to find a way for them to avoid state and federal oversight and to lobby against pending federal legislation that would limit trustee compensation. A few years later, law enforcement personnel searched a secret office safe at Kawaiahaʻo Plaza and found a computer file named "CJ" that contained an astonishing two-page memo from "Nam" to "Speaker." "Nam" was Namlyn Snow, who worked directly for Henry Peters. "Speaker" was Peters. "CJ" was Chief Justice Moon. The memo's subject was "Trustee Selection Process," and it was dated March 21, 1994, immediately after Gladys Brandt had delivered the blue-ribbon panel's list of names to the justices. In this memo, Snow, an employee of a charitable trust, mapped out a plan by which the justices of Hawai'i's Supreme Court could steer the trustee nomination process back onto a more congenial track:

Speaker, events with regard to this appointment may be fast-breaking and there may not be much time to have any meaningful input on strategy with those "under the gun" which is key to an undesired outcome. . . . CJ Moon [should] issue a press release. . . . In the press release CJ Moon can also say that the justices, acting as individuals, accept full responsibility for the final selection in accordance with the provisions of Mrs. Bishop's will and do not wish to shirk that responsibility. A statement to this effect serves to say "The buck stops here" and regardless of any committee recommendations, the justices alone have to make the decision.

CJ and the justices can issue a statement saying that while the committee guidelines excluded . . . politicians, the justices were looking for the most qualified candidate and did not see a person's career in public service *per se* as a disqualifying factor. Those who serve in elected public office were chosen by our citizens to represent us. The fact that they are good enough to represent our citizens should not be used as an indictment against their abilities to sit on the [Bishop Estate] board of trustees. In fact, recognizing the current mood of certain segments of the community and the tremendous pressure which is being applied to exclude the appointment of politicians to the board of trustees, the appointment of this candidate was not an easy decision. The outstanding and exceptional career and performance of this appointee won the unanimous approval of the individual members of the court.

The steps laid out in the secret memo bore a remarkable similarity to the steps Moon and the other justices took at the time: "In certain aspects, the justices' writings and actions closely match reactions and announcements scripted by Snow," according to a confidential report submitted to the attorney general and Campaign Spending Commission in 2000.

The Snow memo was a smoking gun, but there was even more evidence of behind-the-scenes manipulation. Although verbatim minutes of trustee meetings were never taken, investigators eventually gained access to handwritten notes Lokelani Lindsey had made during these meetings. One such note, dated weeks before the justices formed the blue-ribbon panel, listed the names of Pfeiffer, Cornuelle, Brandt, Shim, Richardson, and Takabuki, who were all later named to the panel by Moon. Also among Lindsey's jottings were statements concerning the selection of a new trustee by the justices and the ways in which a screening committee could be used to achieve the desired outcome. Bearing in mind the possibility that the justices already knew who they wanted to pick and that they perceived a need to slow down the selection process, Lindsey wrote: "If they already made up their minds . . . the screening committee will be an excellent way to go." Then she added: "Only mechanism to allow the delay to occur is the committee."

Lindsey's handwritten notes and Snow's secret memo raised serious concerns about the justices' independence and increased the chances that someone would sue them for breaching the fiduciary duties they accepted when they agreed to select trustees. Individuals cannot be forced to select trustees, but anyone who accepts such a power is required to use it to further the trust's charitable mission, not for personal gain or political payback. This legal exposure gave the justices strong personal incentives not to cooperate with any investigation of Bishop Estate trustees. In fact, the justices' personal interests would be best served if any such investigation could be shut down prematurely and the records sealed, incentives that were to play out strongly in events to come.

chapter 8

Five Fingers, One Hand

Matsuo Takabuki's decision to take control of investing marked the beginning of what evolved into a "lead trustee" system, in which trustee functions and areas of responsibility were divvied up among the Bishop Estate trustees. This was a serious breach of trust for a number of reasons. For example, each co-trustee has a fiduciary duty to stay informed and involved, and to petition the appropriate court when confronted with serious, ongoing breaches of trust. Under Bishop Estate's lead trustee system, however, access to information was tightly controlled, even among trustees. A single trustee was able to decide what information would go out from his or her area; when, in which directions, and in what form it would be presented to the board; or whether it would be presented at all.

By 1995 the lead trustee system was both deeply rooted and pervasive. Henry Peters was in control of asset management, Lokelani Lindsey had education and communications, Dickie Wong handled government relations, and Gerard Jervis was in charge of legal affairs. For a while Oz Stender was lead trustee for alumni relations, but then the other trustees took that away, and he was left with nothing.

Stender was constantly surprised by decisions made by single trustees, such as the hiring of Yukio Takemoto to manage contracts. Takemoto had left the Waihe'e administration under a dark cloud. His activities in administering contracts, especially non-bid contracts, were the subject of an extensive investigation and serious allegations. Without Stender's even knowing it was a possibility, Dickie Wong hired Takemoto to administer all of Bishop Estate's contracts. He also gave Takemoto a large budget and a thirteen-person staff.

Immediately after Yukio Takemoto left the Waihe'e administration, Dickie Wong hired him to administer contracts for Bishop Estate.

Stender also was surprised by Bishop Estate's increasingly creative record keeping. Sometimes there would be three sets of minutes for a single meeting. Anything deemed sensitive was stamped "Confidential—Attorney-Client Privilege" and held by Bishop Estate's chief in-house lawyer, Nathan Aipa. For years people whose job it was to keep an eye on the trustees, such as court-appointed masters and lawyers in the attorney general's office, did not even know these documents existed. The trustees took the absurd position that anything said or done in Aipa's presence, as well as anything given to him for safekeeping, was protected by attorney-client privilege and for that reason could be kept secret.

During the 1990s the trustees hired dozens of outside lawyers while adding yet more lawyers to Aipa's in-house staff. Despite the presence of so many lawyers, there was never a written policy on conflicts of interest, and no significant effort was ever made to acquaint the trustees with even the rudiments of their fiduciary duties. On one occasion Stender took it upon himself to arrange a workshop on basic trust law for his fellow trustees. Edward Halbach, the nation's top expert on trusts and someone who cared deeply about Bishop Estate's charitable mission, agreed to fly in to lead the discussion, pro bono. But when the other trustees refused to attend, Stender had to tell Halbach not to come.

The trustees' lawyers produced a long, detailed handbook for Bishop Estate employees, but none of it applied to the trustees. For them there were no rules, and for their actions, no matter how outrageous, no consequences. Henry Peters could swear at or physically intimidate anyone, at any time, in or out of the boardroom, and not have to account for his behavior. Dickie Wong could park in a red zone and not worry about having his car ticketed or towed. Gerard Jervis could demand that a particular applicant be admitted to Kamehameha or that expelled students be reinstated and see it happen. Lokelani Lindsey could spend $128,000 from the school's staff development budget on a special diet program for herself and her friends without board approval or even the school president's knowledge.

Bishop Estate trustees had not always been so arrogant. Staff members talked wistfully about former trustees who would join them regularly for coffee and who cared about them and their families. In those earlier days, trustees had get-togethers when people joined or left the

staff. The company car was a Volkswagen Beetle. Staff members recalled seeing it "blazing down the street with three trustees in it."

Under English common law, trustees were expected to serve without compensation unless the trust document said otherwise. Pauahi's will said nothing about trustee fees. In 1884 the Hawai'i Supreme Court ruled that trustees of any trust could take "reasonable compensation for their time and trouble." In 1927 the legislature established statutory formulas that trustees could use when setting their fees for any particular year. These formulas changed from time to time. In most years the maximum trustee fee was set at slightly more than 2 percent—but of what? Did the formula apply to net or gross income? Gains or net gains? The answers to these critically important questions were never clear. Compounding the uncertainty, the trustees never stated publicly how they were interpreting or applying the formulas. Most years they apparently applied a liberal interpretation of the formulas and then divided the resulting amount among themselves in equal shares. This approach drew scattered criticism but did not produce shockingly high numbers until the mid-1980s, after the U.S. Supreme Court upheld the 1967 mandatory leasehold conversion law. By 1987 trustee fees had grown to slightly more than $925,000 per trustee.

Trustees at prominent private schools in Hawai'i, such as Punahou, 'Iolani, and Mid-Pacific Institute on O'ahu; Seabury Hall on Maui; and Hawai'i Preparatory Academy on the Big Island, took no compensation. Neither did members of the governing boards at well-endowed universities, such as Harvard, Yale, and Stanford. It had always been that way. Why would Bishop Estate be different?

The pat answer provided by Bishop Estate trustees was that, unlike the governing boards at other charitable institutions, the trustees at Bishop Estate functioned as lead trustees, which made them the equivalent of full-time CEOs, rather than part-time directors. Dickie Wong frequently expressed pride in the lead trustee system, describing it as "five fingers acting as one hand." He said it enabled the trustees to do the work of a chief executive officer, chief operating officer, chief financial officer, chief legal officer, and chief communications officer, as well as a board of directors. When asked under oath who held the five trustees accountable for good results, Wong first said, "Nobody," then changed his answer to "Us."

The trustees had effectively hired themselves to run the organiza-

tion, a highly unusual move. There were no job descriptions, performance standards, or annual reviews, and no one except they themselves had the power to conduct such reviews. The trustees of Bishop Estate had power without accountability, a recipe for disaster.

There are people who are responsible for oversight of charitable trusts. The state attorney general, as *parens patriae,* has the responsibility and ongoing power to investigate indications of trust abuse, and to ask the courts to take action when trustee misconduct is found. Even if the attorney general falls short in providing such oversight, the state court with jurisdiction over trusts—in Hawai'i, the probate court—has the power to take action *sua sponte* (on its own) when it sees trust abuse. Hawai'i also provides for a master to review the trustees' accounts each year. Before 1970 masters were hired by the attorney general. Since then they have been selected by the probate judge and given responsibilities and powers of investigation much like those of the attorney general.

Supreme Court justices who selected trustees arguably had an ongoing responsibility to take appropriate action in the face of serious trust abuse by anyone they selected. Also, probate court rules since 1995 have required lawyers to report misconduct by their trustee clients directly to the probate court.

Despite glaring problems at Bishop Estate for many years, all these lawyers, specifically attorneys general, probate judges, masters, justices of the Supreme Court, and trust counsel, acted as though everything was as it should be. Year after year, decade after decade, attorneys general never investigated, and masters appointed by the probate court never scratched below the surface. In fact, many of the masters submitted fawning reports. The high-water mark was reached by master Alvin Shim in his 1988 report. Bishop Estate trustees, he gushed, were doing an "awesome" job. That particular adjective appeared seventeen times in his twenty-five-page, double-spaced report. Although loaded with adjectives, the report entirely lacked the kind of information readers (namely, the probate court judge) needed to agree or disagree with Shim's "awesome" conclusions.

Even masters inclined to take their job seriously would have found the going difficult. Bishop Estate lawyers served as gatekeepers. Speaking on condition of anonymity, one former master described how Bishop Estate lawyers had made sure he saw only what they wanted him to see, and not the rest:

> They would get someone like me and say, "Here's how this is done: you're not entitled to this, you don't get into that." That sort of thing. There's such a sense of history, of tradition, and you know they are the experts on all this; they have been around for a long time and have this huge bank of institutional knowledge, and it's natural for the master to be reliant on them. To some degree you have no choice but to rely on them.

A senior staff member described it from the inside:

> Masters would come in and they'd do a cursory review of the Estate, a cursory interview up on campus, and then they would come in and negotiate what would be in the master's report. Trustees had editing rights over that stuff. They would see it before it went to the court; they got to vet it; they got to go through and say, "We don't agree, that needs to be taken out." And unless the master was just adamant about stuff getting left in, it would go out.

Judging from the reports that were submitted to the probate court, few masters were adamant about anything. In 1988, when the trustees wanted to keep secret the $599,000 annual raise they had just given

Alvin Shim served as a court-appointed master and member of the blue-ribbon panel.

the trustees in arguing to the court that the numbers should remain a secret. Shim's explanation for not telling the public was that Hawaiian cultural modesty weighed in favor of non-disclosure.

𝒻rom time to time Mainland newspapers and magazines printed stories on Bishop Estate. Reporters would come to Hawai'i for a few days, a week or two at most, and go away shaking their heads. Every article they wrote covered basically the same ground: the huge size of Bishop Estate, the concentration of land, money, and power it represented, its reach, its connections with other sources of power, its penchant for secrecy, and its disdain for outsiders. The articles all seemed to be reports of strange happenings in a faraway place, which by some forgotten historical circumstance had come to be under the American flag but did not behave like a state under the American legal system. The tone was one of amazement that such an obvious and extreme situation had apparently been going on unchallenged in Hawai'i for a long time.

Meanwhile, local media coverage tended to be superficial and approving. In the second half of the twentieth century there were fewer than half a dozen serious newspaper analyses of Bishop Estate—approximately one per decade. Two of these were in the short-lived *Hawai'i Observer,* whose circulation never reached more than about five thousand.

Most media executives seemed disinclined to investigate Bishop Estate's shady dealings. There were reasons.

In 1987 the *Honolulu Star-Bulletin* decided to do an in-depth story, perhaps a series. Just minutes after a reporter showed up at Bishop Estate headquarters, though, the *Star-Bulletin*'s managing editor, David Shapiro, got a phone call from Bishop Estate's director of communications, Neil Hannahs, who called the uninvited coverage "an invasion of privacy" and demanded that it be stopped immediately. Roadblocks placed in the reporter's way slowed the *Star-Bulletin*, but his work eventually appeared. Shapiro described the fallout: "After the story was written, there was a lot of pressure not to publish it. After we did, they came down on us in every way they could. They tried to punish us." A $40,000 advertising supplement was canceled, a complaint was filed with the Honolulu Media Council, and a resolution was introduced on the floor of the state legislature denouncing the *Star-Bulletin* for trying to make the trust and its trustees look bad.

A reporter for *The Honolulu Advertiser* did some good investigative work on Bishop Estate nearly a decade later, but then the *Advertiser*'s publisher instructed the reporter's supervisor to redirect those efforts. His explanation was that *Advertiser* readers were tired of reading negative things about Bishop Estate.

This was an era of enormous power for the people who ran Hawai'i's government. What was noteworthy was not the power itself, but its concentration. There seemed to be less and less separation between individual branches of government, which were supposed to act independently—and also between Hawai'i's government and Bishop Estate.

As control became more centralized, accountability suffered. The media did less investigative reporting, not only of Bishop Estate, but of government. Critical thinkers at the University of Hawai'i focused on national and international issues rather than on local politics. Bar association presidents never criticized judicial selection, even at its political worst, nor did they talk publicly about the judiciary's role in politicizing trustee selection at Bishop Estate. Businessmen, conscious of this concentrated power and motivated by a desire for favorable treatment (or wanting to avoid unfavorable treatment), did not say no when asked for political contributions or other favors. Anyone who wanted to get ahead in Hawai'i assiduously avoided being viewed as a critic, or even associating with the relatively few outspoken critics.

Politics in Hawai'i was like politics elsewhere, only more so.

chapter 9

The Education Trustee

In 1988 Bishop Estate needed a new president of Kamehameha Schools. Until then, all the men who ran Kamehameha had been *haole*. Now, 102 years after the Schools' founding, the trustees wanted a Hawaiian. Two graduates emerged as the top two candidates: Hamilton I. McCubbin, class of 1959, who had a doctorate in school psychology and child welfare from the University of Wisconsin-Madison, where he was serving as dean of the School of Human Ecology; and Michael J. Chun, class of 1961, who had a doctorate in environmental health engineering and a bachelor's degree in civil engineering, both from the University of Kansas, and experience in county government in Hawai'i. McCubbin and Chun each had two strong supporters on the board of trustees. McCubbin's supporters had nothing against Chun, except that he was an engineer, not an educator. Chun's supporters saw him as charismatic and politically *akamai* (smart) and were dubious of McCubbin's ability to inspire. After much discussion, the vote went for Chun.

Michael Chun was Kamehameha, inside and out; from kindergarten onward, he had been a credit to the school. He was a star athlete, the first Kamehameha boy ever to be named to the National High School All-American Football Team. He was runner-up for the Quarterback Club of Honolulu's Sportsman of the Year Award, second only to an Olympic weight lifter, and he won the Schuman Award for outstanding sportsmanship, leadership, and academic work, and for displaying high moral and spiritual values. He sang in the boys' glee club and the mixed chorus, made the National Honor Society, was elected boys' student body president, and was a top ROTC cadet, company commander.

Chun replaced Jack Darvill, who had taken early retirement be-

Michael Chun became the first Hawaiian president of Kamehameha Schools in 1988.

cause of controversy over a lottery admissions policy that had been in place since 1979 and that Chun inherited. Lottery admissions had grown out of the ongoing debate over what kind of children should be admitted to Kamehameha Schools. Darvill's idea had been to diversify Kamehameha's student body by eliminating the selective admissions system at the kindergarten level and replacing it with a lottery system open to all qualified Hawaiian children, not just the brightest. Competitive admissions kicked in at the seventh-grade level; to keep their spots, elementary-school students who had been attending Kamehameha had to compete, without being given preference, against bright and interested Hawaiian students from all other schools. The controversy erupted when the majority of a cohort of Kamehameha Schools students who had been admitted by lottery failed to gain entry into the seventh grade.

Takabuki wrote in his memoir, *An Unlikely Revolutionary*, that "the result for these students and their parents was traumatic. . . . There was a feeling that the school did not do enough to prepare these students and that their failure to move on to the seventh grade tainted them as 'inferior' or 'stupid.'" Emotions were almost unbelievably high. Darvill reportedly received death threats.

Soon after his appointment, Chun recommended terminating the lottery system. The trustees agreed. In the future all admissions would be based strictly on competitive tests, but once children were accepted at Kamehameha they could stay as long as they kept up their grades and stayed out of trouble.

As president of Kamehameha Schools, Chun was enormously popular with parents and students. They saw him as a good and industrious person who made himself available to everyone. There was always something going on at Kamehameha, and Chun was always on the scene— at track meets, the prom, ROTC spring camp, the fifth-grade play. He could be seen participating in a student run or riding on the team bus to a Warrior game. The day after each game, he would look for players to congratulate or console. He maintained an open-door policy at his campus home, Hale Pelekikena—students could drop in after school for a soda, sit and "talk story," play music, and raid the refrigerator for leftovers. Chun regularly went with students to volunteer at the Institute for Human Services, a homeless shelter, where they sliced vegetables and helped serve meals. He put part of his salary into a private foundation for youngsters with special needs and never made a public issue of his acts of generosity. He drew students to him without effort or guile; they felt like part of his 'ohana. Many referred to him as "Uncle Mike."

He had equally good relations with his fellow alumni. He was one of them, and although he had achieved much in life, he showed no sign of arrogance or pretentiousness. There was nothing about him that would not have made Princess Pauahi proud.

After nearly five years of smooth sailing, however, "Uncle Mike" was about to hit stormy seas. The newest trustee, Lokelani Lindsey, had just been made lead trustee for education, and she had definite thoughts about what was needed at Kamehameha.

When Marion Mae Lokelani Maples Lindsey joined the Bishop Estate board in 1993 at the age of fifty-three, it marked the first time in the history of Bishop Estate that all five trustees were Hawaiian—and that one of them was a woman. Lindsey had a bachelor's degree in physical edu-

Marion Mae Lokelani Maples Lindsey was the first woman named to the Bishop Estate board of trustees.

cation from Church College of Hawai'i and a master's degree in Pacific Island studies from the University of Hawai'i. She had been one of the first *hula* dancers at the Polynesian Cultural Center and had led her own *hālau*. She had spent almost all of her adult life working in Hawai'i's Department of Education, teaching physical education for eleven years, then serving as vice principal at three different schools in four years, principal at a fourth school in Honolulu for one year, and district superintendent for eleven years on Maui. In 1990 she ran unsuccessfully for mayor of Maui County.

A practicing Mormon, Lindsey said she satisfied the religion requirement in Pauahi's will (that trustees be members of the Protestant religion) because she had been baptized in Kawaiaha'o Church as an infant. Reverend Akaka, pastor of Kawaiahaʻo Church, told reporters that once having been a Protestant was not the test: "Trustees of Princess Pauahi's estate and schools should first of all be faithful, active . . . and exemplary members of their Protestant churches." But Reverend Akaka did not press his point, the justices and the other trustees declined to comment, and the issue died quickly.

The chairman of the state Office of Hawaiian Affairs, Clayton Hee, praised the justices for their wisdom in selecting Lindsey, calling it an inspired choice. Lindsey's credentials as an educator, according to Hee, were "beyond question." Evidently neither Hee nor the justices had checked with Lindsey's co-workers at the DOE, who did not consider her much of an educator. The Lindsey they knew tended to be "self-seeking," "heavy-handed," "unable to work collaboratively," "volatile," "incapable of compromise," "not the kind of person who could motivate the people under her," and "vindictive."

Senior DOE administrators said that Lindsey always made sure the people around her knew both that Governor Waiheʻe was her cousin and that he had taken a personal interest in her career, as if those facts made her someone not to be taken lightly. She bragged to them that for years the state superintendent of education, Charles Toguchi, had wanted to fire her but never could because she was too powerful politically.

Despite Lindsey's interest in politics, her co-workers and her boss were caught off guard by the news of her appointment. Charles Toguchi described how he found out. "I was driving on the Pali and got a call on my cell phone from a woman yelling and screaming, 'I got it, I got it!'"

Toguchi had no idea who the caller was, or what she was talking about, so he asked, "Who is this?"

The person on the other end said, "It's Lokelani Lindsey, and I got it. I'm a trustee!"

"A trustee of what?" asked Toguchi.

"Bishop Estate! I'm a trustee of Bishop Estate!" Lindsey replied triumphantly.

Toguchi said that he almost hit the car in front of him when it slowed to make a turn. He had been trying to picture Lindsey as a Bishop Estate trustee.

Shortly after her appointment, Lindsey's fellow trustees named her lead trustee for education, yet provided no written or even oral guidelines as to what that meant. Oz Stender was not pleased. He felt strongly that the trustees' job was to make the trust estate optimally productive, not to run Kamehameha Schools. Professional educators should be hired to do that. The National Association of Independent Schools agreed; their principles of good practice for trustees stated: "An individual trustee does not become involved in specific management, personnel, or curricular issues." Lindsey saw things differently. She immediately set up an office for herself on campus in the administration building, opposite the office of the president, Michael Chun. From there she involved herself in personnel decisions, issued edicts on curriculum, and virtually took over the school's budget, questioning individual line items all the way down to 250 ballpoint pens at ten cents each.

A few months later the trustees gave Lindsey another lead trusteeship, putting her in charge of communications, not just on campus but also at Kawaiahaʻo Plaza. Soon she was personally reviewing a wide range of written communications. At Kawaiahaʻo Plaza, this included everything from advertising and news releases to social invitations and Christmas card design. At the campus, she perused newsletters, handbooks, administrative forms, bulletin-board signs, teachers' letters to parents, and even the wording on tickets, magnets, and T-shirts.

Whether at headquarters or on campus, Lindsey—for different reasons from Chun—could not be missed. She ordered an extra-large parking stall and regularly engaged in what she called "walking-around management." Wearing a square-shouldered suit jacket with as many as a dozen heavy gold bracelets jangling on one arm, Lindsey would enter classrooms and offices, usually with an entourage, unannounced and uninvited.

Lindsey routinely ordered Bishop Estate staffers to run errands for her—not just small things (shopping, picking up her grandchildren and driving them places), but big ones too. When the renovation of her beach house needed variances from state and county rules, Lindsey ordered two high-level staffers to attend to the matter. They did the necessary work on Bishop Estate time, over a period of thirteen months, totaling 150 hours for one, 30 hours for the other. Then there was travel. Lindsey's inter-island trips typically were taken with an entourage that sometimes took up an entire first-class cabin. There also were numerous trips to the Mainland and Asia, always first class, often with companions added at the last moment, even if the travel budget was already depleted. Lindsey made at least sixteen trips to Las Vegas, the first just six weeks after being appointed to the board. Because she never filed a report on any of these trips, it was not clear what connection they had to her work as trustee. This violated both common sense and the trustee's fiduciary duty not to benefit personally from the trust's resources.

Lindsey did not get along with the popular president of Kamehameha Schools. She insisted that it was not personal; she had the greatest *aloha* for Chun. She considered him a nice man with a good heart—just no good at his work. She told Chun he needed a vice president. Chun disagreed, but Lindsey insisted. Lindsey said Chun could decide whom to hire, with one catch—it had to be someone from her list. Lindsey's list contained two names: Gilbert Tam, a longtime Bishop Estate employee who had no training or experience as an educator, and Rockne Freitas, a former professional football player who had gone on to be an administrator at the University of Hawai'i. Each had close ties to Lindsey, Peters, and Wong. Chun chose Freitas, mainly because the two of them had grown up as neighbors in Lanikai on O'ahu's windward coast and had played sports together at Kamehameha.

Chun drew up an organizational chart in which the educational units at Kamehameha reported directly to the president, as they had always done, with the vice president off to one side. Lindsey rejected that. Her organizational chart had the new vice president positioned between Chun and everybody else at Kamehameha. It was soon clear that she wanted Freitas running the school and Chun merely overseeing curriculum and planning. All major directives went from Lindsey to Freitas and then to staff.

The teachers viewed Freitas as Lindsey's agent, someone who would do what she wanted done without hesitation or complaint. A short time spent working with him convinced them they could not take him seriously as an educator. Once, during a meeting to discuss the curriculum, teachers contended that changes were needed to get students to think more critically and communicate more effectively. Freitas reportedly pointed to statistics showing that more than three out of four Kamehameha graduates were going on to four-year colleges and asked, "If a kid gets into college, what do we care if he can write effectively?" At first the teachers thought he was joking. Then they realized he wasn't.

From the beginning of Michael Chun's tenure as Kamehameha's president, he and his wife, Bina, had used Hale Pelekikena for all kinds of occasions—welcoming to the campus parents, alumni, leaders of Hawaiian organizations, boards of nonprofit groups, and the Kau Kau Club, an exclusive dinner club that included the governor and leaders

Rockne Freitas served as Kamehameha Schools' vice president and reported directly to Lokelani Lindsey.

from the business community. The Chuns entertained one night in every three, year round, and the cost was high—too high, in Lindsey's opinion. She ordered the head of food services to do a spreadsheet on all the costs of entertaining at Hale Pelekikena, with a stern warning not to juggle any figures. It took a week's work. She also had the accounting staff at Kawaiaha'o Plaza print out a computer record of everything the Chuns had ever purchased with Bishop Estate money. The document was six inches thick.

Chun was not the only person who suffered under Lindsey's watchful eye and heavy hand. Teachers and employees all over Kamehameha were feeling the pressure. Lindsey's micromanagerial style reached everywhere, especially into areas of the school where she felt she had special expertise. One such area was the Hawaiian language program—even though she herself did not know how to speak or read Hawaiian.

For many years, Kamehameha's Hawaiian language teachers had been the campus authorities on questions pertaining to the subject. Lindsey did not like that arrangement; the teachers were too accommodating of new words. For example, they chose to use a relatively new Hawaiian word, *kīwī*, for television, rather than use a combination of older Hawaiian words that translated roughly to "box with moving pictures." The teachers saw the introduction of new words as necessary for the language to survive; Lindsey believed they were corrupting the language of her ancestors.

The first skirmish started out innocently, when a parent phoned a thirty-year veteran of the Hawaiian language department to ask what Hawaiian word should be used on a T-shirt for the girls' basketball team. The teacher suggested *pōhīna'i*, a relatively new but commonly used word. Lindsey heard about this and said the word *pōhīna'i* was not acceptable because it had not existed at the time of Pauahi. To support her in such matters, Lindsey formed a Hawaiian language committee. She gave the chairmanship of the committee to her secretary and seemed to make a point of not including anyone from Kamehameha's Hawaiian language department.

The teachers from the Hawaiian language department requested a meeting with Lindsey to discuss the situation. The meeting was to be held in Konia Hall, a building named after Pauahi's birth mother. The teachers were apprehensive. Earlier in the day, Tony Ramos, Kamehameha's high-school principal, had warned them: "Don't try to fight her, 'cause you're gonna lose." After much discussion among themselves, they decided to go forward with the meeting anyway.

The meeting began with *pule* (prayer) in Hawaiian and light refreshments. Then Lindsey walked up to the blackboard and erased the list of issues the teachers had written on it, saying, "I don't like agendas." She sat on a table at the front of the room and told the group that she could trace her genealogy on her father's side to Hewahewa, counselor to Pauahi's great-grandfather, Kamehameha the Great, for whom the school was named. According to Lindsey, one of her responsibilities was to protect the language and culture of her ancestors: "Failure to teach, and thus preserve 'traditional' Hawaiian, could lead to 'cultural genocide.'" Lindsey added that Pauahi's will gave trustees full authority to be "very hands on," which was exactly what she intended to be.

The teachers could see that Ramos had been right. The take-home message was clear: "Stay out of my way."

Lindsey's activities were not limited to curriculum issues. A promoter named Robert Van Dyke had approached Oz Stender in 1995 with an offer to sell a large collection of Hawaiiana—books and photographs—to Bishop Estate for $450,000. When Stender said he was not interested, Van Dyke immediately lowered the asking price to $250,000. Stender then asked the librarian of Kamehameha's Hawaiiana collection to look at a sampling of items. When she told him that Van Dyke's collection had little value to the school, Stender turned down Van Dyke's offer.

Six months later Van Dyke offered the same collection to Lindsey for $500,000. She asked him, "Can't you make it cheaper?" When he lowered the price to $425,000, Lindsey told him not to sell to anyone else; she wanted time to arrange for the purchase. Without checking with anyone at the school or asking that the matter be put on the agenda, Lindsey brought the purchase up at the next trustees' meeting. She told the other trustees that she was an expert on Hawaiiana and that in her opinion the Van Dyke collection was worth much more than the asking price. She strongly recommended that the trustees buy it "for educational purposes."

The board voted four to nothing to make the purchase; Stender was absent. There were, however, two standard conditions: Van Dyke had to prove that the collection was his to sell, and an independent expert had to agree that the collection was worth the asking price. Until proof of ownership and an appraisal were added to the file, the bulk of the $425,000 purchase price would be held in escrow. When Lindsey told Van Dyke about the conditions, however, he said that he probably would not be able to find all the documents of ownership and that getting an appraisal would be a waste of time and money. He said he would cancel the deal and sell the collection to a full-price buyer if he did not get his money right away.

Lindsey pleaded with him to reconsider and then offered to pay him $250,000 immediately, the rest to be paid when the appraisal was done. He agreed, and Lindsey ordered the money transferred from escrow—all without informing the other trustees.

Henry Peters' vote to purchase the collection had come with his own condition: Albert Jeremiah had to do the appraisal. Jeremiah, a lawyer and Peters' close friend, was already receiving a $7,000 monthly retainer to keep an eye on issues of concern at city hall. Jeremiah's sole qualification as an appraiser of the Van Dyke collection was that he had once run a little weekend business buying and selling such things as sports cards, stamps, and milk-bottle tops. When asked why he had been chosen to catalog and appraise the books and photographs, Jeremiah said, "I'm a collector. They needed someone to look at what they bought. What's the big deal?"

Jeremiah reportedly received $35,000 for his opinion that Van Dyke's books were worth considerably more than the purchase price. The transaction was completed, and the entire collection was delivered to the campus. It was then reviewed by Kamehameha's longtime Hawaiiana collections librarian. She said the same thing of the entire collection that she had said of the samples Stender had shown her: it was worth next to nothing to Kamehameha Schools.

In addition to Hawaiiana books and photographs, Lindsey considered herself an expert on educational technology—specifically, the use of computers in the classroom. Shortly after setting up an office at Kamehameha, she arranged for a company named Education Management Group (EMG) to develop a distance-learning plan for the school. EMG, based in Arizona, specialized in supplying curricula by satellite. Lindsey had gotten to know EMG executives while she was still with the state Department of Education on Maui.

EMG recommended that Kamehameha acquire cutting-edge hardware and software, workstations linked across campus, satellite dishes to receive instructional materials relayed from EMG headquarters, and ongoing training and maintenance. There would be a pilot program involving eight workstations in anticipation of what would quickly grow to five hundred computers, plus infrastructure and support, at a minimum cost of $30 million.

A Kamehameha systems analyst criticized the EMG proposal as "vague" and added that it penciled out to a minimum of $41,000 per teacher workstation in the high school. He called that figure "outrageous." When Lindsey saw the analyst's report, she demanded that the analyst have nothing more to do with the EMG proposal. According to her, he was getting in the way of the EMG "point person": Gilbert Tam, the man Michael Chun had *not* chosen from Lindsey's vice presidential short list.

Lindsey liked doing business with EMG. A company saleswoman once arranged for a chartered jet to fly Lindsey and her husband, along with Rockne Freitas and another friend, Ben Bush III, to New Orleans for the Super Bowl. Not every vendor provided such service. Nevertheless, things did not go well with the company. Its curriculum materials were not a good fit for Kamehameha, and the teachers did not want to use them. Because EMG's software was proprietary, Kamehameha personnel could not load other software or modify the system in any way. No contract was ever signed, but EMG billed Bishop Estate on the basis of "verbal purchase orders." Bishop Estate paid the company between $5 million and $6 million before anyone started asking questions. When it looked as though the entire matter might be reviewed, files started disappearing from locked cabinets. Eventually EMG's services were terminated. Some of the hardware was cannibalized; everything else was discarded.

During Michael Chun's first few years as president, the Kamehameha faculty and staff had held numerous meetings and workshops to consider and debate the school's proper role and possible futures. The written product, "Educational Excellence for the Next Century: A Strategic Plan for the 1990s," was completed, a year before Lindsey joined the board, in a bottom-up style with little involvement from trustees or consultants. Essentially, Kamehameha administrators and teachers wanted the school to focus on producing leaders. Hawaiian children who didn't make the cut at Kamehameha could be served through the trust's extension programs.

Lindsey scrapped this plan and hired her own consultants to assess Kamehameha's educational programs, on and off campus. At a cost of several million dollars, these consultants produced reams of statistics and five separate scenarios for the board to consider. On April 17, 1995, the trustees voted unanimously in favor of the scenario entitled "Go Forward." It would be a major change in direction for the trust. At the center of the Go Forward vision were new schools on the islands of Maui and Hawai'i and an expansion of the center-based preschool program. This vision had its costs, though: to pay for the new schools, virtually all the extension programs had to go, immediately.

For three decades programs such as traveling preschools, parent-infant education, and alternative learning centers had been considered a key component of Kamehameha's mission, touching the lives of an ever-increasing number of Hawaiian children who did not attend Kamehameha Schools. The rationale for doing away with so many long-standing programs came from two directions: statistics in the studies done for Lindsey, which concluded that outreach was not cost-effective, and advice from lawyers, who supposedly said that outreach violated the terms of Pauahi's will and jeopardized the trust's tax exemption. As Lindsey described it, Kamehameha's sole charitable mission was to educate children in its own facilities, using its own teachers, and its own curriculum; anything else was just asking for trouble. She noted a 1910 decision of the territorial Supreme Court that any "support and education," as mentioned in Pauahi's will, had to be provided in the Kamehameha Schools. But when citing legal authority, she did not mention a probate court ruling in 1962 that specifically authorized Bishop Estate's off-campus extension programs.

Word of the trustees' decision rocked the organization to the core. For the first time in history, there were layoffs at Bishop Estate—171 jobs, 14 percent of the total workforce. On the sharp end of the cuts, everything about the termination seemed painfully wrong. Programs were closed abruptly, some with as little as two weeks' notice. A plan to help laid-off employees find other jobs amounted to almost nothing. The severance payments offered by the board looked and felt to the affected individuals like an insult, a multi-billion-dollar organization tossing peanuts onto the floor for them to pick up. And to receive even the tiny amount of money they were offered, the terminated employees had to sign a waiver agreeing not to sue the trustees. Such treatment might not be unusual in the business world, but Bishop Estate was a charitable institution, one that claimed to be rooted in Hawaiian values. People believed that working there meant belonging to an *'ohana,* with its relationships of trust, commitment, and mutual support. To be cut adrift felt like betrayal.

Chun had been against building schools on the outer islands. He preferred outreach and learning centers in Hawaiian communities, be-

lieving them to be better designed to serve at-risk children and far less expensive than big bricks-and-mortar campuses with large faculties and staffs. But Chun had been excluded completely from the decision making.

Stender liked the idea of satellite schools, which is what the new outer-island campuses were being called, but he was also for outreach. He voted to terminate the extension programs only because he had been told that Bishop Estate could not afford both. After that decision was made and announced, however, Stender went back through Bishop Estate's finances and came to the conclusion that there was more than enough money for both the new campuses and outreach. He laid out his new figures in a memo, pleading with the others to re-think the decision to terminate outreach. Lindsey, Peters, and Wong ignored the memo. Jervis wrote back, "The five of us agreed. We held hands, prayed and each committed ourselves to that collective decision. And then you stepped outside of that room and went back on your word."

Morale on campus sank dramatically under Lindsey's regime. She declared five-year contracts a thing of the past. These had been standard at Kamehameha; now everyone would have contracts that came up for renewal every year. One year she ordered teachers to return to the campus early from their summer break to redo the entire curriculum. They had two weeks to accomplish something that would normally take months. The teachers managed to meet the deadline, but their work did not please Lindsey. She rejected everything.

That year, 1996, the new campus on Maui opened a week late and in chaos. Lindsey told others it was additional evidence of Chun's incompetence. Chun, who could not hire anyone or purchase anything without Lindsey's express permission, said privately that he had not received the required approvals until seven weeks prior to the scheduled opening. His requests had sat on Lindsey's desk for over a year.

By this time Chun was entertaining far less frequently. He was seen at church on Sundays looking drained and diminished. He missed a deadline for a new educational strategic plan, sick in bed the day he was to present it to the board. When he finally was able to present it, Lindsey threw it into the trash as Chun and others watched.

There was a siege mentality on campus, a belief that Lindsey was out to get people who crossed her, that nobody was safe. The famous words of Martin Niemoller, a German pastor arrested by the Gestapo before

World War II and sent to a concentration camp, were photocopied and passed around:

> The Nazis first came for the communists, and I didn't speak up because I wasn't a communist. Then they came for the Jews, and I didn't speak up because I wasn't a Jew. Then they came for the trade unionists, and I didn't speak up because I wasn't a trade unionist. Then they came for the Catholics, and I didn't speak up because I was a Protestant. Then they came for me, and by that time there was no one left to speak for me.

The sheet's postscript was a quote from the political philosopher Edmund Burke:

> The only thing necessary for evil to triumph is for good men to do nothing.

If there was one event that could take people's minds off what was happening on campus, at least for a little while, it was Song Contest. Year after year, this one-evening event had been the high point of school life. Song Contest had started at the boys' school in 1921 with choral singing, the classes competing with one another. The first girls' school contest was in 1922.

By 1964 Song Contest had grown too big for the Kamehameha campus, so it was moved to the largest indoor arena in Honolulu, where it would be viewed each year by a packed house. Song Contest kept growing throughout the 1960s, 1970s, and 1980s. It came to be the biggest single investment of time and energy at Kamehameha, requiring two months of a modified class schedule to accommodate daily rehearsals. Every high-school student participated. Someone calculated that 41,000 hours of student, faculty, and alumni time went into the 1980 contest, amounting to hundreds of hours of preparation and rehearsal for every minute of performance.

The year 1997 would be special: it was Song Contest's seventy-fifth anniversary. Preparations took over the high school as always: choosing songs for the competition; scheduling rehearsals for the high-school classes, eighteen hundred voices and scores of dancers; organizing the costuming, sound, lights, *lei,* and food service; coordinating parent volunteers; and hiring off-duty police officers for security. The budget was about $250,000, with still more from the TV sponsors.

*Students practicing for Song Contest, an annual event that started at the boys'
school in 1921 and at the girls' school a year later.*

The man in charge was Randie Kamuela Fong, an alumnus who headed Kamehameha's performing arts department. Fong's work in song and dance drew on the traditional past and at the same time broke new ground in performance. He incorporated into his work both the Christian God and the Hawaiian *akua*.

As usual, 1997 Song Contest would be held at Honolulu's Blaisdell Center. There was a full rehearsal on the day before the event, with students massed in their boys' and girls' class groupings for a run-through. There were entrances and exits, sound checks, lighting adjustments, starts and stops and starts again. The morning was long. By midday the students were bored, restless, and ready for some diversion. The student body president, Kamani Kualā'au, went to the microphone to practice his introduction of the board of trustees. The trustees themselves would not be there until the real event. When Kualā'au read the name of Lokelani Lindsey, booing broke out.

There were as many versions of what actually happened that afternoon as there were witnesses—and there was no video or audiotape to check. Some said the booing was organized and sustained. Others, that it was spontaneous and scattered. It was everywhere, from grades nine through twelve. Or it was only the seniors. It was seriously hostile. Or it was just fooling around, the funny thing to do, no malice involved. The whole thing meant nothing. Or it meant everything.

Within minutes some version of the story reached Kawaiaha'o Plaza, and Dickie Wong was heard cursing up and down the trustees' corridor. He said he "didn't give a f——" about Song Contest; if the kids didn't show respect, he would cancel it right now. The next morning, the day Song Contest was scheduled to be held, Wong made a rare trip to the campus to see the high-school principal, Tony Ramos. Wong demanded that Ramos do something about the students. He said the school should not be training "attack dogs" and if there was any more booing of Lindsey, Ramos would be fired immediately.

With Chun at his side, Ramos went from classroom to classroom that day with words about courtesy and common sense. At Song Contest that night there were no boos for Lindsey. She received a polite reception from the audience, as did the other trustees. The most applause, noticeably and predictably, was for Chun, and as usual, the students led it.

In the days leading up to Song Contest, Randie Fong decided to resign from Kamehameha Schools. He felt that he was not getting proper sup-

Randie Kamuela Fong was the first Hawaiian and the first alumnus to head up performing arts at Kamehameha Schools. His threatened resignation sent shock waves through the campus community and helped mobilize opposition to Lokelani Lindsey.

port, but the issue was bigger than that. Fong wanted to make a statement about how badly campus life had degenerated under Lindsey, and he figured resignation was the most powerful way. But Fong's wife still worked at Kamehameha Schools, and his son was a Kamehameha student. Fong worried about retaliation. Because the Fong and Peters families had a number of connections, Fong was able to meet one-on-one with Peters to explain why he was resigning, and to ask for "protection." Peters suggested that Fong meet with Lindsey to work out their differences, and Fong agreed. In preparation for that meeting, Fong wrote down everything he wanted to cover. He had a copy for himself, to help keep him on track, and a copy for Lindsey.

Lindsey had her own agenda. She began by launching into a diatribe against Michael Chun, her voice rising to screams and curses, carrying along the hall. It went on and on, for several minutes. When it finally subsided, Fong told Lindsey this was not about Chun; it was about her: "I need you to hear me. You've got to stop doing these things, hurting people, hurting the school." The two of them went back and forth for hours, past exhaustion to something approaching reconciliation. They both said they would pray on it. Lindsey asked Fong to stay on for another year. She said that when she had first become a trustee, she had promised the other trustees that she would have Kamehameha turned around in five years; she had one to go. She said she wanted Fong to help her make Kamehameha better. Then, suddenly, Lindsey was seized by a fit of coughing that rose to choking. She called to her secretary for her medication, hurried out, and did not return.

After hearing about all this, Stender wrote a memo to the other trustees. In it, he cited Fong's threatened resignation as a clear sign that something was badly broken. He said the problems could be traced directly to "micromanagement"—a code word for Lindsey's rule as lead trustee for education. The solution, according to Stender, was to "return the management of the Kamehameha Schools to President Michael Chun and his staff."

The next meeting of the board of trustees was on April 29, 1997. Michael Chun was not there, but he was at the center of dispute. Was he running the school competently? Lindsey insisted that he was not. She added that all the other administrators were incompetent, too, except for Freitas, the man she had installed as vice president. Stender replied that Lindsey was making it impossible for Chun to do his job. The argument was long and heated, but no conclusions were reached.

After the meeting, Stender wrote another memo, which said that it was an affront to call the staff at Kamehameha incompetent. As for Lindsey's claim that Chun was not doing his job, "I can only respond by saying, the trustees took that job away from him and have given it to trustee Lindsey. You cannot have two people running the ship and then blame one for the sinking."

Lindsey fired back a memo of her own: "It is infuriating that Mr. Stender has ignored our agreement to hold in absolute confidence the details of our Executive Session discussion." According to Lindsey, by writing and circulating his memo among members of his focus group, Stender had moved trustee discussion out of confidentiality and had demonstrated his contempt for the board and its proceedings:

> Rumors, accusations, finger pointing and blame laying have been fueled by deliberate acts coming from the highest levels of Kamehameha Schools/Bishop Estate—from a member of this Board. Mr. Stender continues to manipulate this situation towards his own ends, and encourages certain staff members to carry his disruptive message through our ranks. It is with Mr. Stender's blessing that Mike and Bina Chun are waging their own campaign of innuendo and disinformation against us.

Then Lindsey repeated her mantra that outreach had been wasteful; the campus had no articulated curriculum, no educational plan, and no operating plan—all because of a distressing lack of leadership from the president's office. She acknowledged that Chun was an inspiring figurehead, but what was needed now—and had been needed for years—was not a symbol, but an effective educator: "And what we most certainly do *not* need in the president's office is a manipulative self-serving individual who places his personal interests ahead of those of Kamehameha Schools Bishop Estate—whom he is well paid to serve."

Lindsey was not finished. She went on to re-frame her personal involvement not as micromanaging, but as carrying out her sacred duty:

> I was appointed by the Justices of the Supreme Court to this Trusteeship because of my thirty years experience as an educator, because of my service as a teacher, principal and my nearly eleven years as District Superintendent. Like every Trustee, I swore to uphold my responsibility to perpetuate the testamentary intent of Ke Aliʻi Pauahi; to endure the highest degree of loyalty, care and diligence to this trust legacy, and to prudently administer the educational and business objectives of Kamehameha Schools Bishop Estate within the spirit of the law on trusts. Just like you, it is my responsibility to ensure that the schools run properly and that our students get the education they deserve. . . . I use all of my experience, all of my energy, every capacity I possess for growth and learning, and all of my aloha. That's my job.

Lindsey closed by saying that if anyone was hurting Kamehameha, it was Stender, by characterizing Kamehameha as a "sinking ship." If Stender knew anything about education, he would stop his whining and join her in "sailing forward on a true course, faithful to our Mission, loyal to our Princess and always, always working diligently in the best interests of our students."

chapter 10

"We Must March!"

The Kamehameha ʻohana—students, teachers, parents, and alumni—gradually came to realize that Lokelani Lindsey had transformed their campus into a place of suspicion and fear, a place where no one could act on his or her conscience without fear of reprisal. They saw that the other trustees had done nothing to stop her. Nor had the justices, attorney general, master, or probate judge. This prompted the ʻohana to consider drastic action. Although many of them had a lot to lose, there was too much at stake—their children, their school, Pauahi's legacy—simply to look away. At first one by one, and then together, they acted.

Karen Kaleolani Keawehawaiʻi Farias did not go to Kamehameha Schools, but not for want of trying. Her parents had driven her up to the campus every year to take the admissions test and sat in the car praying with her, holding hands, asking that God would guide their child Kaleolani to Kamehameha. And then every year they got a letter, "Dear Mr. and Mrs. Keawehawaiʻi: We regret to inform you. . . ."

A generation later, Karen Farias' four daughters were admitted to Kamehameha. She was grateful to Pauahi for their education, and especially that they learned to speak Hawaiian. By 1997 two had already graduated. When the younger two brought home the disturbing rumor that Michael Chun would soon be fired, Farias felt moved to do something, so she encouraged her girls to write a petition—not anti-Lindsey, but pro-Chun. It began in Hawaiian and concluded in English, "We the undersigned appreciate and support the work of Dr. Michael Chun. He

Karen Kaleolani Keawehawaiʻi Farias, a professional singer and mother of four Kamehameha alumnae, asked students to sign their names on a petition to show support for the president of their school.

is truly dedicated to the Kamehameha Schools and continues to inspire the children of Pauahi."

Farias took the petition to campus. She was not a protester by nature, but she had told her girls to do what was right, "so if I tell them that, and I sit back and let this happen, then I'm not practicing what I preach." In the parking lot after school, she asked for signatures. When the students heard the word "petition," they kept walking, but when they heard "Dr. Chun," they came back. They signed and got others to sign. Every afternoon, when Farias turned up, students were waiting for her van. More and more students signed, and some wrote notes alongside their names: "We like Uncle Mike." "Hang in there."

In April 1997 Kamani Kualāʻau was at the senior social, near the pool, talking with others in student leadership. All of them would be leaving the school soon, and they did not like the idea of leaving Kamehameha with a cloud hanging over the president's head. They came to a loose agreement to put a letter in the campus paper, *Ka Mō'i*, to be published after graduation. The authors would be Kualā'au, the school's student body president, and James Moniz, the senior class president. It would say how much the students appreciated Chun.

Kualā'au was one to take things on. When he arrived at Kamehameha as a boarder in the seventh grade, he took it upon himself to research the history of Kamehameha and Pauahi, spending time in the school archives after class. Kualā'au walked up to Chun at the party the Chuns hosted every year for the intermediate-school boarders, introduced himself, shook Chun's hand, and made conversation with him. Chun remembered Kualā'au from that night, neat and tidy, shirt tucked in, mature beyond his years.

Kualā'au was not a natural athlete, but he went out for track and field anyway—in the pole vault, an event in which leverage is used to achieve maximum height. Kualā'au aimed high in everything. He could see himself as a Bishop Estate trustee; he talked about it. When Stender was on campus for a panel on drugs, Kualā'au introduced himself to the trustee, then introduced Stender around his dorm. They agreed to keep in touch.

Chun suggested that Kualā'au apply to Princeton where Chun's own daughter, Ka'ili, had gone after Kamehameha. He wrote Kualā'au a strong letter of reference. He also reached out to William "Doc" Buyers, a Princeton alumnus and major donor to that school, who had dined with the Chuns at Hale Pelekikena. With the help of Chun and Buyers, Kualā'au got into Princeton. His family could not afford Ivy League tuition; they lived on Hawaiian homestead land on Maui. But Princeton would provide a financial-need scholarship, and Kamehameha would pay the rest.

A few days after the decision to write something for the school paper, Kualā'au received a phone call from Stender, who had just returned from a long, loud, angry board meeting about Chun. Stender told Kualā'au, "It looks like they're going to get rid of him."

Kualā'au told Stender about the loose plan to write a letter supporting Chun. Given what he had just heard, Kualā'au said, maybe he would send it to the trustees, maybe even to the editors of the daily newspapers. Stender said it would be better to address the letter to the Supreme Court justices, because they were the ones responsible for Lindsey.

Kualā'au and Moniz drafted the letter. At the top they wrote, "A Message to the Justices of the Supreme Court of Hawai'i from Concerned

Students of The Kamehameha Schools." In it, they praised their education, and then focused on Chun:

> Sadly, our president, Dr. Michael J. Chun, the man responsible for bringing Kamehameha to this standard of excellence, may soon be asked for his resignation. He has already been empowered to do nothing, and soon insult may be added to injury. As students who have witnessed the profound aloha that Dr. Chun has extended toward each member of the Kamehameha 'ohana and the community of Hawai'i, we find it deplorable that anyone would question the integrity of his leadership. Though reasons may be cited for Dr. Chun's "resignation," there are other signs that Kamehameha is in a state of turmoil, and that this is not an isolated incident. Several of our best teachers are resigning or retiring at the end of this school year. Many more are dissatisfied with the current board of trustees' new leadership and management styles. All of this is adversely affecting our classmates and our friends. The decline of the quality of the education at Kamehameha will soon show. The best teachers being put in the lowest state of morale will go elsewhere. Something must be done. Many may believe that the Trustees are ultimately responsible for The Kamehameha Schools; we do not. We hold you, the Justices of Hawai'i's Supreme Court, as the selectors of The Kamehameha Schools' Trustees, responsible to ensure the integrity of our Schools. We hold you responsible to put politics aside and ask, is this what Princess Pauahi would have wanted? We leave this to your good judgment.

The next morning Kualā'au read the letter to his homeroom and to two classes. Then he was called out of class and told to go to the principal's office. When he got there, the principal, Tony Ramos, told him that someone wanted to meet with the two of them right away. Ramos drove Kualā'au to Kawaiaha'o Plaza in downtown Honolulu, where they were ushered into Lindsey's *koa*-paneled office. The door was then closed. Lindsey began by telling Kualā'au that she had been getting phone calls about him and his letter. She asked him to admit that the letter was Stender's idea. No, said Kualā'au, he was doing what he was doing of his own free will; he had been planning to write the letter even before Stender called.

Lindsey told Kualā'au that Pauahi's will was "under attack" and that his letter could add fuel to that and create other problems, too. She

Kamani Kualā'au, student body president at Kamehameha Schools in 1997.

talked about rumors and the harm they could do, such as the rumor that she wanted Chun fired. She said rumors like that were hurtful to her. How would Kualā'au like it, she asked, if she called Princeton and described Kualā'au as a "rabble rouser"? She would never dream of doing this, she added—she just wanted him to understand how she felt when people did things behind her back.

Then Lindsey said there were things that she could not tell Kualā'au about Chun, because of personnel law, the implication being that if Kualā'au knew these things, his opinion would change. She added: "Do you know that you are accused of planning the applause for Chun on Song Contest night?" All this was too much for Kualā'au. He felt trapped. His stomach was in knots, and he began to cry. Suddenly Lindsey's tone changed. She told Kualā'au he should go back to school now, and added that she and Ramos would not be telling anyone about the meeting: if word of it got out, they would know who the source was.

As Kualā'au was leaving, Lindsey put her arms around his shoulders and said she loved him.

On the way back to the campus, Kualā'au asked Ramos, "If Uncle Oz said they are going to fire Dr. Chun, and Mrs. Lindsey said they have never discussed the issue, then who is telling the truth?" Ramos did not answer.

Nona Beamer graduated from the Kamehameha School for Girls in 1941 and later taught there. In 1997 she helped mobilize alumni against Lokelani Lindsey.

Nona Beamer, in her mid-seventies and living on the island of Hawai'i, heard about what was going on at Kamehameha. She and her family were closely linked to Kamehameha. Her father had been at the preparatory school when Gladys Brandt was the only girl there. Nona Beamer and all her brothers and sisters had gone to Kamehameha, as had her two sons. She had taught there and had started the *hula* program along with Brandt. Beamer still had many friends and relatives on the faculty and in the dorms. As she listened to them describe Lindsey's behavior, Beamer became upset, then distressed, and finally infuriated. The letter she wrote to the editor of *The Honolulu Advertiser* took her only a couple of minutes to compose:

> Kamehameha Schools trustee Lokelani Lindsey has shamed the Hawaiian people! Her high-handed tactics on campus with students, staff and faculty have completely demoralized the entire Kamehameha 'ohana! The deep concerns have spread through the community, the neighbor islands, and farther. Mrs. Lindsey's micro-management methodology is an utterly diabolical plan of a self-serving egoist! We call for an impeachment and Supreme Court re-dress!

Beamer drafted her letter on May 3, 1997, and then faxed copies to several friends. By chance, the next night there was a meeting of alumni at the home of Leroy and Leina'ala Akamine. Both of the Akamines had strong ties to Kamehameha. Leroy's years there had given him purpose and meaning. He said it was where he learned to be a strong Hawaiian—well grounded morally, trying to live up to the legacy of Pauahi. Leina'ala was a life member of the alumni association and taught *hula* on the Kamehameha campus. Their son taught in the summer school, and their daughter-in-law worked in the admissions office. A grandchild was in kindergarten there.

The gathering at the Akamine home was a meeting for the class of 1952. Such meetings were not customarily political; this one had been called to plan their next reunion. But issues were in the air.

Leroy had also invited several members of the class of 1953, including Oz Stender, a friend of many years. Paulette Moore was there and had with her a copy of Beamer's letter, which she read out loud. The group then discussed the impact such a letter might have and how they could support Beamer's efforts to make things *pono* (right) at Kamehameha. Signing a written statement would show commitment, but names on paper would certainly come under Lindsey's gaze. For anyone who worked at or did business with Bishop Estate, or had children or grandchildren at Kamehameha, there was much to lose. The group discussed whether it was a good idea for the letter to be published right away, or ever. For Hawaiians, letting a Hawaiian issue loose in public was a perpetual dilemma, especially a big one like this. It was agonizing.

The same day as the meeting at the Akamine home, Rochelle "Rocky" Tokuhara was at another meeting of alumni. Tokuhara had been in student leadership during the 1970s, and her style had always been direct. Her roommate, Robin Makua Nakamura, was a Hawaiian language teacher at Kamehameha and had shared stories about how Lindsey was trying to control everything and how it was affecting morale. Tokuhara called together some active alumni, people who had a network of others in their classes. They met at the home of Toni Lee, class of 1959, whose grandparents, mother, and two brothers had all gone to Kamehameha. The group talked for hours about their frustrations and about what they could do that might have an impact. Tokuhara was for action. The people at the meeting were well placed to do something: none of them worked at Kamehameha or Kawaiaha'o Plaza.

Later that night, Tokuhara told Stender about the meeting she had just attended, and he told her about the meeting at the Akamine home. Tokuhara suggested that they join forces. This prompted Stender to set up a meeting for May 7, three days away, at the Pacific Club.

Roy Benham, who graduated with Nona Beamer in 1941, had taught in the high school at Kamehameha when he was a young man. During Benham's first year on the faculty, Stender had been a student in Benham's dorm.

On the evening of May 5 Benham was at yet another meeting of alumni. Stender was there, too. This group was preparing for the May talk-story session with Lindsey. At the April talk story, the Kamehameha *'ohana* had voiced concerns that Lindsey declined to discuss. She said responses would be forthcoming in May.

A talk story in Hawai'i could be anything from relaxed chatter over food and drink to a chance to air whatever might be on people's minds, with the understanding that no one would get heated. At Kamehameha, talk stories had a history, a status. If the May talk story went well, perhaps something could be done without having to "go public." But the next day the group heard that there would be no May talk story. Lindsey had talked to Dickie Wong, and Wong canceled the session, citing "unforeseen schedule conflicts."

Meanwhile, a Hawaiian language teacher at Kamehameha, David Eyre, was talking with Gary Obrecht, an English teacher who had been at Kamehameha for three decades. Both felt that things at the school had become intolerable under Lindsey's rule. Obrecht had stepped forward in one of Lindsey's sessions with faculty and said a prayer about respect and disrespect. This had raised eyebrows and put Obrecht on

Lindsey's list of people to watch. Eyre and Obrecht were especially concerned that Kamehameha was about to lose Randie Fong because of Lindsey. They decided it was time for Kamehameha teachers to organize and express their opposition.

On the morning of May 7 Eyre and Obrecht put meeting notices in faculty boxes. Within an hour the two of them were cautioned against going ahead with the meeting. They were not forbidden to hold it, just warned by their principal that there might be consequences. Later they learned that someone had pulled the notices from the faculty boxes. Even so, word spread, and about thirty people came, about one in eight of the Kamehameha Schools professional staff.

The meeting started with *pule* (prayer) and *mele* (song), both in Hawaiian. A high-school counselor spoke and was followed by Eyre. Others were moved to speak as well. It was almost as if they were witnessing in church. The mood was somber, the tone one of grieving. There were long silences. One teacher talked loudly about the lack of action, about how a real protest would confront the trustees directly and forcefully; at Kamehameha, this teacher said, the teachers were sheep, going meekly to the slaughter. But his was the only such voice. In what others said, and in the silences, there was a sense of risk, of going into harm's way, an awareness that revenge could be exacted. At the same time there was a sense that greatly important things were at stake, a sense of being on the brink, of a dam about to burst. They agreed to meet again, on May 13. Later someone had T-shirts made: "We Are Not Sheep."

That evening, the group summoned by Stender and Tokuhara met at the Pacific Club. About forty people were there, alumni from the 1940s to the 1970s. The youngest was Lei-Ann Stender, Oz Stender's daughter, class of 1973. One after another, each person spoke about why he or she was there. For some, the immediate reason was Randie Fong. Others felt Michael Chun needed support. Stender's daughter spoke about her father: she said that being a Bishop Estate trustee had turned his hair white. Karen Farias was the only person in the room who had not personally gone to Kamehameha. She talked about her daughters and their petition. Robin Nakamura, the only teacher there, talked about the Hawaiian language "war" with Lindsey and the dark cloud hanging over the campus.

Everybody was there because of Lindsey; yet the problems, they knew, went beyond just a single trustee. As Roy Benham put it, Lindsey, in order to be doing what she was doing, must have the blessing of other trustees. The logical conclusion was that getting rid of just one person wouldn't solve Bishop Estate's real problems. Someone said finding a solution could mean that all the trustees would have to be removed, including Stender. Stender told them he was ready for anything; if it had to be, it had to be; this was bigger than the fate of just one person. Then he left, so those at the meeting could talk freely about what actions needed to be taken.

After much discussion and soul searching, the group decided to take everything public, and in the most public way: a march.

The idea of a march came to the meeting through Carmelita "Dutchie" Kapu-Saffery, a 1957 Kamehameha graduate. She had heard about Lindsey being booed at the rehearsal for Song Contest. She had spoken with Randie Fong and with Kamani Kualā'au. She had attended the meeting at the Akamine home, where she listened to Nona Beamer's letter being read. She had gone to sleep that night and awakened at 4:20 A.M. with the vision of a march fully formed, starting at Pauahi's tomb and ending at Kawaiaha'o Plaza, with chants and songs along the way. She had written down what had come to her, but at the Pacific Club she did not need her notes. When people asked, "What shall we do?" she rose without hesitation and said, "We must march!"

It had been more than a quarter century since the last marches against Bishop Estate. Those marches, held at the time of Kalama Valley and the appointment of Matsuo Takabuki, were 1960s-style political demonstrations, and people from Kamehameha were only a small part of them. What was being contemplated now would be a march by the Kamehameha 'ohana, the people for whom Bishop Estate was founded, against the trustees of Bishop Estate. The very idea was shocking, almost unthinkable. It was against tradition, against culture.

Deeper yet was a dark and troubled certainty. There were people in Hawai'i who were always ready to disparage Hawaiians. They would relish the spectacle of Hawaiians divided, openly in conflict with one another, about to turn the biggest, most visible, and most precious Hawaiian institution into a battlefield.

But the strong consensus was that a dramatic gesture was needed. A date was fixed for the march: May 15, 1997, only eight days away.

The morning of May 8 *The Honolulu Advertiser* ran a front-page article by Greg Barrett: "Furor Erupts against Kamehameha Schools Trustee; Teachers Say She Poisons Morale, Should Be Impeached." The story was the first comprehensive explanation of the churning issues at

Kamehameha—Lindsey and micromanagement, the climate of fear, the possibility of Michael Chun's being fired, Randie Fong's intention to resign.

Then word of Nona Beamer's letter reached the Supreme Court justices. Chief Justice Moon was quoted as saying the problem was internal to the trustees; the justices had no authority to act. Beamer was quoted in response, saying that a power to hire trustees logically included a power to fire them—an argument supported by the fact that the justices, while acting in an "unofficial" capacity, had imposed a mandatory retirement age on Bishop Estate trustees. By doing so, the justices indicated that they, too, believed that their power and responsibility did not end with a trustee's appointment.

On May 9 the *Advertiser's* headline was "Protest Planned against Trustees." The Pacific Club meeting and the decision to march were now public.

On May 11 support for Lindsey appeared in the papers in the form of letters to the editor that said she was the best possible choice for a trustee, fair, diligent, outspoken, tough, a delight to be with, a wonderful woman, mother, and grandmother, a female who had what it took "to enter the sanctum of male power brokers." A petition backing her was circulated saying that anyone at Kamehameha—students, teachers, or administrators—who did not like the direction the trustees were taking should leave the school.

Michael Chun also made his voice heard, but not in the way many had been hoping. On May 12 Chun wrote a letter to students instructing them not to take part in the march. Although the march was partly on his behalf, he said, not to take part would be an act of loyalty to him and the duty they owed to Pauahi and God. Further, absence from school would be considered truancy, and the student handbook made it clear that truancy had consequences. Exams and graduation were approaching; each student should stick to academic work: "If you do, we will end the year with dignity and pride, and Pauahi will smile. God bless all of you."

The next day Chun wrote a similar letter to the faculty and staff. He assured them that their concerns were being heard and that he was working with administrators and trustees to improve communications. He said it was best to keep all this within the 'ohana. Citing the employee handbook, he instructed all faculty and staff to be on campus during the march unless they were ill or at an approved activity.

That afternoon the faculty met, called together again by Eyre and

Obrecht. They considered two statements of concern, one written by Eyre, the other by Kēhau Abad, who taught honors Hawaiian history in the high school. Both statements talked of disintegrating faculty morale, a climate of fear, a community in distress. The question before the meeting was how best to use these statements. A few people signed them; most did not. Many expressed strong concerns about retribution. The meeting ended with the signature pages being torn up.

At another faculty meeting the next day, May 14, an anonymous vote was taken: "Do you support the statements?" Forty-eight out of forty-eight said yes. "Are you afraid to sign?" Forty-seven said yes. The group eventually decided that Eyre, Obrecht, Abad, and an art teacher, Charlene Hoe, should deliver unsigned copies of the statements to the trustees at the culmination of the march.

The campus was buzzing with rumors. One said there would be a mass walkout the day of the march, with students forming a procession from campus to the Royal Mausoleum, where they would join up with the marchers. Another rumor said Chun would not last the week.

The day before the march Chun interrupted classes to make his plea for calm via closed-circuit TV. He had an uncanny ability to connect with each student individually, even on TV. It was one of the reasons students liked him so much. This time Chun appeared haggard but still in control. He looked straight at the camera and spoke slowly, remind-

ing students of their responsibilities, with final exams set to begin the following week, and of the important reasons for their being in school. He used earnest words for young hearts, words that touched their deep sense of loyalty. He paused a moment and then leaned forward to the camera. "I urge you not to participate in a walk-out from classes or in a march planned by alumni and parents. To do so would disappoint me greatly and will be a burden which I do not need at this time." The teachers were greatly disappointed by this, but they assumed that Chun had been told that he would be fired if anyone from the school showed up at the march.

As Michael Chun was making his televised address, Roy Benham and Tomi Chong were entering Kawaiahaʻo Plaza for a scheduled meeting. They had been led to believe that all five trustees would be there. But Nathan Aipa, the trustees' chief in-house lawyer, had recently advised the trustees against having a majority present. Only Dickie Wong and Lokelani Lindsey appeared.

Wong greeted Benham and Chong and told them that the other three trustees could not be there because of scheduling conflicts. He then asked them to call off the march. Benham said that they would relay the request to the alumni, but they were not in a position to cancel the march. Wong slammed his hand on the table: "You people don't know what you're doing. You don't know what you're creating."

Wong and Lindsey did not tell Benham that lawyers for the trustees were at that very moment asking the probate court to appoint a retired probate judge, Patrick Yim, as a fact-finder to look into allegations of mismanagement at Kamehameha Schools. The idea of a fact-finder had come from Gerard Jervis, who contended that unless the trustees took definitive action on their own, the probate court would eventually grant legal standing to students and alumni, who would then have the power to bring Bishop Estate–related issues before a judge. Wong, Peters, and Lindsey disliked the idea of a court-appointed fact-finder, but they disliked even more the thought of students and alumni having direct access to the legal system, with lawsuits and other legal actions presumably not far behind.

It looked as if the trustees had chosen safely. During his tenure as probate judge, Yim had approved all the trustees' annual accounts without asking any tough questions. There also was a family connection: Yim was a nephew of Peters' stepmother. Under the circumstances, it seemed unlikely that Yim would do anything that would embarrass the trustees.

Patrick Yim, a retired probate judge, was hired in 1997 as a fact-finder to look into allegations of mismanagement at Kamehameha Schools.

The trustees proposed to pay Yim $250 an hour from trust funds for the facts as he found them. According to the trustees' petition, it had to be Yim or no one, and his findings could not be made public. The trustees did not need the court's permission to conduct this kind of internal inquiry, but they wanted the court to make the effort "official." The probate judge, Colleen Hirai, approved the arrangement.

That evening Wong and Peters met with Leroy Akamine and another alumnus, Joe Travis. Travis had attended the meetings at the Akamine home and the Pacific Club and had known Dickie Wong since Wong's union-organizing days. Unless it was called off, the march would start in about fourteen hours. Wong demanded that it be stopped. For the second time that day he pounded a table. Travis said that if the board pulled Lindsey back from the Kamehameha campus, that would do it. Travis had no authority from the alumni to say so, but he was right.

At that very moment, the march organizers stood outside Kawaiahaʻo Plaza, where the march was going to end, making last-minute arrangements. Even as late as that, ʻohana leaders would have been enormously relieved to have a good reason to call off the march. All Wong and Peters had to do was remove Lindsey from the campus.

Wong and Peters stepped outside to talk. Minutes later they returned and said they would not remove Lindsey. The march was on.

In 1884 Pauahi's casket, draped in red velvet, had been taken in a horse-drawn carriage from Kawaiaha'o Church up to the Royal Mausoleum at Mauna 'Ala. The march on May 15, 1997, took the same three-mile funeral route, but in reverse, from Mauna 'Ala to the doorstep of Bishop Estate's headquarters, Kawaiaha'o Plaza, which stood next to the church.

Roy Benham welcomed the three hundred or so marchers who gathered for the 10:30 A.M. start. Some wore blue-and-white T-shirts with a picture of Pauahi and the words "We Care—Kū'ē Pono" (resist appropriately) on the front. Off-duty police officers were there as volunteers to help with traffic control, and off-duty tour drivers shuttled people from the parking area to Mauna 'Ala, taking the *kūpuna* (elders) directly to the endpoint. They included alumni from classes in the 1930s and even a few from the 1920s.

The marchers stayed two abreast all the way down Nu'uanu Avenue. They marched into downtown Honolulu, past the governor's mansion, where Governor Benjamin Cayetano lived, through the state Capitol atrium, and onto the grounds of 'Iolani Palace. As they marched, their numbers grew, eventually to more than a thousand. There was no yelling, no rancor, no protest signs. They sang the songs they had sung as Kamehameha students.

In front of the statue of Lili'uokalani, they chose the hauntingly beautiful "Queen's Prayer," composed by Lili'uokalani while she was under house arrest following the 1893 overthrow of the Hawaiian kingdom. As conch shells sounded, the marchers crossed King Street to the statue of Kamehameha the Great that stood in front of the Supreme Court building. Benham led a delegation that presented a document to Chief Justice Moon.

Moon said to Benham, "I really admire your folks' deportment, you know, the way you're doing this. It's really terrific. No signs, no rabble-rousing, just ——." Before he could finish, Benham said: "Yeah, well, we have some concerns and hopefully you can be supporting our efforts to address them." Moon said it was out of his hands, that it was the probate judge who decided trust matters. "But you're the one who selects the probate judge, aren't you?" asked Benham. Moon just nodded.

Meanwhile Fred Cachola, who had been head of outreach services

On May 15, 1997, members of the Kamehameha 'ohana marched from Princess Pauahi's resting place at Mauna 'Ala to Bishop Estate headquarters at Kawaiaha'o Plaza. As they marched, their numbers grew.

for Bishop Estate until it was eliminated in 1995, found himself called into service. He had not expected to take a leadership role during the march, but a preschool teacher, Pualani Akaka, Reverend Akaka's daughter, asked Cachola to deliver to the trustees a document signed by parents at the school in Nānākuli where she taught. Then Cachola ran into his own daughter, Kēhau Abad, at the march. Because she and other Kamehameha teachers were not supposed to be there, Abad was wearing dark glasses and a pulled-down baseball cap. She asked her father to deliver the statement from the Kamehameha teachers.

As the marchers neared the first entry point to the Kawaiahaʻo Plaza courtyard, they saw that the opening was blocked by Henry Peters and Dickie Wong. The two trustees were standing shoulder to shoulder with a group of their families and friends, apparently ready for a confrontation. Rather than try to break through, the marchers just kept going and entered on the opposite side of the compound.

From her darkened third-floor office, Lindsey could watch the marchers without their seeing her. Soon it became apparent to her that marchers were waving to Stender, who was standing at the window in his office, which was next to hers. She went to Stender's office and demanded that he turn out his lights and step back from the window, but he refused.

A staff member had asked Lindsey if there should be refreshments, especially for the *kūpuna*, who might be tired and thirsty. Her response was immediate: "Absolutely not! They are marching against trustees!"

About fifty staff members gathered in the shadows of the parking structure, where—as long as they did not stand close to the railing —they could look down at the marchers without being seen. One of these staffers took the added precaution of standing behind a pillar, not watching, but listening as co-workers described what they were seeing: "I see your mom! I see your auntie! Oh, there's your dad!"

Bishop Estate staffers were not the only people looking for familiar faces. At some point Lokelani Lindsey went into Henry Peters' office, where, together with members of the communications department, they wrote down the names of people they recognized in the crowd below. Lindsey also had staff members downstairs with cameras. Dickie Wong eventually stepped forward to greet the assembled marchers, which outraged Lindsey; but the alternative was to look as though he was hiding.

Wong listened without expression as Cachola read from the documents he had been given. The one from Kamehameha teachers explained that they had been prohibited from attending the march and from even sending a small delegation. The crowd applauded loudly when Cachola read the last line of the teachers' statement: "Let our absence here today speak louder than words ever could."

Then Benham told Wong that the marchers had three major "concerns," a polite word for demands: return management of the school to the president, reinstate the talk-story sessions, and lift the cloud of ret-

Fred Cachola (right), who headed up the trust's extension services before those outreach programs were abruptly terminated in 1995, handed several documents to Bishop Estate chairman Dickie Wong at the culmination of the May 15, 1997, march.

ribution and vindictiveness. Wong's only response was, "We'll look it over and get back to you."

A staff member who had watched all this from the parking structure described what happened after the marchers left: "We all went to our respective desks and pretended to work." She said there was a lot of soul-searching. She remembered asking herself, "Am I a coward that I was afraid to be out there marching? What was wrong with me that I wasn't willing to stand up and be counted and have my face photographed?"

chapter 11

A Tinderbox Waiting for a Match

While others were marching, Toni Lee, who had hosted an alumni meeting during the march's organization, was in Miami Beach attending the Miss Universe pageant. Her daughter, Brook, also a Kamehameha graduate, was a contestant. More than a contestant: she won.

Lee was back in Hawaiʻi on May 25, the day of the Kamehameha graduation ceremony. Normally she would be at the always-packed Blaisdell Center, where she had worked as a volunteer usher for every graduation over the last thirty-three years. This year was different. Being sighted at alumni meetings leading up to the march put Lee on Lindsey's watch list. Lee was told that she would not be ushering this year.

The graduation ceremony itself was typical in most ways: When Chun was introduced, he got his usual standing ovation. Perhaps because everyone knew his year had been difficult, the ovation lasted longer than usual, for several minutes, thousands on their feet. That might have been a subject of conversation in its own right, but all people could talk about afterward was that Lindsey had refused to stand during the ovation. She appeared to be the only one in the entire auditorium who remained seated throughout. Trustee Jervis could be seen trying to coax her out of her chair, but Lindsey would not budge.

Though Chun could do no wrong in the eyes of Kamehameha students and alumni, the teachers had concerns. His management style sometimes seemed more suited for a business or military organization than for a school. The big concern now, however, was his failure to stand up to Lindsey and the other trustees. Throughout the 1996–97 school year,

Kamehameha teachers pleaded with Chun to tell Lindsey that she could not continue to ride roughshod over the entire campus community. In time they concluded that he was not going to stand up to Lindsey anytime soon, at least not openly, and maybe never. They resolved to find their own direction, and seek their own leadership.

Eyre, Obrecht, Abad, and Hoe, the four teachers who had been chosen to deliver a statement at the culmination of the march, assumed leadership roles in an organization that was still forming. Abad suggested a name: Na Kumu o Kamehameha, the Teachers of Kamehameha.

Members of Na Kumu talked about ways to improve the situation, but every idea seemed risky. The employment contracts they had signed prohibited unapproved contact with the media; any public criticism of Bishop Estate trustees could bring disciplinary action, perhaps even termination. Deciding that risks nonetheless had to be taken, the four went public at the end of the school year with a two-page, single-spaced statement issued to the media. It pointed out that there were real and pervasive problems at Kamehameha the teachers had been trying to address for years, and that the trustees, by petitioning the court for a handpicked fact-finder, were working against a shared resolution of issues.

Meanwhile, the organizers of the May 15 march gathered at Kawaiaha‘o Church to discuss what should come next. The atmosphere at that

Leaders of the May 15, 1997, march formed a non-profit organization, Na Pua a Ke Ali'i Pauahi (the Children of Princess Pauahi), whose membership quickly grew to more than four thousand. From left to right: Beadie Dawson, Roy Benham, Tomi Chong, Marion Joy, and Jan Dill.

meeting was charged. Talk centered on the march and the news coverage it had gotten. When Gladys Brandt arrived late, the crowd rose without a word to honor her presence.

Everyone agreed that the energy and focus of the march had to be maintained. For that to happen, however, there had to be leadership and a collective voice. They agreed to organize themselves as a nonprofit organization: Na Pua a Ke Ali'i Pauahi, the Children of Princess Pauahi.

Roy Benham was to contact Dickie Wong on Na Pua's behalf to set up a meeting. He tried repeatedly over the next two days but received no response. Then he got a call: there would be a meeting. Just hours later, though, it was canceled. Eventually another meeting with all five trustees was scheduled for May 24.

Benham reported to Kawaiaha'o Plaza for the meeting along with other members of Na Pua, including Leroy Akamine, Dutchie Kapu-Saffery, Joe Travis, Toni Lee, Fred Cachola, Gladys Brandt, and a former trustee, Myron Thompson. They were seated in the boardroom and told that the trustees would be there momentarily. A few minutes later, in walked Wong, and then Jervis. When Wong asked if anyone wanted to say a prayer, Benham said to hold it, that the meeting had not started. "Where are the other trustees?" he wanted to know. Wong started talking about how much the trustees loved Kamehameha. "Dickie," said Benham, "stop preaching to the choir. Where are the others?" Tied up, said Wong; other things to do. The Na Pua representatives did not believe him, and they walked out. As the group left the building, Bishop Estate's director of communications, Elisa Yadao, was telling reporters how nice it was that the family had gotten together and that now the healing process could begin. Benham was not pleased. "Oh, give me a break," he said later. "She wasn't even in the room, and here she is saying the healing process has begun. It made me sick to listen to it."

Within a week, Benham heard from Wong in writing: "Further discussions with Na Pua will not be productive at this point."

Karen Farias had managed to get thousands of signatures on her petition, a solid basis for the formation of Na Pua. But at the organizational meeting many people expressed uncertainty. They had marched; now what else could they do? There was hesitancy, a feeling that ordinary Hawaiians could not take on Bishop Estate trustees. Someone suggested that a lawyer might be helpful.

There were dozens of Kamehameha graduates who were members of the bar, but for whatever reason, none of them stepped forward. However, one Hawaiian lawyer did offer to help: Beatrice "Beadie" Kanahele Dawson. She had gone to Punahou, but two of her sisters and many friends had gone to Kamehameha. Dawson had entered law school at the University of Hawai'i nearly two decades before, at the age of fifty. Prior to law, she had been in public relations and had worked a while for Myron Thompson.

Dawson suggested that Na Pua get involved in the fact-finding process that the Bishop Estate trustees had arranged in probate court. She also suggested that Na Pua become a voice for the Kamehameha 'ohana, whom she described as "the beneficiaries of Pauahi's trust." The group liked Dawson's suggestions.

While serving as Na Pua's lawyer, Dawson stayed in contact with Deputy Attorney General Kevin Wakayama to make sure she understood the trust law issues, which were new to her. What was not new to her was the job of explaining things to reporters. Dawson had the experience and ability needed to sum up complex issues in simple language, which proved to be invaluable over the coming months.

On the legal front, Dawson moved to intervene on behalf of Na Pua in the fact-finding matter, and she argued that Yim's report should be made public. Most earthshaking from the trustees' point of view, Dawson argued that Na Pua should have legal standing to bring suit against Bishop Estate trustees at any time and for any reason.

One of the trustees' outside trust experts, Robert B. "Bruce" Graham, and Bishop Estate's director of communications, Elisa Yadao, argued in and outside of court that Kamehameha students, teachers, alumni, and parents were not Pauahi's beneficiaries—the school itself was the only beneficiary—and so none of them could sue. This made no sense to the leaders of Na Pua. How could bricks and mortar be Pauahi's beneficiaries, and not the people who gave purpose to the trust? Graham told them he was ready to argue his position through every court-room in the judicial system, and he had the seemingly unlimited resources of Bishop Estate at his disposal.

Na Pua had one lawyer—a volunteer—and no budget. If the trustees wanted Graham to draw out the argument indefinitely, the fact-finding could also be delayed indefinitely. Looking at its options, the Na Pua board reluctantly agreed to set aside the question of legal standing for the time being and turned its attention to making Yim's fact-finding work properly.

The group set up a hotline for members of the Kamehameha ʻohana and recruited facilitators to walk potential witnesses through the experience, getting them ready to tell their stories to Yim. Beadie Dawson told Yim about the group's activities and even gave him a copy of the facilitator's manual. She also explained that Na Pua was keeping a record of what he would be hearing. What she was really saying was that if his report deviated from what the witnesses would be telling him, Na Pua would know.

On July 6 *The Honolulu Advertiser* ran another long front-page story by Greg Barrett, this time about Lindsey's interrogation of Kamani Kua-lāʻau, the Kamehameha student who had co-authored a letter in support of Michael Chun. A week later, on July 13, the *Advertiser* published a letter to the editor by the four Na Kumu representatives that was highly critical of Lindsey and also of their principal, Tony Ramos, for his role in the interrogation.

Lindsey immediately demanded that the four teachers be fired. The legal opinion at Bishop Estate was that this could be done under the employment contract each had signed. Ramos and Chun argued that such drastic action would be hard to defend, that progressive sanctions were standard. After a heated debate, the trustees agreed not to fire the four just yet. Chun and Ramos issued a formal reprimand and personally urged Abad, Eyre, Hoe, and Obrecht to pull back. They warned them that additional violations would result in harsher sanctions, including the very real possibility of termination.

Meanwhile, Lindsey redoubled her efforts to get Chun off the campus. She had convinced Wong, Peters, and Jervis that Kamehameha was floundering, and all because of Chun. The practical concern was, how would the Kamehameha ʻohana react if the trustees fired their beloved president?

Lindsey, Wong, Peters, and Jervis finally worked out a plan one evening over dinner at Ruth's Chris Steak House in Honolulu, and Jervis was given the assignment of proposing it to Stender. The idea was straightforward: kick Chun upstairs and cut him off from the campus entirely. He could be given "some fancy-sounding title, perhaps chancellor," an office at Kawaiahaʻo Plaza, and freedom to interact with alumni, which was "his strength." The only alternative, according to Jervis, was outright termination. Stender responded that he would not support an attempt to push Chun off campus and predicted that the Kamehameha ʻohana would riot if Michael Chun were fired for no good reason.

The exchange with Jervis convinced Stender that sooner or later the other trustees would fire Chun unless something prevented them from doing so. Stender and the other trustees had made an agreement not to comment publicly about the turmoil at Kamehameha until Yim's fact-finding report had been filed. But after going back and forth many times in his own mind and getting feedback from his focus group, Stender decided to talk. He called Greg Barrett, the *Advertiser* reporter who had been following the controversy closely. A meeting was arranged, and the two of them talked for hours, for the record, with the tape recorder running. The next day, Stender had second thoughts. He called to plead with Barrett not to run the story. Barrett said it was too late for Stender to take back what had been said. The story ran the next morning, July 20, on the front page. Barrett quoted Stender at length about micromanagement, mistrust, and a Gestapo atmosphere at Kamehameha Schools. Some of this had been printed before, but never had it been attributed to a Bishop Estate trustee.

Behind the bolted doors of Kawaiahaʻo Plaza, the reaction was explosive. Jervis threw a rolled-up copy of the Sunday *Advertiser* at Stender.

Then Peters berated Stender, calling him a traitor. Peters looked like he was going to hit Stender, but then Jervis stepped between them, cursing Stender and shouting, "Get the f—— out of here. You're not part of the team."

Stender went to his office and composed a memo to his fellow trustees:

> I did not appreciate the abusive language Trustee Jervis used in his shouting at me and his throwing the newspaper at me. This is precisely the sort of behavior that does not belong in the boardroom of this institution, however, it is typical of trustees' behavior. . . . It is also the sort of behavior that is extended to staff members of this organization. It is this way of dealing with people that has brought us to this point. How much more pain from this sort of treatment can our people endure before we will see a revolution for change?

The alumni had marched; Na Pua and Na Kumu had formed; Stender had gone public. The situation was a tinderbox, just waiting to be ignited.

chapter 12

Time to Say "No More"

On August 9, 1997, the *Honolulu Star-Bulletin* published an essay in its editorial section under the banner headline, "Broken Trust." The essay began: "The community has lost faith in Bishop Estate trustees, in how they are chosen, how much they are paid, how they govern. The time has come to say 'no more.'"

The essay went on to cover virtually that entire section of the paper, a head-on, 6,400-word attack charging that underqualified and overpaid trustees had been selected in a rigged political process, had engaged in loose and self-serving financial management, and had distinguished themselves mostly by conflicts of interest, disdain for accountability, greed, and arrogance. "Broken Trust" reached beyond Bishop Estate to indict the whole interlocked system of cogs and wheels that had produced the trustees and allowed them to operate with impunity: Hawai'i's political machine, the Judicial Selection Commission, the Hawai'i Supreme Court justices.

Names were named: Dickie Wong, Henry Peters, Lokelani Lindsey, Gerard Jervis, Chief Justice Ronald Moon, Associate Justices Steven Levinson and Robert Klein, Governor John Waihe'e, union leader Gary Rodrigues, former court-appointed master Alvin Shim, political insider Larry Mehau, and more.

Stories were told: How Mehau had almost become a trustee. How Waihe'e manipulated the judicial selection process to get his men, Levinson and Klein, onto the Supreme Court. How Rodrigues had badgered other members of the blue-ribbon panel in an unsuccessful attempt to get Waihe'e onto the Bishop Estate board. How the justices rejected that panel's selections and then picked the ultimate political insider, Gerard

Jervis. How Waiheʻe, after failing to get onto the board, went straight from the governor's office to a law firm that was paid seven-figure legal fees to preserve the right of Bishop Estate trustees to pay themselves excessive compensation. How Yukio Takemoto had been hired at Bishop Estate after having been seriously compromised in a legislative investigation of his activities in the Waiheʻe administration. How Lokelani Lindsey used Bishop Estate staffers for her own private purposes. How Henry Peters negotiated a transaction on behalf of a group buying real estate from the Estate. How trustees improperly put their own money in a Bishop Estate oil deal.

A few of these stories were already known, but most were not. All together in one place, they had a thunderous effect in a state that, in the words of the authors of "Broken Trust," "has a tradition of tolerance and quiet acceptance of others. In the island way, it often is considered disruptive—even rude—to speak out." According to the authors, the situation at Bishop Estate screamed for attention. The system as it was now operating was producing trustees who were perverting Pauahi's vision: "The princess intended a sacred trust. What we ended up with is a political plum."

"Broken Trust" ended with a story about a school in New York where the trustees had operated with conflicts of interest and the president

was grossly overpaid. A group of angry faculty, students, alumni, and former trustees had made enough noise to prompt an investigation that resulted in the removal of all but one of those trustees. The state attorney general filed a lawsuit to hold each of those trustees personally accountable, legally and financially, for mismanagement of assets and violations of fiduciary duty. "If it can happen in New York," the authors concluded, "why not in Hawai'i?"

Five people had submitted "Broken Trust" to the *Star-Bulletin*. Gladys Brandt, a former principal of the Kamehameha Schools and former chairwoman of the University of Hawai'i board of regents; Walter Heen, a retired judge of the State Intermediate Court of Appeals and a former state legislator and city councilman; Monsignor Charles Kekumano, a retired Catholic priest and chairman of the Queen Lili'uokalani Trust; Samuel King, a senior Federal District Court judge; and Randall Roth, a professor at the University of Hawai'i Law School.

All the authors of "Broken Trust" were active in civic affairs; two had been active politically. King had once headed the state Republican Party and in 1970 was its candidate for governor. Heen was a staunch Democrat who would go on to head the state Democratic Party. Kekumano stayed away from secular politics, but he was no stranger to public service: he had been a regent at the University of Hawai'i and Chaminade University and president of the Association of Hawaiian Civic Clubs, had been named Humanitarian of the Year by the Hawai'i chapter of the American Red Cross, and was a longtime member of the Police Commission. Brandt had been named Woman of the Year, Educator of the Year, Alumnus of the Year, and Hawaiian of the Year by various groups. Roth had been a member of the faculty of three law schools and had been named Professor of the Year at all three.

A former Kamehameha principal, two judges, a professor of trust law, and a Catholic priest. Four of the five were Hawaiian: Brandt, Heen, Kekumano, and King. And these four were also *kūpuna*, Hawaiian elders, with the wisdom of age: Heen was sixty-nine; Kekumano, seventy-eight; King, eighty-one; and Brandt, ninety. These did not seem like people who would try to garner publicity for themselves or hurt the sacred trust of a Hawaiian princess, an *ali'i nui*.

Gladys Brandt had been deeply involved in events leading up to the march and in Na Pua's formation. Kekumano, Heen, and King had been hearing from her and other Hawaiians about the intolerable situation at Kamehameha Schools. Heen and King were primarily concerned about the way trustee selection appeared to be corrupting the judiciary. Heen knew firsthand that Judicial Selection Commission members were asking candidates for the Supreme Court to say whom they would be inclined to appoint to future vacancies on the Bishop Estate board of trustees. This appeared to be affecting the selection of justices and the quality of the court.

Roth, forty-nine, was a Mainland *haole*. He had arrived in Hawai'i from Kansas seventeen years earlier to join the University of Hawai'i faculty of law as a specialist in taxation, trusts, and legal ethics. During his first few years on the faculty, he had tried to learn as much as possible about Bishop Estate so he could refer to it when discussing tax-exempt charitable trusts in the classroom. He was surprised that so little information was available. The annual financial statements and masters' reports were woefully inadequate.

By the mid-1990s Roth had come to believe that the trustees were committing serious breaches of trust. Some of these breaches, such as excessive compensation and inadequate pursuit of the trust's charitable mission, were obvious even to the public. Yet no attorney general, court-appointed master, probate judge, justice of the Supreme Court, or trust

counsel appeared likely to do anything about it. To Roth, this amounted to reckless endangerment of the trust's tax-exempt status.

Roth was also the volunteer host of a Sunday morning talk show on Hawai'i Public Radio called *The Price of Paradise*. Shortly after the march on May 15, 1997, he decided to devote several weekly broadcasts exclusively to Bishop Estate. As was his usual practice, he would place a companion essay in *The Honolulu Advertiser* on the day of each broadcast. Working closely with the *Advertiser*'s editorial-page editor, Jerry Burris, Roth had done this many times before.

Roth asked dozens of knowledgeable insiders to talk with him about Bishop Estate on deep background, not to be quoted by name without permission. They included former Supreme Court justices, current and former Bishop Estate trustees and court-appointed masters, current and former senior staff members at Kawaiaha'o Plaza, Kamehameha Schools officials, leaders of the alumni association, and current and former members of the Judicial Selection Commission, along with current and former legislators, deputy attorneys general, and judges. Many of Roth's sources talked at length and candidly, although none allowed a tape recorder, and five said if anything were ever attributed to them, they would deny having said it. Three retired jurists encouraged Roth to widen his inquiry, telling him the issues were bigger than just Bishop Estate.

Roth met with Burris in late June to show him what he had so far. Burris called it explosive and said anything this big would have to be approved by his boss, Jim Gatti. Burris said he would show the draft to Gatti and set up a meeting.

While Roth was waiting for an appointment to meet with Gatti, he asked Judge King to critique the draft. After reading it closely, King said he liked what Roth had written, but he had two major concerns. First, Roth would be painting a target on himself. Second, it was doubtful that one *haole* acting alone could accomplish meaningful change at Bishop Estate, which had always been considered a Hawaiian trust and Hawaiians' business. Roth asked if King would consider co-authoring the essay, but he was not optimistic. After all, King was a federal judge. Most people in that position would keep their distance from something as controversial as this. To Roth's delight, King did not hesitate: "I'll do it if it's okay with my wife."

King had met his wife, Anne, during World War II, when both were U.S. Navy officers training to be Japanese interpreters. Just prior to meeting King, Anne had graduated Phi Beta Kappa from Smith College, majoring in classical Greek language and literature. They married in 1944. Now King would be asking her if he could get involved in something that might become highly controversial. The fallout from it could have a big impact on both their lives and the lives of their children and grandchildren. Her response did not surprise him: "Yes, I think you should."

King told Roth that more co-authors were essential. He suggested Gladys Brandt. Roth had interviewed Brandt for the essay and had come away enormously impressed. The next day Roth took the draft essay to Brandt's apartment. She read it slowly and carefully. When she finished, she had one question. "You say Sam King is with you on this?"

"Yes," said Roth.

Brandt said, "Then count me in."

Roth told Brandt that ideally another person or two would be added. She immediately said, "Let me call Monsignor Kekumano," her good friend of many years. Kekumano read the draft later that day with Brandt and Roth sitting quietly in the room. But Kekumano hesitated. It might not be a good time to drop such a bombshell on the public; maybe it would be best to wait until the situation on campus at Kamehameha was clarified. Roth started to debate the point but stopped when Brandt gently placed her hand on his arm. Brandt encouraged Kekumano to elaborate his concerns and listened patiently as he did so. Roth had another appointment. As Brandt walked him to the door, she whispered, "Don't you worry. Leave the Monsignor to me." She called Roth a few hours later to say that Kekumano had signed on.

The next day, Roth asked the three whether it would be all right if he invited Walter Heen to join the group. He had long thought highly of Heen, and when Roth interviewed Heen for the essay he had been impressed by Heen's level of knowledge about Bishop Estate and the judiciary. The others also knew Heen well and respected him. Roth went to Heen's home to make the pitch. It did not take long: when Heen heard that King, Brandt, and Kekumano were already in, he was ready to sign up.

Five was a good number. It had weight. It matched the number of trustees, and the number of Supreme Court justices. The group had come together in less than forty-eight hours. By contrast, things could hardly have moved more slowly with Jim Gatti at the *Advertiser*. Burris had given Gatti a draft to read, but Gatti said he was too busy to read it. Then, once he had, Gatti said he was too busy to meet with Roth to discuss it—and after a meeting was finally scheduled, Gatti canceled. The meeting was rescheduled, and Gatti canceled again.

"Broken Trust" authors, from left to right: Walter Heen, Samuel King, Gladys Brandt, Charles Kekumano, and Randall Roth.

Meanwhile, the five co-authors were re-working the essay together. They discussed at length each of the points that needed to be made and the best way to make them. Heen was the most politically sensitive and the most legally minded in his approach to a finished document. King was for less legalese and more plain talk. Kekumano was adamant about the precise words and images he wanted on the page. As Brandt put it, he was the most willing to be "persnickety." Brandt herself had fewer wholesale suggestions than did King and far fewer than Heen and Kekumano, but by regularly suggesting a single word change here or there she was able to set the perfect tone.

As the essay came to take final shape, Roth was calling Burris daily, sometimes as often as four times a day. The most Burris could say was that Gatti had thumbed through the pages of the latest draft and had expressed "concerns." Gatti said the essay was "trying to be both journalism and opinion," and he "had a problem with that." When the long-delayed meeting with Gatti finally took place, he said the essay was much too long and that a lot of the content was nothing more than "old news." If anything were going to appear in the *Advertiser*, it would have to be in the form of a scaled-down opinion piece. Roth said that might be acceptable to the authors, but only if the deleted information could be included in a companion news story, written by an *Advertiser* reporter. Out of the question, said Gatti. If the opinion piece ran, it would run alone: no companion piece, and no lead story. When Roth suggested that the authors might be inclined to offer the essay to the rival *Star-Bulletin*, Gatti said the *Star-Bulletin* had far fewer readers than the *Advertiser*, and besides, the *Star-Bulletin*'s editor would have the same concerns he had. Refusing to make any promises, Gatti suggested that some version of the essay could probably run a week or two from the coming Sunday.

Roth felt indebted to Jerry Burris, with whom he had worked closely for years and who had already added his editing touch to the essay. Roth also wanted to reach as many readers as possible. So he agreed to keep working with the *Advertiser*, provided it was all right with the other authors.

When Roth reported on this meeting to Brandt and Kekumano, they saw the decision as an easy one. They didn't care if the *Advertiser* had double, triple, or ten times the number of readers. They said that Gatti had given Roth "the run-around" and that time was running out. In the last few days Brandt and Kekumano had become convinced that Lokelani Lindsey was on the verge of firing Michael Chun. They believed the essay could stop that, but only if it appeared before Lindsey took action. That would probably not happen if Gatti had anything to say about it. Brandt and Kekumano were adamant: "Take it to the *Star-Bulletin*."

King and Heen did not feel as strongly, but they concurred. So late in the afternoon of Thursday, August 7, Roth called Burris to tell him of the group's decision and then took the essay to the *Star-Bulletin*'s offices, where he found David Shapiro, the managing editor, about to leave for the day. Roth described the situation to Shapiro, who agreed to read the essay that night at home and to meet with Roth first thing the next morning. From home, Shapiro called the *Star-Bulletin*'s editorial-page

David Shapiro and Diane Chang, the Honolulu Star-Bulletin's *managing editor and editorial-page editor, respectively, made the decision to publish the "Broken Trust" essay.*

editor, Diane Chang. The two of them were waiting for Roth when he showed up at the *Star-Bulletin*'s offices the next morning.

Shapiro and Chang peppered Roth with questions about sources and about the authors' ability to back up statements in the essay. Roth showed them his notes and explained which sources would be willing to step forward if necessary. Shapiro and Chang knew that publishing the essay could be extremely good for the struggling *Star-Bulletin*—or extremely bad. The stakes were high, and the *Star-Bulletin*'s publisher and editor, John Flanagan, was out of town and unavailable. Shapiro asked Roth to step out of the room for a few minutes so he could talk privately with Chang. Less than a minute later, Chang emerged from the room, smiling. The piece would run, as is, immediately. If Brandt, King, Kekumano, Heen, and Roth were willing to put their names on the essay, Chang and Shapiro were willing to publish it.

Within minutes staffers began to prepare a lead article, headlines, a companion editorial, artwork, and a political cartoon. As Shapiro copyedited the essay, Roth heard him say under his breath, to no one in particular, "God, I love this job."

A few minutes later Shapiro assigned a reporter to get comments on the essay from Bishop Estate trustees and Supreme Court justices. The plan was to include their comments in the lead article. Chief Justice Moon never returned the reporter's call. The call to Kawaiahaʻo Plaza was returned immediately, but directly to Shapiro. Bishop Estate's director of communications, Elisa Yadao, wanted publication postponed until she could review the essay thoroughly with the trustees, and she wanted time to prepare a detailed, point-by-point response. Shapiro refused. He thought "Broken Trust" was important news that needed to be brought to the public's attention and feared any delays could go on endlessly as trustees threw up new barriers. He told Yadao the trustees could comment in the lead article now and could have as much space as they wanted at a future date of their choosing for a rebuttal essay of their own. Yadao declined both offers.

The next day, Saturday, August 9, 1997, "Broken Trust" appeared in the *Star-Bulletin* with a front-page lead story, an editorial cartoon, and an editorial that said four trustees—Wong, Peters, Lindsey, and Jervis—had betrayed the trust vested in them by the will of Princess Bernice Pauahi Bishop and should resign.

Eight days after "Broken Trust" appeared in the *Star-Bulletin*, the Sunday *Advertiser* ran front-page articles and a banner headline, "Bishop Estate Firestorm." Slightly smaller headlines read, "Months of Criticism Batter Venerable Trust" and "Justices, Head Trustee Reject Critics' Charges."

The *Advertiser* editorial section had been expanded to include a long response to "Broken Trust" signed by the chairman of the Bishop Estate board, Dickie Wong. He denied that there were problems on the Kamehameha campus, and he denied the breaches of fiduciary duty at Kawaiahaʻo Plaza. Wong said that Bishop Estate had never been bigger or better financially; its credit rating had the highest grade possible. Educationally, he said, Kamehameha was excellent. For the trustees, Pauahi's will was the bible, and it put them in charge. The trust, her gift, was not broken. What threatened its very foundations was the "frenzy of challenges," "baseless and unprovable charges," mud thrown by critics who had "gone into the gutter."

Also in the *Advertiser*'s editorial section were a long critique of "Broken Trust" by *Advertiser* staff and a scathing commentary by Gatti, who said that "Broken Trust" had been inaccurate and unfair and that its authors had acted precipitously and irresponsibly.

Rounding out the *Advertiser*'s section that week was a large picture

By 1994 all five state Supreme Court justices were Waihe'e appointees (left to right): Associate Justices Paula Nakayama and Robert Klein; Chief Justice Ronald Moon; Associate Justices Stephen Levinson and Mario Ramil. © Gary Hofheimer Photography, Haleiwa, Hawai'i

of the five Supreme Court justices in their robes: Chief Justice Ronald T. Y. Moon and Associate Justices Steven H. Levinson, Robert G. Klein, Paula A. Nakayama, and Mario R. Ramil. Below the picture were their considered thoughts on the "Broken Trust" essay. They wrote that it was "factually inaccurate, distorted, irresponsible," and it had "expressly and impliedly impugned the integrity, honesty, ethics, intelligence, qualifications, competence and professionalism not only of the five members of the Hawai'i Supreme Court as individuals, but also of the court as an institution." The justices said they selected Bishop Estate trustees with solemnity and seriousness out of respect for Pauahi's wishes and "a sense of historic duty that cannot be minimized."

Then the justices defended their treatment of the blue-ribbon panel several years earlier and gave themselves the highest grades for scrupulousness and fidelity to duty. Any statement of "purported fact, innuendo or suggestion" that they were otherwise motivated was "unfounded, reckless speculation" on the part of the "self-sanctified" co-authors of "Broken Trust," "whose motivations should be seriously questioned."

Star-Bulletin commentaries that appeared later that month reflected what people across the state were saying about the justices:

> Citizens rely on the state's highest court to find justice in the most obscure cases. Why, then, can't the Hawai'i Supreme Court see something as plain to the average person as the mustache on John Waihe'e's face? When they appoint as Bishop Estate trustees powerful politicians, who themselves appoint members of the Judicial Selection Commission, who in turn nominate candidates for the Supreme court, etc., our esteemed justices lower themselves into base politics. (August 23, 1997)

> Instead of filling the Bishop Estate with qualified CEOs, which they say is their goal, justices gave three of the last five lucrative appointments to two legislators who appointed members of the Judicial Selection Commission and one member of the commission. (August 30, 1997)

"*Broken Trust*" set off other strong reactions. One of the trustees' lawyers, Michael Hare, criticized the authors for "throwing mud" and "tarring people with rhetorical questions and faulty logic." Hare said it was wrong for the authors to reveal that his firm received over $10 million in legal fees from Bishop Estate in the years following his term chairing the Judicial Selection Commission. He did not question the statement's accuracy; he simply argued that it might lead readers to assume a connection.

John Waihe'e told reporters he was disappointed that the "Broken Trust" authors had not had "the courtesy to call to check the facts." He gave his version of the blue-ribbon panel story and of a subsequent meeting he had had with Kekumano to discuss the matter. Kekumano subsequently said Waihe'e's story was "not the same as my clear recollection of what transpired."

U.S. Senator Daniel Inouye declined to comment on the essay, calling the situation "rather tragic and sad." The other senator from Hawai'i, Daniel Akaka, defended the trustees. He said the level of compensation

was not too high; if anything, the trustees deserved to be paid more. His elder brother, Abraham, still pastor of Kawaiahaʻo Church, delivered a completely different message from his pulpit. He said that the moral character of the trustees needed to be carefully weighed.

The Bishop Estate communications department characterized the essay as an attack on Pauahi's legacy. They placed full-page newspaper ads defending the trustees, with Pauahi's portrait prominently placed. Wong insisted that the essay was the work of Roth, a Mainland *haole*. The trustees' chief in-house lawyer, Nathan Aipa, picked up on this, repeatedly referring to the "Broken Trust" authors as "the Roth group." Aipa also told reporters that Sam King was probably just sore because nobody ever made him a Bishop Estate trustee. Those reporters called King for a response, and King was happy to oblige: "Nathan Aipa is an ass."

Robert Midkiff, a successful businessman with strong family ties to Kamehameha Schools, criticized Bishop Estate's management structure and its financial performance. He said publicly that it would be in the trust's best interests—and the best interests of Kamehameha Schools—for Bishop Estate to re-structure itself into a nonprofit corporation. According to Midkiff, this would involve bringing its governance structure into the twenty-first century, with a board of directors rather than a board of trustees—something Bishop Museum had already done to its advantage. He added that a Bishop Estate board of directors should include outstanding individuals from outside Hawaiʻi.

Henry Peters did not appreciate Midkiff's outspokenness. Peters saw Midkiff, who was then in his late seventies, one day on the practice green at the Waiʻalae Country Club and started after him as if he were going to assault Midkiff with his putter. Peters stopped only when his golfing partner grabbed his arm and held him back. The next time Peters sighted Midkiff was in the club's locker room. Peters exclaimed in a voice that could be heard throughout the room that he would put his investment portfolio up against Midkiff's at any time. Midkiff, said Peters, was nothing but a "white-ass *haole*."

Peters also took aim at the four Hawaiian co-authors of "Broken Trust," calling them "high muckety-muck, country-club Hawaiians" and "a very arrogant group."

The May 15 march by Na Pua had put a spotlight on the problems at Kamehameha Schools. The "Broken Trust" essay expanded the zone of

attention. The public now knew that the problems at Bishop Estate were greater than just the work of one heavy-handed trustee on the Kamehameha campus, and they involved more than just Bishop Estate.

A topic that had previously received surprisingly little media coverage was suddenly front-page news every day. The *Advertiser* and the *Star-Bulletin* each poured more and more resources into coverage of the unfolding events, as if they were at war over who "owned" the story. George Chaplin, the *Advertiser*'s editor from 1953 to 1986, called "Broken Trust" and the follow-up coverage the biggest news story to hit Hawaiʻi since Pearl Harbor. The *New York Times*, the *Wall Street Journal*, the *Washington Post*, *USA Today*, *60 Minutes*, and many other national and international media outlets said basically or exactly the same thing. In an interview for a Mainland publication, Oz Stender wearily described the media coverage as constant: "The whole community has come unglued."

Everybody was talking about Bishop Estate, and not in glowing terms. More than talk, these events galvanized action, a chain of events that would never be forgotten by those who took part in them, and whose ultimate outcome seemed at every turn uncertain.

chapter 13

Like Investigating the CIA

Governor Benjamin Cayetano and his attorney general, Margery Bronster —who, as *parens patriae*, was supposed to watch out for the interests of the beneficiaries of charitable trusts—did not get involved when trust abuse was obvious, nor when the Kamehameha *'ohana* marched. They also chose not to intervene when Na Pua and Na Kumu formed and asked for their help. But the political climate had just changed. Community reaction to "Broken Trust" signaled that the public—including the Kamehameha *'ohana*—would support an investigation, even demand it. Political observers did not know what to expect. Cayetano was a Democrat, and there were undeniable connections between Bishop Estate and the Democratic Party. But Cayetano was also an independent thinker, and he felt little *aloha* for Waihe'e and Waihe'e's crowd, including the justices. Theoretically it was the attorney general, not the governor, who decided whether to investigate a charitable trust. But this was not just any charitable trust.

Then, on August 12, 1997, three days after the publication of "Broken Trust," Cayetano made a blockbuster announcement: He had just instructed his attorney general to begin an investigation. Serious accusations raised by prominent leaders could not be overlooked, said Cayetano. Asked by reporters why he had not called for an investigation sooner, the governor explained there had always been an unspoken understanding in the community that Bishop Estate business was the business of Hawaiians. Cayetano, a non-Hawaiian, said, "If the beneficiaries don't get excited, why should we?"

Bronster's investigation would not be the only one. Patrick Yim had started his fact-finding research into problems at Kamehameha Schools

*Colbert Matsumoto fit the profile of the typical court-appointed
master: a political insider with no background in trust law.*

several weeks earlier. He declined to talk to reporters, however, so the
public knew little about that investigation. The master's report was also
due to be filed, in just one month. The master, Colbert Matsumoto, had
been reviewing the trustees' annual accounts for months.

Prior to the publication of "Broken Trust," there was no reason to expect Matsumoto's report to be out of the ordinary. He fit the usual description of a Bishop Estate master: a political insider with little or no
background in trust law. Matsumoto had been Cayetano's staff attorney
in the legislature and had also been prominent in Cayetano's successful
run for governor.

After reading "Broken Trust" and hearing that Cayetano had instructed Bronster to investigate, Matsumoto told friends, "It's a whole
new ball game." He requested an extension and sought help from Ed Halbach, his former law professor at Berkeley and the same trust expert who
had agreed to conduct a workshop that four trustees refused to attend.
In addition, Matsumoto hired a local certified public accountant, Steven
Sakamaki, to help make sense of the numbers. Matsumoto also took a

closer look at new probate court rules that applied to official investigations of charitable trusts in Hawai'i. He found that these gave him the legal authority to inspect anything at Bishop Estate—anything—whether or not the trustees approved. At Kawaiaha'o Plaza, when Dickie Wong first heard what Matsumoto was demanding, he asked his lawyers to put these complex new rules into layman's language. They said it boiled down to this: "Whatever Colbert wants, Colbert gets."

Although Matsumoto was looking as deeply as possible into the workings of Bishop Estate, the media reported little about him or his work. This suited Matsumoto just fine. Like Yim, he felt strongly that the courtroom, not the newspapers, was the proper place to present his findings and make his recommendations.

Also proceeding under the public radar was an Internal Revenue Service audit of the trust and its for-profit companies. The audit had begun in 1995, the same year a *Wall Street Journal* article had appeared in which it had been suggested that some of Bishop Estate's dealings would never withstand IRS scrutiny. By the time "Broken Trust" was published, agents from the IRS had been working at Kawaiaha'o Plaza for the better part of two years. They were few in number but easy to spot. They all dressed and acted like Mainlanders engaged in serious business. They did not socialize or do much more than nod as they entered and left Kawaiaha'o Plaza each day. The door to their office opened only to allow documents to be taken in; it was then shut and locked again.

A glance at the newspapers of the time would give the impression that there was only one investigation: the attorney general's. And, whatever that investigation did or did not accomplish in the legal realm, it made great press and completely captured the public's imagination. Margery S. Bronster was one of only a few female attorneys general in the nation. Highly visible women in public life were a distinct minority in Hawai'i; young, *haole* women in high places were an even smaller group. Here was a *haole* woman, still in her thirties, going after the powerful, all-Hawaiian board of Bishop Estate, seemingly alone. This unique position, along with Bronster's confrontational style, invited vivid metaphors. She was portrayed, in print and in editorial cartoons, as a fearless dragon slayer. The *Star-Bulletin* ran a half-page headshot of Bronster with a headline that asked, "Who Is This Person Who Dares Go Eye to Eye with Bishop Estate?" The companion article quoted the state's budget director, Earl Anzai: "She's not going to be intimidated, that's for sure." He added that she was principled "to a fault." To illustrate his point, Anzai described how Bronster made him leave the room when she briefed Cayetano on the status of her investigation, just because Anzai's wife had been a Bishop Estate lawyer during the years under investigation and had been named as a defendant, along with the trustees, in a large lawsuit that arose out of a Bishop Estate investment. Bronster was equally direct and unbending in other arenas, including the courtroom. In the words of a prominent Honolulu attorney, she was a Rambo, the kind of lawyer who would tie on the headband, pick up the machine gun, and go. Another lawyer described her trial tactics as "scorched earth."

Bronster was a litigator by training and temperament. She had no background or apparent interest in wills, trusts, taxes, or charities. Before "Broken Trust," she did not even know what authority she had, if any, to investigate Bishop Estate. When Cayetano told her to investigate, she turned to Kevin Wakayama, the only deputy attorney general with experience in the area, for help. Wakayama explained the nature and extent of her *parens patriae* powers and responsibilities and advised her to conduct the investigation under the new probate court rules that Colbert Matsumoto was employing so effectively in his own efforts. Wakayama added that Bronster could not automatically publicize confidential information acquired in this way, but the probate court would allow her to do so if the request was reasonable.

Bronster told Wakayama that she intended to take a different route. She did not want to fool around in probate court or be constricted by probate court rules; her plan was to use subpoenas to force cooperation and then make public whatever she found. Wakayama believed that the trustees would use every legal maneuver available to stall such an investigation, and that Bronster would get bogged down trying to enforce the subpoenas for information she could easily obtain under the probate rules. In an effort to get Bronster to change her mind, Wakayama arranged for her to meet with Matsumoto, who told the attorney general he did not understand her thinking. If the goal was to get information, why not go through the probate court? But Bronster had already made up her mind, and so the meeting was short. After Matsumoto and Wakayama left Bronster's office, Matsumoto asked, "Whose side is she on, anyway?"

Bronster took the route that invited a head-to-head confrontation, and she got it. To battle her, the trustees hired Bill McCorriston to head up an all-star legal team made up of a half dozen or more large firms. McCorriston's reputation among lawyers was that of a skillful advocate who "played to win."

Stender knew of McCorriston's reputation, and that six other firms already had been contacted to provide support to McCorriston's efforts. Stender expressed grave concerns about this development in a memo to the other trustees.

It appears to me that we have engaged a battery of attorneys to declare "war" with the state's attorney general. Not being an attorney, this tactic is puzzling to me. It would appear to me that we as trustees—in the interest of protecting the trust—would want to cooperate in every way with the attorney general to determine the truth. And, if in the investigation of these allegations, we find that there have been transgressions against or mismanagement of the trust, we would want to know and do what is necessary to correct it.

Stender's memo ended with a question: "Are we engaging the services of these attorneys to protect the legacy or to protect trustees?"

At times the legal battlefield looked tilted indeed. Bronster assigned a team of deputies to investigate, but Wakayama was the only one with expertise and experience in trust law. She hired an outside law firm to provide trust-law expertise. Within just a few weeks, her team had issued more than a hundred subpoenas, then two hundred, then three hundred, with more to come. There was a limit to her resources, however. Other state agencies started complaining about not getting needed legal help from Bronster's office, and the arrangement with the outside law firm proved too expensive to maintain. Bronster's deputies were stretched to the breaking point; in financial and manpower terms, McCorriston had her hopelessly outgunned. Anyone reading the newspapers, however, was only vaguely aware of the supporting cast on either side of the developing legal showdown.

What reporters saw—and therefore what they reported—was Bronster and McCorriston going head-to-head in public. Blow-by-blow accounts of their encounters filled the newspapers and TV newscasts, and the public loved it. As Matsumoto, Yim, and the IRS were quietly gathering the explosive information that would ultimately drive events to their conclusion, the public watched Bronster and McCorriston lobbing grenades at one another.

The edge between the two lawyers was sharp, and it quickly grew personal. When Bronster subpoenaed McCorriston's billing records, he had her served with a subpoena of his own, at her home, early on a Sunday morning. Bronster told her deputies that she would not have hired

Attorney General Margery Bronster and Bishop Estate lead lawyer Bill McCorriston both had a reputation of being ready to do what it took to win. Each spent more time with reporters than in court.

McCorriston or any of his lawyers to work for her: they fell short on competence and character. McCorriston let it be known that he had declined even to interview Bronster a few years earlier when she had expressed interest in joining his firm.

Bronster and her deputies complained of "stonewalling" on the part of McCorriston and his clients. Bronster marveled at how they acted as if Bishop Estate's very existence depended on the maintenance of absolute secrecy. The trust's chief in-house lawyer, Nathan Aipa, unwittingly and hilariously embodied this mentality when he showed up in court one day with the minutes of completely routine board meetings in a briefcase that he had handcuffed to his wrist.

Bronster and McCorriston talked daily to reporters. He claimed that she used "weasel words," engaged in "character assassination," and had a "hidden agenda" to get Cayetano re-elected and lay the groundwork for her own future in elective politics. McCorriston also complained that Bronster's subpoenas were creating an unreasonable overload of work for Bishop Estate: six staffers copying full time, a quarter of a million pages of documents that had been produced already, and "truckloads" more to come.

Bronster countered that what McCorriston provided was too much of the wrong thing and not nearly enough relevant information. On Lokelani Lindsey's purchase of the Van Dyke book collection, for instance, McCorriston produced five thousand photocopies of title pages that nobody at the attorney general's office cared about, but he did not offer up Lindsey's crucial two-page memo that ordered payment of trust funds without board authorization; Bronster found out about it only through documents subpoenaed from the escrow company that had been holding the money.

In a potentially crippling blow, Circuit Judge Kevin Chang ruled that Bronster could not force production of privileged documents, at least not by issuing subpoenas as she had done, and that it was too late to start over in probate court. Bronster immediately appealed to the Supreme Court, where several years' worth of cases were already backed up. Judge Chang had hobbled Bronster's investigation in a single stroke.

Bronster was able to get literally tons of non-privileged materials, but even that did not come quickly or easily. McCorriston found reasons to contest each key subpoena and to appeal adverse rulings. Each subpoena had its own story, often bizarre or petty. There was the time Mc-Corriston provided only four boxes of requested documents when Bronster expected twelve. Deputy Attorney General Hugh Jones asked the court to hold the trustees in contempt for not providing the other eight boxes. McCorriston said the requested items would actually require at least fifteen to twenty boxes, and that he needed more time. When Mc-Corriston eventually produced a total of only twelve boxes, he explained that the documents had been moved from one type of box to another; that's why there were fewer boxes. Not willing to accept McCorriston's word on this, Jones put a fellow deputy attorney general on the stand with the two kinds of boxes and a tape measure.

Thousands of hours of expensive lawyer time were spent on such skirmishes. Each time a judge issued a ruling, the losing side appealed. Appeals could have been expedited, but the Supreme Court justices declined to do so.

At the rate things were going, it would be years before Bronster had the documents she was seeking, if she got them at all.

While Bronster and McCorriston bloodied each other in public, neither gaining a clear upper hand, progress was occurring on other fronts. By mid-November, shocking developments were raining down at a breakneck pace. The master, Colbert Matsumoto, although far from finished with his work, had decided to issue a preliminary report, which would serve two purposes: he wanted to put pressure on Patrick Yim, who he feared would whitewash the problems at Kamehameha Schools, and he wanted to demonstrate to the IRS that the probate court was taking the troubles at Bishop Estate seriously, in the hope of heading off the grave federal action he was afraid would come.

Matsumoto submitted his preliminary report on November 17, 1997. It was 119 pages long, carefully structured, clearly written, and remarkably direct in its assessment: Bishop Estate trustees were nowhere near compliance either with the law or with Pauahi's will. The investment decisions had been haphazard; conflicts of interest were evident; strategic planning was sorely lacking; the basis used for calculating trustees' fees was flawed; minutes of board meetings were woefully deficient; and annual reports fell short in ten major ways. Matsumoto had been "taken aback" by the level of secrecy he found at Kawaiahaʻo Plaza; he said he could not help feeling as though he were reviewing the Central Intelligence Agency's finances rather than those of a charitable educational organization. And he was amazed by what a close look at the books revealed. With Sakamaki's assistance, Matsumoto determined that the trustees had not generated the substantial investment returns they had claimed. In fact, for the year under review—July 1, 1993, to June 30, 1994—Bishop Estate investments actually lost $135 million. Matsumoto was especially critical of the lead trustee system of governance, which, as he explained thoroughly, violated basic principles of trust law. The system's abolition was just one on a list of twenty-one recommendations Matsumoto made to the probate court.

Hours before making his report public, Matsumoto took copies to Kawaiahaʻo Plaza for Bishop Estate's attorneys, Nathan Aipa and Bruce Graham, to read. When he returned an hour later to see if they had any questions, he found them speechless. This was unlike any master's report they had ever seen.

Matsumoto wasn't the only one who feared a whitewash by Yim. The "Broken Trust" authors shared his concern and decided there should be a second public essay, this one focused exclusively on Lindsey's impact on the education side of Bishop Estate.

On November 27, 1997, the *Star-Bulletin* published "Broken Trust II." The headline read: "Schools' Gross Mismanagement Must Stop Now—Tyranny, Distrust, Poor Decisions Reign at Kamehameha." The opening words were: "We are appalled by developments at Kamehameha Schools since the appointment of Lokelani Lindsey as 'lead trustee' for education." The body of the essay, like that of "Broken Trust," piled up evidence of things gone terribly wrong, beginning with the firing of the 171 outreach workers in 1995 and going on to describe Lindsey's public statements that Kamehameha teachers were incompetent, her closed-door interrogation of a student leader, her threat to fire Na Kumu representatives for speaking out, and more.

Like "Broken Trust," this second essay had five authors, and only Brandt was a member of both groups. All were noted experts on education, and a majority were Hawaiian and had been intimately connected with Kamehameha Schools: Isabella ʻAiona Abbott, Ph.D., professor of botany at the University of Hawaiʻi and a 1937 graduate of the Kamehameha School for Girls; Winona K. D. Rubin, former assistant to the president of Kamehameha and former state director of human services; Nona Beamer, former student and teacher at Kamehameha and author of the incendiary letter that helped get the marchers rolling; and Roderick F. McPhee, president emeritus of Punahou School and the group's only *haole*.

Over the course of three and a half months, Patrick Yim, the trustees' handpicked fact-finder, conducted 160 interviews and collected twelve hundred completed questionnaires, all under the watchful eye of Beadie Dawson, Na Pua's lawyer. People from all walks of campus life stepped forward to tell their stories, which were overwhelmingly critical of Lokelani Lindsey.

Yim wanted to keep things contained, to resolve them internally, quietly, perhaps using *ho'oponopono*, a Hawaiian form of mediation. On November 10 he met with the trustees to make an offer: He was prepared to submit a detailed report of his findings and to recommend that Lindsey be removed as a trustee, but there was another option. He was willing instead to report back a single word to Hirai: *pau* (completely done). All she or the public would ever know was that the matter had been resolved. For him to do that, however, Lindsey had to step down as lead trustee for education, apologize to the people she had offended, and agree to stay away from the campus.

On hearing Yim's conditions, Lindsey cried, Wong protested, and Peters erupted. Despite the uproar, Yim never raised his voice, nor did he retreat. The meeting ended without an agreement.

Over the next few days, Yim tried to reach Dickie Wong by phone, but his messages were not returned. Stender managed to talk at length with Wong and tried his best to convince him that Lindsey's retreat was the best option, but Wong would not even consider it. He said Yim was asking for too much, that it would be disloyal for Wong not to support Lindsey now.

Yim reached Lindsey and arranged a one-on-one meeting. She listened to him go over all the reasons why she should accept his offer, but again she refused to budge. As the exasperated Yim was leaving, Lindsey thanked him for meeting with her. "Don't thank me," he told her. "I'm going to be your worst nightmare."

Yim's comment convinced Lindsey that she needed to unleash a full-on counteroffensive. Some time ago she had ordered staffers to compile all kinds of statistics from the years Michael Chun was president of Kamehameha Schools. As organized and presented, these would give the appearance of lamentable failures: reading and math scores that got worse as students moved from first grade to fifth grade; roughly half the sixth-graders of 1995 failing the promotion examination to seventh grade; more than half the graduating class of 1997 with SAT scores that would not qualify them for admission to the University of Hawai'i; and median scores far below those of rival private schools Punahou and 'Io-lani. The overarching message was that Kamehameha was falling behind as a school. As Lindsey would later put it, "The longer students were at Kamehameha, the worse they performed." And that wasn't all. Lindsey also had documents supposedly showing that Chun and his wife had spent money extravagantly and without proper authority, amounting to hundreds of thousands of unauthorized dollars.

Lindsey organized all these materials in three-ring binders, labeled them "An Imperative for Educational Change," and distributed them at a trustees' meeting in late November—the day after "Broken Trust II" appeared, and one week before Yim was scheduled to submit his report to the probate court. On top of each binder was a two-paragraph statement in boldface type about the critical need for confidentiality. Lindsey read this statement aloud to the board and explained that a leak of this report to the media could be devastating to Kamehameha students. At Dickie Wong's request, Nathan Aipa stamped each copy "Confidential—Attorney-Client Privilege." Oz Stender, who had been accused of leaking information from the boardroom, asked Aipa to keep the copy Stender had been given, so any leaks couldn't be blamed on him.

Nevertheless, just one week later the contents of Lindsey's confidential report was on the *Advertiser*'s front page. They had been provided to Greg Barrett, along with a three-hour interview, by none other than Lindsey herself. Even Peters and Wong could hardly believe what she was doing. She had sought their permission to "tell her story," but they had no idea what Lindsey had planned. Missing from the copy Lindsey furnished to Barrett was the cautionary language about confidentiality that she had stressed seven days before. In her interview, Lindsey told Barrett there were serious problems at Kamehameha that she was determined to correct; she wanted people to understand that the problems were Michael Chun's doing, not hers; she was just the messenger; the criticisms of her in "Broken Trust II" were mere allegations, not facts; like Yim's report, that essay had been based solely on rumors and malicious gossip. According to Lindsey, Stender and other alumni had formed a conspiracy against her, all because they did not want people to know the truth about how bad things were at Kamehameha Schools because of Chun.

JONES

CHUN

LINDSEY

HUMAN SHIELD

Patrick Yim had filed his report under seal, presumably not expecting it to ever see the light of day. But when Lindsey's report showed up in the *Advertiser*, the probate judge, Colleen Hirai, made Yim's report public. It read like an indictment. It was like "Broken Trust II" again, and then some—from someone who had been handpicked by the trustees. The words Yim used to describe Lindsey's behavior read like a dictionary of disastrous management: Lindsey had been "abusive," "arbitrary," "controlling," "disrespectful," "hostile," "insensitive," "intemperate," "intimidating," "oppressive," "presumptuous," "rash," "threatening."

Yim detailed the many ways administrators had been bullied, admissions decisions manipulated, and informants used to maintain absolute control over all aspects of campus life. He also described how Lindsey had undermined the school's zero-tolerance drug policy by intervening on behalf of relatives and children of her friends; had decreed that kindergartners learn by Christmas of each year to identify all the trustees by picture and name; and had seemingly gone out of her way to insult teachers and staff, individually and collectively, calling them overpaid, underworked, and hopelessly incompetent.

Yim, who held the same dim view of the lead trustee system as Matsumoto, recommended that authority at Kamehameha be returned to the school's president, Michael Chun, and that Lindsey give up any position of control or direct oversight of the schools.

That afternoon, Wong and Peters stood by Lindsey's side at a press conference as she defended herself, repeating again and again that she was just the messenger. If people did not like what they were hearing, they should look to the school's president for answers. Then Wong stepped to the microphone. Only four months earlier he had insisted that Kamehameha was educationally excellent; now he was saying the opposite. The problems at Kamehameha were so troubling that Lindsey had done the right thing in going public with her report.

What happened next surprised a lot of people. Wong got misty-eyed, and acknowledged that more was at stake than just Lindsey's future. "Dickie Wong," he said, "ain't going down without a fight."

Wong's emotions were understandable. By the time the Yim report was released, on December 12, 1997, the trustees had already been sent reeling by the public release of the Matsumoto report in probate court the month before, and they could see that the IRS audit was headed in a direction in which they did not want it to go. The "majority" trustees were used to controlling situations, but now they were in a desperate state of damage control.

The trustees' initial reaction to Matsumoto's harsh assessment was to circle the wagons. They and their lawyers accused Matsumoto of being factually wrong on any number of matters. They also blamed Steven Sakamaki, the accountant who had helped Matsumoto analyze the trust's financial records. They said that Sakamaki was a small-time pencil pusher who had taken a small-minded approach. Bishop Estate was too big for such a minor-league player; Sakamaki could not begin to understand the complexities of their situation. They compared him to a blind man feeling only one part of an elephant but trying to describe the entire animal.

At the probate court hearing on Matsumoto's report just two days later, however, it turned out that Sakamaki was not blind. Acting on advice from their lawyers, the trustees formally accepted all but one of Matsumoto's twenty-one recommendations. It was a complete turnaround, one the trustees hoped would buy them a little more time. One of their twenty concessions was an agreement to implement a traditional organizational structure, in which a hired, well-qualified CEO would run the trust and the trustees provide only oversight. In private, though, Peters told members of his asset-management team that they would always report only to him. When asked by a senior staff member whether that would not violate the agreement to end the lead trustee system—an agreement that had just been communicated to the master and attorney general—Peters explained, "These are not honorable people. One does not deal honorably with dishonorable people."

O*z* S*tender* had been absent from the trustees' emotional news conference after the release of the Yim report, but this was no surprise. Also conspicuously absent was Gerard Jervis, who until only recently had stood firm with Wong, Peters, and Lindsey, as one of the "majority" trustees.

Soon after Matsumoto had intensified his investigation, however, Jervis began to talk privately about possibly joining forces with Stender.

By the end of October, he had done so. The *Star-Bulletin* called it "an about-face," and that was exactly what it was. The week before "Broken Trust" appeared, Jervis had been cursing and throwing things at Stender. Prior to that, he had even hired a private investigator, paid for with trust funds, to dig up dirt on Stender. But now, just a few months later, Jervis was on Stender's side.

In newspaper commentary, Jervis was portrayed as opportunistic, but Stender welcomed the companionship anyway. The minority side of the table had been lonely. Wong often told people that power boiled down to numbers: "Five beats four; three beats two; two beats one." For years Stender had been the odd man out in a four-beats-one Bishop Estate boardroom. Now, with Jervis at his side, Stender was one vote away from controlling Bishop Estate. And he had a plan to get that final vote.

$\mathcal{B}y$ 1997 Stender had been a Bishop Estate trustee for eight years, and he had often spoken privately about what he perceived to be serious misconduct by the other trustees. He had shared some of these concerns with a series of masters and had met with lawyers in the attorney general's office in 1992 and again in 1995, trying unsuccessfully to get them to launch an investigation. Although he was duty bound to do more than just complain privately about serious abuse, the advice he had gotten from a well-placed lawyer was that a lawsuit against his co-trustees would cost Stender at least $2 million, and that he probably would not prevail in any Hawai'i court.

In addition to the financial cost of filing a lawsuit, Stender knew that he could be inviting his own removal. This potential grew greater with each passing year. How could he explain not having petitioned the court for eight years when by his own admission there had been serious breaches of trust from the beginning? Worse yet from Stender's standpoint: There was not a single allegation in Matsumoto's master's report that would not apply as much to Stender as it did to the others. In fact, because Stender had been in the Bishop Estate boardroom longer than anyone except Peters, his personal exposure was relatively great.

This legal equation for Stender changed in December 1997, however, with the publication of the Yim report and Lindsey's leaking of her own "confidential" report. Rather than having to seek the ouster of all of his fellow trustees, it opened a door for Stender to ask the court to remove a single trustee—Lindsey—based solely on her behavior as lead trustee

for education. The climate was right to single Lindsey out; the Kamehameha *'ohana,* deeply offended by Lindsey's actions, would enthusiastically support any effort to remove her.

Stender and Jervis wrote to Lindsey shortly after the Yim report became public. They said that they had arrived at the sad but certain conclusion: she must resign as a trustee, immediately.

> We cannot stand by and allow you to continue to bring harm
> upon our school and our children for whom you have the most
> sacred duty. You have breached your duty and are unfit to serve as
> a Trustee of the Bernice Pauahi Bishop Estate. We urge you to do
> the right thing by immediately resigning your position as Trustee.
> If not, we will petition the Probate Court for your removal.

Lindsey, predictably, refused to step aside, and the fight was on.

The year's stunning series of unprecedented events ended with one final blockbuster announcement. Seven months after the march of the Kamehameha *'ohana,* four months after the publication of "Broken Trust," one month after the release of the Matsumoto report, and two weeks after Yim submitted his sealed report, the *Advertiser* published Lind-

sey's "confidential" report, and the majority trustees switched overnight from ridiculing Matsumoto's recommendations to promising to
abide by them, the Hawai'i state Supreme Court did its own about-face.
Four of the five justices announced that, beginning immediately, they
would no longer select Bishop Estate trustees.

Four months earlier, in their response to the "Broken Trust" essay,
the justices had indignantly defended their sacred and historic duty
to select trustees. Now the justices said their continued participation
would "promote a climate of distrust and cynicism and . . . undermine
the trust that people must have in the judiciary."

When they made this thunderclap of an announcement, the justices
insisted that they had never acted politically or done anything wrong.
The *Star-Bulletin*'s editorial board didn't buy it:

> Trustee selections made by the justices have been lamentable be-
> cause political motivation was evident. The impropriety of the
> justices hearing cases involving trustees they had appointed is
> obvious. (December 22, 1997)

The *Advertiser* saw that problem and more: the justices' actions had
been driven completely, and even openly, by politics:

> By giving up the responsibility for naming trustees, the four jus-
> tices have broken a key link in the arrangement that kept the
> state's dominant Democrats in power for generations. The late
> Gov. John Burns and his army of loyalists . . . made no secret of
> their agenda. . . . In order to pursue their goals . . . they needed
> to exert control over the key institutions. Influence over Bishop
> Estate was part of the plan. And that influence was played, rather
> openly, through the governor's office to the judiciary and then
> on to the board of trustees of the Bishop Estate. (December 23,
> 1997)

Four justices put their names on the blockbuster announcement—
Moon, Levinson, Nakayama, and Ramil. Klein, the only Hawaiian of
the five justices, dissented in the strongest of terms. He called the decision unwise, untimely, and uncharted. If something was wrong with
justices' deciding the legal controversies of trustees they selected, the
answer was to appoint substitute justices, according to Klein. Klein was
prepared to continue selecting trustees "as a majority of one." That was
not likely, but what would happen was not clear. The probate court had
jurisdiction, which meant the probate judge had the power in his offi-

cial capacity to select trustees. But there was no reason to expect that one probate judge acting officially would necessarily do a better job than had five Supreme Court justices acting unofficially.

Cayetano was adamant: the selection of Bishop Estate trustees "cannot be left to one judge." Many people agreed. But if this function could not safely be left in the hands of five Supreme Court justices or one probate judge, how *should* future trustees be selected?

That would be a question for a new year.

chapter 14

Mistrust and Paranoia

If 1997 *had been* an earth-shattering year for Bishop Estate trustees, it had been equally unsettling, in different ways, to the trust's employees at Kawaiahaʻo Plaza and Kamehameha Schools. During the reign of the current trustees, employees had become accustomed to living by the proverb Japanese immigrants brought to Hawaiʻi: "The nail that sticks up gets pounded down."

The trustees' close monitoring of the march in May 1997 added paranoia to the atmosphere of fear within Kawaiahaʻo Plaza. Few dared, however, to say a word about it. The paranoia sprang from, as much as anything, the photographs that had been taken of the marchers. When asked about it, Dickie Wong said the photos were for the historical record. But Wong had never been known for his stewardship of institutional history, and the photos were not lodged in the Kamehameha archives with all the other historical items. Instead, they were last seen in Lokelani Lindsey's office, laid out on her desk, with her informants pointing at faces while Lindsey wrote down names on her yellow legal pad.

When "Broken Trust" appeared, the atmosphere at Kawaiahaʻo Plaza darkened even more. A senior staff member said it was "like being in a tomb, or a bunker." There was anxiety about computer files and e-mail. Was it really true that files could be retrieved from a central location even after they had been deleted from an individual computer? And what about e-mail? Could it be monitored without the user's knowing? Some people stopped using e-mail altogether.

Many believed that the phones were bugged. They thought they heard clicks and buzzes on the line. Sometimes they would finish a call, put the phone down, pick it up again, and hear no dial tone. Was that because the tap had not disconnected yet?

Oz Stender just assumed that his office was bugged. He would turn up the volume on his radio whenever he had something important to say.

Staffers received word one day that Kawaiahaʻo Plaza was going to be swept for electronic listening or viewing devices. This alone would be highly unusual, but there was more. The "sweep" was scheduled for a weekend, in the middle of the night. The reason given for the unusual scheduling was that it would not disrupt work. But to some, the middle of the night with no one around seemed like a perfect cover for installing bugs, rather than removing them. Staffers noted that there was no purchase order for the sweep. This was not standard procedure; it meant there was no way to check who authorized it or exactly what was requested. Payment was made on the basis of a nondescript invoice with a note that had been typed, not handwritten: "To Accounting: Confidential!" and an unreadable signature. The invoice was for "20 Phone Lines Surveil." It came from Special Systems and Services International, which turned out to be a storefront in a small shopping mall in ʻAiea that sold all kinds of surveillance devices.

Outside Kawaiahaʻo Plaza the nastiness had started early and spread, and it was still going on. Greg Barrett of the *Advertiser* received a threatening visit at home from a man who said it was his job to "make nice" with people before they got hurt: "You know what I mean, brah." Margery Bronster received direct threats, two of them serious enough to warrant security at her house. Beadie Dawson, the unofficial voice of Na Pua, received typewritten threats. Stender got anonymous phone calls at home, and someone slashed one of his car tires in a downtown parking garage.

A deputy attorney general received word one day that Lindsey had been seen at Kawaiahaʻo Plaza over the weekend, ordering files deleted from an office computer. Laurian Childers, an information technologist in charge of the Estate's computer network, told deputies that she had been instructed to make sure that the deleted files could not be restored. Childers swore to this in an affidavit. Sixty minutes after Childers made this statement, her husband received an anonymous phone call at home. A man's voice said, "Tell that f—— *haole* bitch if she knows what's good for her she won't testify."

Lindsey insisted that the deleted files were a collection of Hawaiian songs and some information about a trip to New Zealand and had nothing to do with the attorney general's investigation. She did not explain why, in the middle of an investigation, such innocuous items would need to be deleted from a computer over the weekend and carefully wiped clean from the server.

Childers wanted only to tell the truth and then be left alone. It was not to be. The threats continued. Bronster arranged for armed guards at the Childers' home and an escort for their three-year-old daughter to and from preschool. Childers loved her job at Bishop Estate, but the situation became intolerable. After several weeks of living in the company of armed guards, she and her family sold their home and moved away from Hawai'i. She never testified.

Morale at Kamehameha Schools was at an all-time low. Lindsey's leaked report felt like a punch in the stomach to many teachers and students. Nobody trusted Lindsey's version of the truth, but the report left them wondering what the real truth was.

When Patrick Yim turned in his fact-finding report, he strongly recommended that Bishop Estate get an independent assessment of the Kamehameha Schools' administration. The majority trustees—Peters, Wong, and Lindsey—were eager to comply. In short order they retained Peterson Consulting of San Francisco for the job. The non-bid contract, for an estimated $400,000, was awarded even before Peterson sent in its proposal. To Stender, it looked like the fix was in. He wrote a series of memos pointing out that the majority trustees had completely ignored a staff report on the subject and had picked Peterson without proper due diligence. He concluded: "No business in its right mind would select a consultant this way in light of the magnitude and importance of this project."

Stender was not alone in his discomfort with Peterson. The teachers had not been consulted, and according to Na Kumu, of the nineteen client areas listed on Peterson's own Web site, none had anything to do with education. By Na Kumu's definition, only two of the five team members had a background in education, and neither of them had specialist skills that justified the money Kamehameha was paying them, which eventually grew to $540,000.

Unsurprisingly, the Peterson report rehashed material from Lindsey's report and repeated Lindsey's primary message: the longer students were at Kamehameha, the worse they performed. Also as expected, the report drew a bead on Michael Chun. After first acknowledging that he had some fine qualities and good intentions and was loved by students, the Peterson Group gave Chun what amounted to a flunking grade: He lacked "the educational background and leadership skills the Schools need to take them successfully into the next century." He also had "lost the confidence" not just of the trustees, but also of the Kamehameha staff. One of Lindsey's personal attorneys, Michael Green, used the occasion to call Kamehameha "a factory of failure."

In an open letter, Chun reassured the *'ohana:* "The outstanding quality of our educational programs is found not only in our graduates but also in the pride and inspiration of all who have been touched by our schools. Let there be no doubt that Kamehameha is a great institution!" Na Pua and its spokesperson, Jan Dill, a classmate of Chun's at Kamehameha, echoed that assessment and expressed total confidence in Chun. Dill questioned the data and the motives behind the Peterson report, saying that the report was just "another example of how the trustees continue to manipulate the truth to serve their own personal interests rather than the interests of the students and the legacy of Pauahi."

Who, then, was responsible for the troubles at Kamehameha?

Patrick Yim, Na Pua, Na Kumu, "Broken Trust II" authors, Stender, and Jervis all blamed Lokelani Lindsey for whatever Kamehameha's problems might be. Lindsey and the Peterson Group, along with Wong and Peters, blamed Michael Chun. Chun didn't blame anyone, but neither did he stand up to, or for, anyone. Meanwhile, the teachers had to go in to work every day and explain to their students why the newspaper headlines were calling their beloved school a "factory of failure"— and why most of the Bishop Estate trustees, whose names and faces they had learned in kindergarten, seemed to agree.

The teachers had banded together as Na Kumu O Kamehameha because of Lokelani Lindsey. As events unfolded, they widened their sights. On June 6, 1997, the *Star-Bulletin*'s front-page headlines read, "Kamehameha faculty goes public; Risking their jobs, more than 200 teachers organize and issue a two-page statement blasting trustees."

Unlike the teachers, Kamehameha administrators did not complain publicly. They continued to follow orders (as required by their employment contracts), even when Lindsey, Wong, and Peters targeted Na Kumu and especially its leaders, Abad, Eyre, Hoe, and Obrecht. Two

Julian Ako was one of two renegade Kamehameha administrators who openly supported Na Kumu. He went on to become principal of Kamehameha High School in 2005.

administrators, however, became convinced that the situation was so abnormal, so perverse, that a higher duty required them to support the teachers, and to do so openly. These renegade administrators were Julian Ako and Kathy Kukea.

Ako had worked for Bishop Estate since 1979, first in outreach, then on campus as head of social studies, and finally as dean of student activities. Everyone in his family had gone to Kamehameha, and he himself had finished his senior year in 1961 at the head of his class, slightly ahead of Michael Chun. Ako's valedictorian's speech was on the biblical text, "For unto whomsoever much is given, of him shall be much required."

Kukea had spent nearly all of the preceding twenty years as the coordinator of curriculum and instruction at the Kamehameha high school. She had looked forward to having a woman trustee at Bishop Estate but had come to view Lindsey's appointment as a huge mistake.

Distance immediately developed between Ako and Kukea, on one side, and their boss, Tony Ramos, on the other. As the divide widened, fellow administrators found it increasingly difficult to keep one foot in each camp. Meetings grew more and more strained and stressful. One longtime senior administrator started holding prayer meetings in her office. Ramos reorganized the administrative team, pushing Ako and Kukea to the outer edges. Their personnel evaluations got stuck for a long time somewhere between Ramos' desk and Lindsey's, and meetings were held without their knowledge. Ramos stated in their presence that anyone who did not support trustee policy could always leave.

Ako and Kukea did not leave, but a number of teachers did, five for Punahou School. Roderick McPhee, who had served as Punahou's president for twenty-five years and had coauthored "Broken Trust II," described those five as truly outstanding teachers. Many teachers who were still at Kamehameha were now looking into other options.

Na Kumu decided that a teachers' union might improve the situation and hired a lawyer to help sort through the possibilities. These efforts drew financial support and encouragement from members of the statewide public-school teachers' union, but the Kamehameha teachers had little interest in being part of a large labor organization. They just wanted respect and protection.

Although deeply divided on other issues, all five trustees and Michael Chun were absolutely united in their desire to stop the teachers from forming a union. They hired a labor lawyer and a labor "consultant." Michael Chun wrote to Na Kumu that the two were being brought in to promote communication and help with "the healing process." Na Kumu quickly discovered, however, that the lawyer the trustees had hired specialized in sharp-edged advocacy for employers, and the consultant was known around town as a union buster.

The trustees said that the teachers could not hold organizing meetings on campus, but this was eventually ruled to be in violation of federal law. Then the trustees asserted that the Kamehameha teachers could not form a union because they all were part of the management *'ohana*. This, too, was determined to be without merit. Chun argued that a teachers' union at Kamehameha would be divisive. He campaigned against the idea with letters and memos and had an anti-union video running on the schools' closed-circuit TV system right up to the day of the union vote on March 13, 1998. When the secret ballots were tallied and certified, the result was 186 for a union, 36 against.

During the last few days of the union campaign, something else of great significance was happening on campus. A team from the Western Association of Schools and Colleges (WASC) was on an accreditation visit to the secondary school. There could hardly have been a worse time for

WASC to be taking a close look at Kamehameha. Even if WASC decided to re-accredit the school, the WASC team could not fail to observe that the campus was in turmoil. A report critical of teachers and students could be yet another serious blow to morale at Kamehameha. The WASC team worked non-stop, sitting in on classes, looking at portfolios of student work, talking with teachers and staff, and at night comparing their personal observations with the school's own self-study.

On the day of the union vote the WASC team gave the faculty and administration an hour-and-a-half preview of the report they planned to submit. In it, they said, they intended to describe teachers and staff as capable and committed, both to the school's mission and to the students. As for the students, they were "some of the nicest, friendliest, most energetic, capable, and promising youth in the world." Then the members of the WASC team outlined their thoughts about trustee governance. They called it a "perverse application of top-down management which openly undervalued, if not scorned, the professional expertise, talent and commitment of the non-administrative staff, and created an oppressive, intimidating, and fear-drenched climate." It was, in a word, "dysfunctional."

IN KAMEHAMEHA SCHOOLS, NEARLY EVERYBODY READS THE WASC ACCREDITATION REPORT...

When the WASC team finished the preview, there was complete silence. Then came bursts of applause, and, finally, a standing ovation. The teachers felt vindicated and hopeful.

The printed WASC report came out labeled "confidential," but the substance of it immediately turned up in the Honolulu dailies, where it reverberated for quite some time. WASC re-accredited Kamehameha for only three years. This was a flashing red light: something was wrong. Punahou had been re-accredited at almost the same time for six years, the maximum. So had eleven public schools; only three other schools in the state had been limited to three years. To many, this did not look good: Kamehameha, a private school with enormous financial resources, was at the bottom of the pile with a sad handful of struggling public schools.

The trustees' response was to order an investigation—not into any of the substantive areas faulted by the report, but to find the person who had failed to honor their order that the report be kept confidential. Chun assigned the investigation to Ramos, who eventually submitted a three-page report that was inconclusive. The majority trustees demanded a re-investigation. Pushing hardest was Lindsey. This time she wanted McCorriston's law firm to do the investigating. Jervis and Stender opposed this move, but they were outvoted.

McCorriston's people quickly established a campus presence and started calling in selected teachers and administrators. They questioned them on short notice, under oath, with a court reporter taking everything down. For a brief period, Stender and Jervis got a temporary restraining order from the circuit court after finding a woman staff member weeping under interrogation, "scared to death."

"One thing is certain," McCorriston said at the time, "the investigation will proceed." He called it standard business practice. The employee handbook prohibited unauthorized release of confidential material, and it would be wrong for the trustees not to get to the bottom of this, he said. When someone pointed out that Lokelani Lindsey had without authorization released a confidential report on education, McCorriston replied that that was different. Lindsey was a trustee, not an employee; the handbook did not apply to her.

The investigation of the leaked WASC report dragged on for months, at great expense to the trust, and never uncovered the source of the leak. The teachers said little publicly, but in private they were outraged. Outsiders had invaded the campus, commandeered office space, ordered teachers out of their classes for interrogation, and even threatened to subject them to lie-detector tests. And the president of their school had not stepped forward to stop it.

The teachers wanted Chun to stand up for them, even if it meant getting fired. That would make him a martyr to principle and rally Hawaiians to support him in sustained righteous rage. They saw Chun as the one figure who could mobilize and sustain that kind of passion.

Chun had chosen not to put his job on the line. If he had begun to lose the confidence of his faculty—or if, as the Peterson report said, he had already lost it—that was the reason. In private, Chun had sought guidance from others. Stender advised prudence and patience. He said the majority trustees had all the rope in the world with which to hang themselves, and that was what they were doing. Let them go on knotting the nooses around their necks; when those trustees kicked the trapdoor open beneath their own feet, Chun would still be standing. It was essentially the same advice Stender had been following himself for the past eight years.

Douglas Ing, Chun's personal attorney and longtime friend, also advised a cautious approach: what good would it do for a leader like Chun to get himself fired?

Gladys Brandt saw things differently. She told Chun that leadership was needed on campus, now. The situation had become intolerable for the teachers; it was just a matter of time before the students were affected, if that had not happened already. Brandt asked Chun, "Why be president if you don't act like a president?"

Confronted with conflicting advice, Chun turned to God. For years Chun had been a churchgoer at St. Andrew's Cathedral, but comfortable Episcopalianism was now insufficient. He became an evangelical Christian, born again. He prayed together with his wife, with staff members in their offices, and on the phone with alumni. He handed out WWJD bracelets—What Would Jesus Do? When it fell to Chun during these difficult times to summon up words of comforting guidance for his teachers and students, the message he most powerfully wanted the children of Pauahi to receive, above all else, was the need to draw closer to God.

chapter 15

A World Record for Breaches of Trust

As the investigations mounted, it became abundantly clear that Bishop Estate trustees, over time, had violated numerous fiduciary duties, perhaps even criminal laws. As the IRS eventually put it, they were treating Princess Pauahi's legacy like "a personal investment club," theirs to do with as they pleased, with shockingly little apparent concern about the trust's charitable mission. The trustees never had an overall investment plan and sometimes did not appropriately investigate before making investment decisions or monitor deals after they were made. Matsumoto, Sakamaki, and accountants from the Arthur Andersen firm eventually compiled a list of forty-seven Bishop Estate investments that each lost at least $2 million between 1994 and 1996.

Diversification, a cornerstone of prudent investing, did not seem to be a concern, much less a priority, for Bishop Estate trustees. At a time when they already owned 262,000 acres of land on the Big Island of Hawai'i, a promoter told Henry Peters about "the real estate deal of the century." That was his description of 30,500 acres of Big Island land formerly owned by Hāmākua Sugar, a former sugar plantation about to be sold at a bankruptcy auction. For years investment advisers had been advising that the trustees diversify more, not less, but Peters wanted to add this non-income-producing land to the trust estate anyway. He was determined, and he was in charge. Lawyers cautioned Peters not to bid more at the auction than the land's appraised value, so he checked to see what that was. Bishop Estate staffers familiar with the Hāmākua land initially said that acreage might be worth as much as $8 million to

Bishop Estate. After receiving a visit from Peters, however, they upped their estimate to $15 million. Evidently not satisfied with this, Peters hired an outside appraiser who, without inspecting the property, said he thought the land was worth $20 million.

An in-house staff report said if the Hāmākua land was to be acquired, the purchase should not be financed through borrowing; otherwise, the annual cost of servicing the debt would have to come out of income from other trust properties, and that would reduce the amount of money available for Kamehameha Schools. Yet, without even a vote from the trustees, Peters bought the land for $21 million—almost all of it borrowed. Nothing was recorded in minutes, not even the fact of the purchase. In the years following the purchase, the Hāmākua land generated operating losses well in excess of $1 million a year. This included the cost of security, which was provided by Larry Mehau's company.

Matsumoto's list of forty-seven separate transactions that each lost at least $2 million between 1994 and 1996 began with Kukui ($49,395,947); Montrose Group ($47,205,472); SoCal Holding ($34,459,800); JMB Cadillac Fairview ($29,000,000); and Rock Real Estate ($22,535,000). Before Matsumoto discovered this information and made it public, most people only knew about investments that either worked out well (because the trustees would talk about those) or that ended up in litigation outside Hawai'i (where courts rarely seal records). This second category included not just the oil and golf course deals previously mentioned, but also an Internet start-up called KDP Technologies.

KDP said it provided a computer dating service and software that allowed actors, entertainers, and models to display their talents on the Internet. This investment had been presented to Bishop Estate by Ben Bush III of California, whom Lindsey had met when they were both involved in an effort to buy gold hidden in the Philippines for resale to rich Arabs at a big profit. Lindsey had said nothing to the trustees about her personal business dealings with Bush, and Bishop Estate's staff did not look into his background. The staff member responsible for due diligence on the KDP deal took the view that because Bush had been introduced by Lindsey, his credibility was not to be questioned. If there was any field riskier than methane gas exploration or luxury golf course development, it was Internet start-ups. Bishop Estate initially committed only $500,000, but that quickly grew to $1.3 million. Bush got a finder's fee, reimbursement for a loan, and a salary of $90,000. Dickie Wong's brother-in-law, Randy Stone, received a $150,000-a-year consultancy, plus stock options.

The trustees eventually learned that Bush, in another part of his investment-advising activities, had been laundering money and committing fraud. He was indicted, tried, convicted, and jailed. Bishop Estate's entire investment in KDP, whose business product was described by a lawyer in the attorney general's office as "soft-core pornography," was lost completely. The personal money that Bush and Lindsey put into their gold scheme—$800,000 for Bush, $400,000 for Lindsey—also disappeared.

One high-profile investment, though, did turn out exceptionally well—Goldman Sachs. Even it, however, was not what would normally be called a "prudent" investment. This story began in December 1991, when Jon Corzine asked Matsuo Takabuki if he would be interested in putting Bishop Estate money into Goldman Sachs. Goldman Sachs wanted Bishop Estate as a partner in order to extend its global reach. Takabuki and Corzine negotiated back and forth over how big an interest the trust would get for $250 million, and the deal came together fairly quickly.

Corzine was back two years later, however, asking for another $250 million. The Goldman Sachs strategy was misfiring: Partners were quitting the firm and taking their money with them. That had never happened before, and it was an ominous turn. There was a real chance, when Bishop Estate agreed to double up on the original investment, that the company would implode. Fortunately, that did not happen. Goldman Sachs turned the corner and did very well when the global economy started to boom. On the day the company went public in 1999, Bishop Estate's $500 million investment was worth $1.5 billion. That was before taxes had been paid and only half the figure reported when the decision to go public was first announced, but still a big gain.

Media reports seemed to assume that this was tax-free money, but because the investment in Goldman Sachs generated what the tax law calls "unrelated business income," the gain was actually fully taxable. In fact, because the trustees had used a for-profit corporation to hold the stake in Goldman Sachs, the gains when the firm went public did not even qualify for favorable capital gain rates, but instead were taxable at the highest state and federal corporate rates. In essence, the trustees in 1992, and again in 1994, were betting that the total return on Goldman Sachs would be at least 40 percent higher (the applicable tax rate) than they could get from a diversified, professionally managed portfolio, or from any other passive—and therefore tax-exempt—investment opportunity. In this case the gamble paid off.

Dickie Wong had argued against putting in the second $250 million in 1994, but he eventually decided to vote for it, along with the other trustees. Some years later he acknowledged in a deposition that Goldman Sachs had been a risky investment. He recalled thinking to himself as he voted in favor of making the investment, "Dickie, you're going to roll the dice. Let's see what happens." At another point in the deposition, he said, "Sometimes I guess it's better to be lucky than right."

The reason the trustees put money into Goldman Sachs in 1992 was simple: Takabuki wanted it to happen. By 1994, however, Takabuki had retired, and Henry Peters was lead trustee for asset management. When Corzine asked for the second quarter-billion dollars, Peters put himself in charge of negotiating the details. The story of the final negotiation session was to become legend at Goldman Sachs. Corzine had just been named board chairman and CEO and was flying all over the world, sharing his vision for the firm. Within Goldman Sachs it was considered a big deal that the man in charge of the entire organization would fly in for this final meeting with "the Bishop people." At the designated hour, Corzine entered the conference room with his retinue, expecting a short meeting. His private jet was on the airport runway, waiting.

Peters was supposed to speak on behalf of Bishop Estate, but now that all eyes were on him, he just sat there. Finally, after a long, uncomfortable silence, Peters said, "I'm not really prepared for this." The Goldman people were dumbfounded. Then Peters added, "My assistant can explain it." Everyone listened closely as the assistant explained that the trustees' approach for setting the price had not changed since 1992, when Takabuki was there. Within fifteen minutes the terms were set: Bishop Estate would put in another $250 million and own just over 9 percent of Goldman Sachs.

People at Goldman Sachs held Matsuo Takabuki in high regard. They believed that he understood their business and the nature of the investment he had made on behalf of Bishop Estate. Peters, though, appeared to them to be in over his head.

He was also in over his head when negotiating an arrangement with Robert Rubin, the man who had been co-chairman of Goldman Sachs in 1992 when Bishop Estate first became a partner in that firm. When Rubin left Goldman to join President Bill Clinton's administration, he exchanged his partnership interest for the firm's promissory note, in an amount that reportedly approached $50 million. He then offered to pay $200,000 per year to Bishop Estate for the trust's guarantee that he would collect the full amount of the promissory note, plus interest, no matter what happened to Goldman Sachs. On the basis of that one phone call, the deal was made, and then for five years Bishop Estate received Rubin's check annually.

Goldman Sachs did not default on the note, and Bishop Estate did not have to make good on the guarantee to Rubin. Talking about it after the fact, Oz Stender described the deal as "almost like free money."

Like the investment of half a billion dollars in Goldman Sachs, this smaller transaction worked out well; the trust made a million dollars pure profit just for guaranteeing a note. The way the decision was made, however, could hardly be described as prudent. It did not fit into an overall plan, and the trustees lacked the expertise to measure the risk or set an appropriate price.

From 1994 to 1996, the period of time eventually reviewed by the Bishop Estate master Colbert Matsumoto, Bishop Estate's investments lost 1 percent overall. During the same period of time, the Dow Jones industrial average went up 72 percent. In 1995, when the trustees terminated 171 Estate employees, they said it was because the outreach programs were inefficient.

Bishop Estate's communications department took out full-page newspaper ads claiming that the trustees had made a great deal of money during this period. Peters said the same thing in his own way: "At the end of the day, when all of the net gains and losses are added up, we made money. I'm not one to brag, but that's what we did."

What Peters and the communications department did not say was that the trustees' numbers included the rent from old leases and capital revenue from the mandatory leasehold sales that had been forced upon them. These sources of cash put Bishop Estate in the black, but they had nothing to do with the current trustees' financial acumen. It was the rising value of Princess Pauahi's land that had turned Bishop Estate into the financial colossus it became.

Although trust law requires trustees to make a reasonable effort to determine market values, Bishop Estate trustees during the 1970s, 1980s, and 1990s did not appraise trust land. On financial statements, they listed it at 1965 values, which were dramatically lower than current values. When asked about this, they said there was no need to know current values. In 1990 Stender estimated that the trust estate had a minimum market value of $10 billion. He described this number as "very conservative."

During the 1990s trustees at prestigious universities such as Harvard, Yale, and Stanford typically expended 4 to 5 percent of their endowment value each year on education. The same was true of local educational institutions such as Punahou and 'Iolani. Because Bishop Estate trustees did not reveal current values, there was no way to determine what percentage of the trust estate was devoted each year to the charitable mission. Had current values been known, the public would have seen more clearly that Kamehameha Schools was being shortchanged. Based on Stender's "very conservative" estimate of Bishop Estate's market value, the amount spent on Kamehameha while he was a trustee never approached even 1 percent. This was one of the main reasons the IRS would later conclude that Bishop Estate looked more like an investment club than a charitable organization.

In 1987, when mandatory land sales were producing a tsunami of cash, the trustees started to accumulate large amounts of income, rather than spending it currently, as required by Pauahi's will. Within ten years they had withheld nearly $350 million of such income from Kamehameha Schools—five times a single year's operating budget. The five trustees did this without telling any master, attorney general, or probate judge. Even if any of these "watchdogs" had been inclined to take action, an accounting change in 1987 made it difficult for anyone to detect exactly what the Bishop Estate trustees were doing.

Prior to that time, Bishop Estate's financial statements reported the income and principal accounts separately, making it easy for interested parties to determine the existence and amount of any accumulated income. Although the 1987 accounting change was of great significance, the trust's longtime outside auditor, Coopers and Lybrand, evidently never insisted upon disclosure either of the change or of the ever-growing accumulation.

Hoarding income may seem as prudent as putting money in the bank for a rainy day, but charitable trusts are not supposed to operate that way. They exist, and enjoy their tax-exempt status, in order to pursue their charitable missions, not to grow into financial empires. Trust

LAND OF CHARITABLE TRUST

law, tax law, and the terms of Pauahi's will all required that the Bishop Estate trustees focus on educating children. While secretly accumulating income in the hundreds of millions of dollars, the trustees, citing financial constraints, turned away upward of eleven out of twelve applicants to Kamehameha Schools and dismantled virtually all the outreach programs.

Most private schools across the nation, even those with large endowments, seek tax-deductible contributions to expand their charitable reach. Asked under oath whether the trustees had tried to do this, Dickie Wong said, "No, I don't think it ever crossed our minds."

At the same time that the trustees were shortchanging Kamehameha Schools, trust funds flowed generously toward other people. Trustees reportedly instructed executives and school administrators to hire individuals handpicked for unbudgeted positions and outside consulting work—much of which seemed to require hardly any real work at all. The attorney general's removal petition eventually provided examples: Three unnamed former Bishop Estate trustees were paid consulting fees "disproportionate to the services, if any, actually rendered." George K. Lindsey Jr. received a $3,120 monthly retainer for providing "negligible,

U.S. Congressman Neil Abercrombie (left) and Office of Hawaiian Affairs Chairman Clayton Hee (right) worked closely with Dickie Wong (center) before and after the justices gave Wong his Bishop Estate trusteeship.

if any, legal services to the trust." The chairman of the Office of Hawaiian Affairs, Clayton Hee, received an undisclosed salary to be a cultural affairs researcher, "with negligible duties." Larry Mehau's company got a non-bid oral contract to provide front-gate security at Kamehameha for $40,000 a month. Dura Constructors, a company that had Peters on its payroll when he was serving in the legislature, got non-bid contracts worth millions. Rhino Roofing, a company headed by Peters' nephew, received more than a million dollars of non-bid and subcontracting work. Albert Jeremiah received $7,000 monthly, "without regard to whether any work was performed," and additional amounts for occasional chores, such as appraising the Van Dyke book collection.

Peters called any suggestion of favoritism "hogwash" and added, "Why not give a job to someone you know?"

Nor did Peters' friends see anything wrong with such an approach. When asked if his friend Henry Peters helped get him the job, Jeremiah's immediate response was, "I sure hope so."

It is illegal for charities to involve themselves in political campaigns—but Bishop Estate staffers sold fund-raiser tickets for many politicians, including Henry Peters' protégé, Marshall Ige. And that was just the beginning. According to lawyers in the attorney general's office, Ige wound up his successful 1994 campaign for re-election to the House of Representatives still owing $18,262.71 to Ryan's Graphics, a company that had done printing for him. He could not pay the bill, so Yukio Takemoto made a call to Ryan's office and an arrangement was worked out. Ryan's sent a false invoice to Kajioka, Okada, Yamachi Architects, a firm that had been awarded non-bid contracts from Bishop Estate; one of its partners, Allen Kajioka, had once been Dickie Wong's campaign manager. Although the invoice was for goods and services they had never received, the Kajioka firm paid it in full, zeroing out Ige's debt. This cost Kajioka $18,262.71—a small percentage of the non-bid work it received from the Estate.

The campaign financing reports of state Senator Milton Holt, a Kamehameha graduate who worked in Bishop Estate's government affairs office while he was a legislator, drew similar attention because of unusual transactions, such as $9,800 paid from "petty cash" and an $11,000 "loan" of campaign funds for his personal use, even though such transactions were illegal. Investigators also discovered that Bishop Estate had provided to Holt the same kind of creative financial help extended to Ige.

Holt had been the target of a separate federal criminal investigation in 1994 unrelated to his job with Bishop Estate. After securing a legal opinion from Michael Hare of the Cades law firm, Bishop Estate's Nathan Aipa authorized use of trust funds to pay Holt's attorney fees. The total was $14,948. Not many employers would pay the legal expenses of a staff member under investigation for public corruption. That this employer was a tax-exempt charity made the payment all the more disturbing.

Employees who questioned Bishop Estate's doings were not treated so well. Bobby Harmon was a prime example. Harmon began working at Bishop Estate in 1988 in the area of risk management. He had solid credentials and worked hard. For eight years his job evaluations were excellent, and he was promoted to president of P and C Insurance, a wholly owned subsidiary of Bishop Estate. Harmon's job required him to evaluate risks, decide on insurance coverage, and negotiate with brokers of independent companies for the best prices. It was important work involving big money.

During the two years Harmon headed up P and C, from 1994 to 1996, Henry Peters was lead trustee for asset management. Between Harmon and Peters was Nathan Aipa. Harmon came to believe that serious breaches of trust were occurring, exposing Bishop Estate to potentially large lawsuits and putting its tax-exempt status at risk. For example, the trust's tax counsel had stressed to Harmon the need for Bishop Estate to keep its for-profit subsidiaries, such as P and C, at arm's length in order to preserve the trust's tax-exempt status. Yet, Harmon knew from experience that although he was president of P and C, it was Peters and Aipa who effectively ran the company.

Harmon also was concerned about decisions that seemed to go against the best interests of both P and C and Bishop Estate. Against his recommendation, a big insurance contract was given to a favored vendor at a cost more than double what Harmon thought he could have secured through competitive bidding. Harmon also found instances in which trustees had not brought in the Estate's insurance carrier to defend the claims. This meant the trust would unnecessarily pay its own defense costs, and trust funds would be used to pay any damages that the insurance company would refuse to pay. This subjected the trust estate to big risks without any compensating benefit that Harmon could see. What Harmon did not realize at the time was that trustees had their own reasons for keeping under wraps the details of certain trust investments—such as the McKenzie deal in which four trustees secretly held personal interests.

In November 1996 Harmon made a list of things he had witnessed that made no sense to him or that appeared wrong and presented it to Aipa and Peters. They told him not to concern himself with these matters; he should just do what they told him to do. But Harmon believed that his role as president of P and C required him to do more. He knew that new IRS regulations permitted someone in his position to be fined if a charitable trust incurred unnecessary expenses, and he saw no reason to subject himself to personal liability.

Harmon reported his concerns to the trust's outside auditors, Coopers and Lybrand. Shortly thereafter Harmon received the first formal reprimand he had ever had in his working life. By the end of the following month, Harmon had been fired for "wrongful actions" and hit with an injunction that forbade him from discussing the circumstances of his firing with anyone. This was about six months before the publication of "Broken Trust."

Harmon tried to find a job elsewhere in Hawai'i, but without suc-

Bobby Harmon was president of P and C Insurance, a wholly owned subsidiary of Bishop Estate, until Henry Peters fired him in December 1996 after Harmon pointed out serious irregularities to the trust's outside auditors.

cess. Prospective employers wanted to know why he had left Bishop Estate, but he could not tell them without violating the terms of his employment contract (which itself was labeled "confidential"). No Hawai'i company wanted to hire him for a responsible job under these circumstances. And because the file said he had been fired for wrongful actions, he could not even collect unemployment benefits.

Harmon went to eight different local law firms asking if they would be willing to sue Bishop Estate. Because he had modest savings and no income, the law firm would have to advance the litigation costs and work for a contingent fee, which would be payable only when and if Harmon won the suit. All eight firms turned him down. Then Harmon sent a long memo to several government officials and media reporters, saying he wanted them to know what had happened. Within hours, Bishop Estate lawyers hauled him into court for breaching the confidentiality clause in his employment contract and violating the terms of an injunction. Judge Bambi Weil ordered everyone who had received materials from Harmon to return them to Bishop Estate. The director of communications, Elisa Yadao, declined to comment other than to say that Harmon was under injunction "because of his unauthorized removal of Estate property."

Harmon had personally witnessed what he believed to be serious wrongdoing within a charitable trust. He had tried to get help from within the organization, then from its outside auditors. When he was punished for doing this, he expected the judge to encourage him to tell all. Instead, she muzzled him.

Harmon had blown the whistle, and for his trouble he lost his savings and his home. He declared bankruptcy and moved to the Mainland.

Henry Peters often said that the only thing that could hurt Bishop Estate was government. So it made perverse sense that the trustees devoted an entire department at Kawaiaha'o Plaza to making sure government was happy with them: the Government Relations Department, which insiders called GRD. Peters said it just made sense to help politicians in ways the politicians would appreciate. "I don't think," he said, "we're any different from any institution in this town." There was one big difference, however: Bishop Estate was a charitable trust.

GRD began in the early 1990s with Namlyn Snow, Henry Peters' right-hand person. Snow had worked for Peters before he was a politician, as far back as his days with the Model Cities program in Wai'anae. GRD grew quickly to a staff of six. People in other departments at Kawaiaha'o Plaza had only vague notions of what GRD was doing. Snow kept sensitive GRD materials in a locked safe in her office. Years later when special investigators obtained the materials, they detailed their findings in a confidential report submitted to the attorney general's office and Campaign Spending Commission.

The report explained that GRD had been staffed with people possessing extensive experience in government and lobbying. There were indications that these individuals, on behalf of Bishop Estate, had tried to influence government actions by creating activist organizations seemingly unconnected to Bishop Estate but actually controlled by GRD personnel. Moreover, GRD operated an ongoing intelligence-gathering apparatus and released damaging information on opponents to reporters, legislators, and other parties; and actively opposed specific legislative measures, including proposals to reduce trustee compensation.

One of the special investigators compared Snow's tactics to those used by the CIA operating covertly within a banana republic. GRD would reach out quietly to locals through intermediaries, gather intelligence, and on that basis set people in places where they could operate independently, with no tracks back to GRD. Questioned by investigators, one GRD staff member insisted that she had engaged in political activities as an individual—not as someone on the Bishop Estate payroll, but as a graduate of Kamehameha. Yes, she had joined Hawaiian community groups, sought leadership positions, and worked to accomplish the trustees' goals—but not in her official capacity. She had steered people to testify at hearings, chauffeured them to rallies, drafted letters to the editor for them to submit, and raised money for politicians—but only to fulfill her civic duty, not because she worked for Bishop Estate. Materials later found in Snow's safe, however, suggested a different story. This staffer's activities were listed in her annual job performance report under the heading "Highly Sensitive and Confidential Subject Matter."

Another member of the GRD staff also insisted that what he did was not lobbying. Yes, he attended many political fund-raisers and entertained politicians frequently, but this was just "establishing a friendly relationship." Asked why a charity would pick up the tab for elected officials if it did not expect someday to ask for something in return, he said it did not work that way in Hawai'i. In his words, "If you and I are friends, and I have an issue that's up, that you are involved with or you are on the committee or you're in the legislature, whatever it is, it's almost like I feel I don't need to ask you to vote for my stuff already. It was like, uh—what would you say?—understood. That if you're my friend you're gonna, you know, do it. I don't have to ask you." When asked to identify the people in the legislature he considered "friends," this staff member named twenty-two of the twenty-five senators and thirty-nine of the fifty-one representatives.

A third GRD staff member described to investigators how Snow would call her at home to be at a political fund-raiser on two hours' notice, or to go out and campaign for certain candidates. When asked under oath whether this was done on her own time, the staffer said, "No, I had to attend . . . it was part of my job."

It was later found that GRD staffers had used their Bishop Estate credit cards at least 780 times between 1992 and 1997, and that the majority of these occasions were in connection with government officials such as state legislators and county councilmen.

Political activity was not limited to GRD personnel. Under oath, a

Bishop Estate lawyer, Colleen Wong, described how Nathan Aipa, her boss, would get her to campaign for a favored candidate. Did she not feel that she could just say no? "I know Nathan wouldn't have asked me to do something like that unless he felt he really needed me to do it, and so I didn't voice my [reservations]. Quite frankly, . . . if I had my way I wouldn't have done it."

On August 28, 1991, Oz Stender wrote a memo to Namlyn Snow saying, "We should have a systematic program for making political contributions with a defined budget for trustees and management participation." He also suggested guidelines "for attending fund-raisers and staff participation in political activities." Snow apparently followed up on these suggestions. One of the documents discovered in her safe was a policy and procedures statement on political fund-raising. For example, it directed that all tickets for political fund-raisers be sent to Snow's office. These often arrived in bulk. One stuffed manila envelope from Honolulu's mayor, Jeremy Harris, contained twelve hundred tickets at $25 each.

Snow personally recorded each batch of tickets by the name of the candidate and then logged them out under the names of the individuals who were to arrange their sale. As contributors were located, checks and cash would come to Snow to be recorded, bundled, and then sent on to each candidate's campaign fund. Copies of the checks were put in a binder and locked in the safe each night.

Nowhere on the candidates' reports did the name Bishop Estate appear. The targeted buyers of the tickets were firms that did non-bid business with Bishop Estate. In turn, the contact person at the firm would try to pass along the tickets to companies and people beholden to that firm, such as subcontractors and employees, who in turn would unload tickets, if they could, on family, friends, and anyone else they could find to help pay the cost of the tickets they had been asked to buy.

The bulk-sale ticket business was primarily with developers, contractors, engineers, architects, and lawyers. Because Sam Hata headed up facilities and support services for Bishop Estate, Snow had him selling tickets to vendors and contractors. Nathan Aipa selected outside counsel for the trust's legal work, so Snow made him responsible for selling tickets to lawyers.

Bishop Estate was far from the only place in town where fund-raiser tickets were trafficked. In Hawai'i, paying for these tickets had become part of the political price of doing business. Everybody knew it; Bishop Estate simply had taken it to a new level.

$\mathcal{C}$ompensation was always a sensitive subject at Bishop Estate. Henry Peters, who relished his role as lead trustee for asset management and contended that he earned every penny he received, put himself on the boards of fourteen different companies. One of these companies, Mid-Ocean Insurance, reportedly gave more than $200,000 in fees and stock options to each of its directors. Critics said because Peters was already collecting $1 million a year for his services as a trustee, he should turn any additional director fees and stock options over to Bishop Estate. Peters declined, contending that he was a director of Mid-Ocean because of his personal expertise, not because he was a Bishop Estate trustee.

When the topic of compensation came up, Peters sometimes would explain that Bishop Estate trustees had to pay for their own health insurance, provide for their own retirement, and pay a 4 percent state excise tax on self-employment income. When you considered the magnitude of the job, said Peters, Bishop Estate trustees were underpaid.

In 1994, when staff members discovered that the trustees had been paid more compensation during the preceding year than could be justified under any interpretation of the statutory formula, Peters told them to take another look at the numbers and "be creative." The trustees ended up claiming additional trustee fees, totaling $615,844, by extending the statutory formula to money spent on campus improvements. A current court order prohibited exactly what they had done. Predictably, the recalculations were stamped "Confidential—Attorney-Client Privilege."

In 1995 Guido Giacometti, the former head of Bishop Estate's asset management group, described for the *Wall Street Journal* some equally "creative" tax planning that had involved moving assets back and forth between the tax-exempt trust and its wholly owned for-profit companies, which Giacometti called "a repository for the dogs." An independent tax expert was quoted in the article as saying that this was "beyond creative" and suggesting that it would never withstand IRS scrutiny.

The IRS began its in-depth audit of Bishop Estate that year.

$\mathcal{T}$here were more than 1.5 million tax-exempt organizations in the United States by the late 1990s, and they controlled more than a trillion dollars of wealth. In any given year, IRS agents audited only a few thousand of these organizations. When they uncovered abuse, their options were limited to one: revocation of the organization's tax-exempt status. Only a few dozen audits in any given year uncovered violations serious enough for the IRS to take such drastic action. Because revocation of a charity's tax-exempt status tended to punish the people who relied upon a charity rather than the actual wrongdoers, the IRS seldom used its only weapon.

In 1995 leaders of the nonprofit community and senior officials with the IRS asked Congress to give the IRS the option of punishing the individuals who abused their positions of power within a charity. Under the proposal, the IRS would have the option of imposing "intermediate sanctions" on the actual wrongdoers, rather than having no choice but to revoke the charity's tax-exempt status. For example, trustees who paid themselves $900,000 when their services were worth only $100,000 could be fined 25 percent of the $800,000 "excess benefit." The fine in this example would be $200,000 per trustee, per year. Such trustees would also have to pay the excess benefit amount back to the charity. Finally, if a trustee did not make both of these payments within sixty days of being ordered to do so, the penalty would increase from 25 percent to 200 percent.

Charitable organizations from all over the country had only good things to say about the intermediate sanctions bill—with a notable exception. One charity said that being able to punish individual wrongdoers was a terrible idea. This charity lobbied against the enactment of intermediate sanctions, spending nearly $1 million of trust funds in the process. This charity was Bishop Estate.

Despite the trustees' efforts and behind-the-scenes support from Hawai'i's congressional delegation (except for Representative Patsy Mink, who stood up to the trustees), Congress passed the intermediate sanctions bill in 1996. There was, however, one consolation for the disappointed Bishop Estate trustees: the new law would be effective only for periods after September 1995. This meant intermediate sanctions would not be available to IRS agents for most of the years currently under audit. For those years, the only sanction the IRS could apply would be revocation; and the trustees knew that the IRS almost never took such a drastic action. The flip side was staggering: if the IRS revoked Bishop Estate's tax-exempt status retroactively to 1989 (as the IRS was empowered to do), it could cost Kamehameha Schools upward of $1 billion.

chapter 16

"That's Just the Way You Do It"

Hawai'i's Supreme Court justices insisted for years that there was nothing wrong with selecting trustees while acting as private citizens and then putting on their robes and deciding cases involving the very same trustees. The five authors of "Broken Trust" contended that although private citizens are always free to say no, once they agree to select trustees of a charitable trust, they assume a duty to make a good-faith effort to select trustees who will further the trust's charitable mission. In a luncheon speech to the Rotary Club of Honolulu in September 1997, Monsignor Kekumano declared that the justices had not acted in good faith: their action "reeked of political maneuverings and manipulations."

For Supreme Court justices to be so overtly political was unseemly, even if they were acting "unofficially." However, there was another problem: because the justices claimed to be acting unofficially, they could be sued personally (arguably without the benefit of judicial immunity) if trustees they negligently selected went on to harm the trust. Such exposure gave the justices a personal stake in any legal controversy involving Bishop Estate trustees. It was a classic conflict of interest.

Over the years, bar association leaders never said anything about this, at least not publicly. One former bar president said it was a simple oversight: "I had lost sight of the obvious—the Supreme Court was ruling on all these cases involving the trustees they appointed. That was a real problem." Another former president admitted he had recognized the issue but did not want to be the one to point out that the justices were violating their code of judicial ethics.

When Cayetano instructed Bronster to investigate allegations made by the "Broken Trust" authors, he specifically said he wanted her to look into the way trustees were being selected. But when she met with the justices to discuss how best to proceed with this inquiry, they said that they would agree to be interviewed only as a group. Otherwise, said the justices, lawyers from the attorney general's office might try to "trick us" into telling different stories.

Bronster said she was prepared to subpoena the justices, if necessary, to hear their individual accounts. Justice Levinson took particular offense at this. He argued ardently that although the justices had acted unofficially in selecting trustees, they were still justices; it would not be proper to force them to cooperate in an investigation; the integrity of the judiciary was at stake—case law said so. By the time he finished, he had gone red in the face.

According to Bronster, the justices' message to her was clear: "We'll just see whether your subpoena power goes so far. If we're the ones to decide it (which we probably will be), we don't think so." After weighing all the pros and cons, including the possible impact this fight would have on other important cases her office had pending before the Supreme Court, Bronster decided not to subpoena the justices.

The justices had won the standoff. It left them above the fray, which was where they wanted to be. But in the process of getting their way, the justices had engaged in a private, *ex parte* (without the other side present) discussion with the attorney general about her subpoena power in the Bishop Estate investigation. Judicial ethics are very clear in this situation: any justice who participates in such an *ex parte* discussion has no choice but to step aside and let substitute justices decide cases related to that issue. But these five Supreme Court justices appeared to have every intention of continuing to preside over Bishop Estate cases, including the many appeals that were already stacking up from Bronster's investigation. Bronster described the situation delicately, from her point of view:

> I thought perhaps they would realize that they didn't want to rule on something related to a discussion they had already had with one of the participants, so I wrote them a letter suggesting that they might want to recuse themselves from hearing that particular issue. They answered, "You want us to recuse ourselves, you make a motion." They probably thought I'd wise up and go away, but I did make that motion. They sat on it for a couple of months, and finally they sent it off to the judicial conduct commission with a suggestion that the "appearance of impropriety" justified or ne-

cessitated recusal. The commission agreed; but nobody seemed to mention the fact that these conversations had occurred.

Sure enough, when the justices announced that they would not personally decide cases arising out of the Bishop Estate investigation, they said nothing about the *ex parte* communication that had forced them to step aside. Instead, they cited "overheated circumstances." The justices also said nothing about their refusal to cooperate with the state's top law enforcement officer in an official investigation of a matter in which they had participated—as they had earlier insisted, over and over, they had done—as private citizens.

The justices continued to maintain that they had no responsibility to explain or discuss their actions, either in their official capacity as justices or as ordinary citizens. But, ironically, justices engaged in behind-the-scenes communication with people who were, or were likely to be, in front of them as litigants. Investigators working for the attorney general found evidence of numerous *ex parte* communications between justices and trustees, including phone messages taken by the trustees' secretaries. In the days leading up to the march, for example, Jervis' secretary left this message for him: "Steve Levinson desperately needs to talk to you." Lindsey's handwritten notes several days later indicated that Jervis had just met with at least two of the justices to discuss legal issues, and a host of phone messages from Levinson to Jervis suggested a close personal relationship between the justice and the trustee: "Says to please call him tomorrow. Wants to share happy stuff about the school and other stuff cause you're his good buddy"; "says you owe him a phone call (putting it mildly)"; "Lynn out of town Wed. Good time to have boys nite out"; and "No excuses for no phone call except if you're dead!"

The Supreme Court justices were not the only ones with ethical issues. Dozens of lawyers were being paid millions of dollars from Bishop Estate trust funds for legal services supposedly rendered on behalf of "the trust." They called this the "enterprise" theory. Under traditional trust law, however, a trust is a relationship between trustees and beneficiaries, not a separate enterprise. In Hawai'i, lawyers for "the trust" were actually representing five individual trustees—not one trust. The difference is more than semantic. Lawyers have a duty to represent the interests of each client to the fullest possible extent of the law. When the interests of individual clients begin to diverge, problems arise for

Nathan Aipa served as the Bishop Estate trustees' chief in-house lawyer from 1986 to 1999.

lawyers who supposedly represent them all. For example, the duty of confidentiality owed by a lawyer to an individual trustee-client may be impossible to reconcile with that lawyer's equally important duty to communicate fully with each of the other trustee-clients.

In the case of Bishop Estate, this meant that so-called lawyers for the trust had to choose which of their duties to honor at the expense of the others. When Stender asked Aipa for information that Stender needed to carry out his fiduciary duties as a trustee, Aipa sometimes told Stender that the requested information could not be provided because it was "confidential." It is a breach of duty for a lawyer to intentionally deny vital information to a client, and yet, had he provided that information, Aipa might well have breached the confidentiality he owed to another client.

With the Bishop Estate trustees' interests in serious conflict with one another, lawyers like McCorriston, Hare, Graham, and Aipa found themselves in a virtually impossible situation. McCorriston claimed to have gotten three outside legal opinions essentially saying that Bishop Estate was an enterprise and his client was the board. When asked why it was, then, that his own court documents listed all five trustees as his clients, McCorriston replied, "That's just the way you do it."

Each trustee also hired lawyers to represent the personal interests of only that one trustee. Although the trustees personally hired dozens of such lawyers, most of the fees, which totaled millions of dollars, came out of Bishop Estate's coffers.

In August 1998 it appeared that Bill McCorriston had stalled the attorney general's investigation. It had been a full year since the publication of the "Broken Trust" essay, and all Bronster had to show for her efforts were hundreds of subpoenas that were still being questioned in court and truckloads of materials that never seemed to include the documents she really wanted. Then, in September, newspaper headlines signaled a dramatic new turn: "Trustee Case to Be Examined by Grand Jury; Investigation Could Lead to Criminal Charges." Citing sources familiar with the proceeding, the newspapers reported that Bronster had convened an investigative grand jury. It would be the first criminal investigation of Bishop Estate trustees in the trust's 113-year history.

The attorney general's office declined to confirm or deny any of this. Nor did a spokesman for Bishop Estate have anything to say. With no one to quote, the *Star-Bulletin* suggested that the trustees might see this as part of a grand plan: "In the past, trustees have described the state's

Judge Michael Town ruled that Attorney General Margery Bronster could simultaneously conduct civil and criminal investigations of Bishop Estate trustees, but then Town repeatedly rejected criminal indictments on procedural grounds.

investigation as politically motivated and said the timing is intended to boost the re-election efforts of Governor Ben Cayetano." At the time Cayetano was running for a second term, and he was behind in the polls.

Bronster's investigation of Bishop Estate had begun as a matter of civil law. Now there was talk of possible crimes. Because it would be improper to use a civil investigation to bolster a criminal investigation, and vice versa, the two had to be legally separated. Bronster could have accomplished that easily and cleanly by referring the criminal investigation to the Honolulu city prosecutor, who had said he would be willing to take it over. Bronster chose instead to keep both investigations. For separation, she erected a conceptual wall, with the civil investigation team on one side and the criminal investigation team on the other. Bronster was in charge of both teams.

Lawyers for individuals targeted by the criminal investigation complained that Bronster's wall was more like a chain-link fence. They complained that it was not realistic to expect lawyers in one office not to communicate with other lawyers in the same office about their respective investigations, and that having Bronster heading up both sides was improper. They asked Judge Michael Town to order Bronster to transfer the criminal investigation to the Honolulu city prosecutor. Town refused.

On the civil side of the "wall" in the attorney general's office, Bronster had only recently decided to seek the immediate removal of all five trustees. On the criminal side, she was now putting together cases against Wong, Peters, and others. The alleged criminal acts had to do with the sale of Bishop Estate land to a group that included Dickie Wong's brother-in-law, Jeffrey Stone. Stone and his partners had allegedly gotten "a sweetheart deal" when they acquired the upscale 229-unit Kalele Kai condominium project in Hawai'i Kai, from which they made a $40 million profit. Stone allegedly reciprocated by helping Peters and Wong sell their condominiums at inflated prices. Peters reportedly sold his Makiki unit—two bedrooms on the second floor—to a company controlled by a friend of Stone's for $575,000 and then turned around and bought a penthouse unit in the same building—three bedrooms on the twelfth floor—for the same dollar figure. Stone then bought Peters' old second-floor unit back from his friend for $575,000 and sold it for $395,000. To the attorney general's criminal investigation team, it looked as though Stone had personally paid for Peters' "upgrade." At about the same time, Wong sold his Makiki apartment to Stone for $613,800. According to Bronster, the appraised value at the time was only $485,000. Bronster saw this as more than simple charity to one's brother-in-law; she saw a connection to Kalele Kai.

Bronster's grand jury indicted Peters for first-degree theft; Stone for bribery and criminal conspiracy, and as an accomplice to theft and perjury; Wong for first-degree theft, criminal conspiracy, and perjury; and even Wong's wife, Mari Stone Wong, for criminal conspiracy and hindering the prosecution by making a false statement. All these indictments related to the Kalele Kai allegations.

Convinced that Peters, Stone, and the Wongs had been denied a fair and unbiased grand jury, Judge Town dismissed all the indictments. He said that jurors had improperly heard the testimony of Nathan Aipa, Bishop Estate's chief in-house lawyer, and of Richard Frunzi, a former lawyer for Stone. According to Town, what Aipa and Frunzi told the grand jury should have been protected by the attorney-client privilege; it did not matter that nobody asserted the privilege at the time. Town also ruled that the attorney general should have made clear to the grand jury that Frunzi was no longer a practicing lawyer in good standing with the bar. By the time of his testimony, Frunzi had been disbarred and was serving time in federal prison for laundering drug money. Another witness before the grand jury had been Patrick Keller, hired by Stone to appraise Wong's apartment. By the time Peters, Stone, and the

Wongs were indicted, Keller was in prison for tax evasion. He also had a record of fraud and misrepresentation.

That two of Bronster's leading witnesses were felons did not help her case. On the other hand, that Stone's lawyer and appraiser were now in jail for unrelated crimes did not speak well for his ability to select honest professionals.

Because Town dismissed the indictments on procedural grounds rather than on the merits of the allegations, the attorney general had the option to re-indict—which is what happened. But when Town threw out the second round of indictments, again on procedural grounds, the attorney general convened a third grand jury. It too voted to indict.

Wong could hardly believe what was happening. In a comparison that was not flattering to himself, he told reporters that even Al Capone had never had his wife indicted.

Lawyers for Peters and Wong claimed that Bronster was using the criminal indictments to pressure their clients into resigning as trustees, and that it was all part of a desperate effort to get Cayetano re-elected. They also complained of Bronster's "heavy-handed tactics" and "media grandstanding." To determine the value of Henry Peters' penthouse apartment in Makiki, Bronster had sent four investigators, unannounced, with a search warrant, a locksmith, an appraiser, and a video camera. Peters' lawyer called this "Gestapo tactics" and "a burglary under the guise of a search." Wong's lawyer said Bronster had run "amok."

Whatever Bronster's motives were, she clearly was playing hardball. Bronster was proving to be McCorriston's equal in her willingness to do what it took to win.

chapter 17

Public Pressure Forces a Political Shift

Bronster and her deputies took a special interest in Milton Holt, the Bishop Estate special projects officer whose legal fees had been paid by the trust several years earlier when he was the target of a federal criminal investigation for public corruption.

In his youth, Holt had seemed destined for great things. He graduated from Kamehameha in 1970, spent a year at Phillips Academy (an exclusive private school in Andover, Massachusetts), and then went on to Harvard, where he quarterbacked the football team. After graduating from Harvard, Holt returned to Hawai'i and went into politics, getting elected to the legislature at age twenty-six. He quickly established himself as a major force in the state senate and was being talked about as a future governor.

In 1987 Kamehameha hired Holt as an assistant athletic director, which came as a big surprise to the Kamehameha president, Jack Darvill. He was not aware that an assistant athletic director was needed or even what the job might entail. Another surprise was that Holt got rent-free housing on campus, at a time when this kind of housing was being phased out. Holt was later brought to Kawaiaha'o Plaza as a special projects officer, another position created just for him. Even staffers with offices close to his did not know what Holt did all day.

By the early 1990s, though, Holt's life was unraveling. In 1992 he was jailed for two days for misdemeanor spouse abuse. In 1993 he was arrested in New Orleans for public drunkenness. He sometimes looked disheveled and was spending increasing amounts of time in Las Vegas

Milton Holt was a powerful politician who for years simultaneously received full-time paychecks and other perks from Bishop Estate.

and Reno; while there he charged personal entertainment on his Bishop Estate credit card, thousands of dollars.

At home in Honolulu, Holt used the same credit card at what were called "hostess bars." These strip clubs charged two or three times the normal price for a beer; other services cost more. In a single night at the Crystal Palace, Holt signed for $540.50; another night, at the Monte Carlo, he ran up a $751 tab; and his evening at New Secret cost $1,500. Holt's credit card statements raised the eyebrows of low-level staffers in the accounting department at Kawaiahaʻo Plaza, but Henry Peters took care of things. For years he reportedly instructed the accounting staff to pay the bills and not tell the other trustees about the charges.

When word of this finally got out, the trustees decided that the trust should be reimbursed. However, there was a problem: Holt did not have anywhere near the amount of money involved. A creative solution was devised. Holt would be given a bonus exactly equal to what he owed, as well as state and federal taxes on the bonus itself, calculated to the penny. It was all done on paper; no money changed hands. Holt's personal obligation to reimburse the trust simply vanished.

When investigators arrived to collect Holt's credit card records, those records were nowhere to be found. It later was learned that they had been removed the day before on Henry Peters' instructions. Peters' explanation was that these particular records were moved because the large number of requests for documents had gotten him confused. According to Peters, Holt's use of a Bishop Estate credit card at strip clubs and Las Vegas casinos had been blown way out of proportion. "What's the problem?" asked Peters. "He paid the money back."

It did not matter what Milton Holt was called at Bishop Estate— associate athletic director, special projects officer, community relations officer—his main service was in gathering political intelligence and exerting political influence for Bishop Estate. Holt's credit card statements indicated that he had picked up the tab for many meetings with lawmakers and appointed government officials, including "meetings" that had taken place in strip clubs. When the *Star-Bulletin* tracked down and published details, it caused a stir. Elected officials were named in print and on television news in the same breath with Crystal Palace, New Secret, Misty II, and Saigon Passion: Joseph Souki, speaker of the house of representatives; Calvin Say, chairman of the House Finance Committee; Terrance Tom, chairman of the House Judiciary Committee; Norman Mizuguchi, president of the senate; Joe Tanaka, senator and former Maui councilman; and Robert "Bobby" Bunda, state representative. Days of political comedy followed. Lawmakers claimed they had no recollection of any such meetings; it had not been marked on their calendars; Holt had their names mixed up; if they had met with him, it had been at restaurants, not strip clubs. Joe Tanaka said that if he was at a strip club with Holt, it was only to look after Terrance Tom, who was blind; Calvin Say said the same. Tom said he had searched and searched his thoughts and had no recollection of these meetings.

All of this raised an important question: Was entertaining government officials on his Bishop Estate card just a matter of Holt's having a good time with old colleagues? In that case he should never have charged the expenses to his employers' card. Or was he trying to influence these government officials on matters important to Bishop Estate? In that case Holt and the trustees were skating on extremely thin ice with respect to the laws governing the lobbying activities of charitable trusts.

For Bishop Estate, the question of lobbying—private advocacy with a goal of influencing a government body—was sensitive. Like other charities, Bishop Estate could legally try to influence government officials only in limited ways. The wrong kind of influence, or even too much of an acceptable kind, could bring trouble. If violations were serious, and especially if they were premeditated and repeated, the trust could lose its tax-exempt status—and Holt's extensive entertaining of legislators was coming to light just as the IRS was actively investigating the trust.

There also were rules on the receiving end of attempts to influence. Politicians were generally required to report campaign contributions and gifts. But none of the annual disclosure forms submitted by politicians whose names turned up in Holt's documentation ever mentioned a strip club.

Three years earlier, shortly after John Waihe'e left the governor's office in 1994, state Representative Ed Case had thought the time might be right for reform at Bishop Estate. He drafted a wide-ranging bill that, if passed, would change the way Bishop Estate trustees were selected, limit trustee compensation, and secure legal standing for Kamehameha alumni so they could hold trustees accountable. In the months preceding the 1995 legislative session, Case painstakingly met with each of his colleagues, one at a time, explaining the bill and why it was needed. These efforts paid off: thirty-one of the fifty-one members of the house signed the bill as co-sponsors, a clear majority.

Then Bishop Estate went to work. Alumni protested, and trustees huddled with their friends in the house. GRD staffers prepared testimony against the bill, recruited people to present that testimony as their own, and arranged for their transportation to the Capitol. On the day the bill was to be considered by Case's committee, Hawaiians flowed into the hearing room, outraged by this "attack" on Pauahi's legacy. Emotional testimony in opposition to the bill went on for many hours.

By then, Henry Peters was no longer speaker of the house, but his successor, Joe Souki, had his own relationship with Bishop Estate: a $132,000 "consulting fee" for services rendered when the trustees bought land in upcountry Maui. As speaker, Souki had the power to hurry a given bill through to a vote on the floor or bury that bill in a committee. To get his way, Souki could offer individual deals that were hard to refuse, such as his support for a legislator's favorite bill, or a committee chairmanship.

Case watched helplessly as the thirty-one co-sponsors of his bill were picked off, one by one, until there were none.

Simply defeating the bill was not enough; the trustees wanted to teach Case a lesson. So they had friends in the legislature propose a house resolution that essentially said the trustee selection process was just fine the way it was. Case argued that the current arrangement had a corrupting influence: "I am confident that, within the bowels of the Bishop Estate, there are those, much more accustomed to the ways of

power and influence than I, who are deeply covetous of the direct pipeline into the inner workings of the Supreme Court afforded them by this process, a pipeline afforded virtually no other person or entity in Hawai'i."

Despite the fact that thirty-one representatives had co-sponsored a bill that was in a key way the exact opposite of this new resolution, the resolution passed overwhelmingly.

Legal guidelines for setting trustee fees did exist: the judge-made law in Hawai'i said trustee fees always had to be reasonable, and there were statutory formulas that set maximum fees. But it was never clear whether the statutory "maximum" was automatically considered "reasonable."

Undefined terms were another source of ambiguity. One statute set the compensation cap at 2 percent of "all moneys received in the nature of revenue or income." Another statute said trustees also could take up to 2.5 percent of "cash principal received after the inception of the trust." Did the first formula refer to net or gross numbers? And—a seemingly small distinction that could radically affect the final sum—to what extent, if at all, should capital losses offset capital gains in applying the second formula? Opinions differed. Edward Halbach, the trust law expert who had helped Colbert Matsumoto, criticized the formulas, calling them "incomprehensible" and "absurd as applied to Bishop Estate's circumstances."

Representative Ed Case, whose attempt to rein in trustee compensation failed miserably in 1995, was ready to try again when the 1998 legislative session opened. Because of the May 15, 1997, march and everything that followed it, the political winds had clearly shifted.

Case believed conditions for reform had ripened. There was now widespread support for a revision of the statutory formula. Among the many voices, Cayetano said trustees should not be making more than the state's governor, whose salary was less than one-tenth of what Bishop Estate trustees were paying themselves. Halbach and other independent experts favored a bill that required fees to be "reasonable under the circumstances," an approach that could be found in a number of federal and state statutes, including one in Hawai'i having to do with fees paid to executors.

Henry Peters was the only trustee who testified at legislative hearings on this bill. Naturally, he strongly favored leaving the old formulas in place. He said they provided an appropriate incentive: "People who raise the question want us to apologize for the success of our portfolio. If we had zero returns, guess what our compensation would be." Experts testified differently. One pointed out that under the current formulas, $10 billion invested in a simple savings account, with no additional effort from the trustees, would still result in annual compensation of $2 million per trustee. Another expert noted that according to the trustees' interpretation of the current formulas, they could have paid themselves $11 million in a year during which they experienced net investment losses in excess of a $250 million.

Peters shot back, "I've had it up to here with experts." Indeed, his experiences with compensation experts had not been positive. In 1993 the trustees paid a national firm $105,000 to prepare a compensation study. But when the trustees submitted this study to the IRS in an attempt to resolve questions about the reasonableness of trustee fees paid between 1990 to 1992, the IRS responded that the study was deficient. For $269,000 more, the trustees commissioned another study by another national firm, but its report was also found to be flawed by IRS standards: neither study, for instance, had taken into consideration compensation levels paid by other nonprofit organizations, and neither addressed the actual qualifications or performance of the five trustees whose compensation the IRS was reviewing.

Peters attributed the IRS position to prejudice: "Nobody talked about commissions when this institution had nothing but *haoles* here. I've been sitting back and taking all of this bull for too long and I'm personally very sick and tired of it."

Meanwhile, the question at the legislature was: could any reform get passed into law, or would the trustees' friends stop it? A potential roadblock was the House Judiciary Committee, chaired by Terrance Tom, one of the politicians alleged to have visited a strip club with Milton Holt. Tom also received $4,000 each month from Bishop Estate to provide legal services—an arrangement that had been in place for years —but there was no record of Representative Tom having been called upon to render any services. Tom claimed that he was able to separate completely his work as a lawmaker from his Bishop Estate monthly retainer fee, but he agreed anyway to delegate work on this particular bill to his vice chairman, who kept it bottled up in the committee. It was later discovered that Tom stayed in direct communication with Bishop Estate's Namlyn Snow via faxes labeled "Confidential." The plan was to

Two years before "Broken Trust," Ed Case was encouraging fellow legislators to reform the way Bishop Estate trustees were selected, paid, and held accountable.

prevent the reasonable-compensation bill from getting out of committee and to pass a bill calling for a task force that would study the issue further. Critics of the trustees in the senate, however, managed to keep alive a reasonable-compensation bill in that chamber, which made it possible for Ed Case to force a floor vote in the house. This caught the trustees and their supporters by surprise; they appeared confused.

The media reported all this to a riveted public. Despite the trustees' undeniable power in the legislature, with a public vote about to be taken, it was conceivable that this bill would pass.

Coming up to the day of the vote, there was a lot of head counting. It would be close. The difference between approval and rejection could be a matter of one or two votes—the votes, for example, of Tom and Souki, and of Representative Robert Herkes, who was on the full-time payroll at Bishop Estate. Was it a conflict of interest for someone who was on monthly retainer, or who was collecting either consulting fees or regular paychecks—in each case from Bishop Estate—to vote on this measure? Souki could have said it was, preventing himself, Tom, and Herkes from voting, but he did not. They all voted, and the bill failed to pass by one vote: twenty-six to twenty-five.

Speaking on behalf of Na Pua, Jan Dill expressed "dismay and disgust that so many legislators failed to vote their consciences." Gladys Brandt urged members of the house "to revive this issue before the close of the legislature." She also suggested that representatives "carefully consider how they vote, because voters of this state will not forget who in the legislature was brave enough to take a stand, and who was not." Both daily newspapers listed the phone numbers of the representatives who had voted no, and these individuals were deluged with calls from their districts. Sensing an opportunity, Case forced a second vote several days later in a seldom-used procedure that bypassed leadership. Souki called it anarchy.

This time the vote was fifty to one in favor of the bill. The public had spoken so loudly, even Souki voted for the bill. The lone dissenter, Calvin Say, would go on to replace Souki as speaker.

The compensation bill passed on May 10, 1998. Five days later would be the first anniversary of the march on Kawaiahaʻo Plaza. To observe the occasion, Na Pua was planning a second march.

Gladys Brandt shared with friends a secret fear: what if Lokelani Lindsey made an appearance at the march and in front of the massed Kamehameha ʻohana gave a tearful public apology, or even just a promise to do better? It would be Hawaiian to forgive Lindsey, and that could effectively stop the push for additional reform.

She needn't have worried. The day before the march, the trustees announced that they would not allow the marchers onto Bishop Estate property at Kawaiahaʻo Plaza unless Na Pua arranged for insurance—$2 million worth. The demand infuriated the organizers of the march, but it pleased Brandt. It was a sure sign that Lindsey and the other majority trustees would continue to resist, all but guaranteeing that the ʻohana would remain steadfast.

The next day Bronster stood with Cayetano as the marchers passed the governor's residence. Toni Lee, on behalf of Na Pua, hugged them both. At the Capitol, leaders of the march thanked the legislature for passing the reasonable-compensation bill. There were gifts for the leaders of the senate and the house, Norman Mizuguchi and Joe Souki, but neither was there to accept. At the Supreme Court building, Walter Heen, one of the co-authors of "Broken Trust," spoke, crediting Na Pua and the 1997 marchers with starting to turn the state right-side up again. There were gifts for the justices, but they were not there to accept them.

At Kawaiaha'o Plaza, leaders of Na Pua and representatives of the new Kamehameha teachers' union filled the courtyard. In time, Dickie Wong, Oz Stender, and Gerard Jervis joined them to accept ceremonial gifts: taro and breadfruit, *lei* of *kukui* nut and plumeria, and Bibles. This was the first time since before the 1997 march that more than two trustees had been face to face with leaders of the reform movement. The respectful exchange had come too late to divert the *'ohana* from doing what it believed needed to be done. According to Jan Dill, Na Pua and the other organizations were now focused on nothing less than the removal of all five trustees.

Toni Lee was direct when asked by reporters whether she had anything to say to the trustees: "Stop the stonewalling, stop the legal maneuvering, open the doors to the truth." Wong talked to reporters too. He said he thought the marchers had learned some lessons over the past year—that they had been less arrogant this time.

Two weeks after the march, Lokelani Lindsey was quoted in *Honolulu* magazine as saying, in effect, that Bishop Estate was looking into moving away from Hawai'i: "We don't want to work in a place where we're not wanted." This was a staggering thought. Bishop Estate was a uniquely Hawaiian institution. Surely this was just Lindsey expressing her frustration. Surely the trustees would never actually consider moving out of Hawai'i. But in fact they were seriously looking into moving the headquarters of Princess Pauahi's trust to the Cheyenne River Sioux tribal reservation, a nation-within-a-nation established in 1889 by an act of Congress. The reservation consisted of 2.8 million acres of rolling prairie fifty miles northwest of Pierre, South Dakota, and was home to about twelve thousand Native Americans. It had its own legislature, court system, and executive branch of government. With an unemployment rate of about 60 percent, the reservation would appreciate a new employer— and since the trust's beneficiaries did not include members of the tribe, the Sioux might be inclined to ask few questions.

Dickie Wong admitted this later, under oath, and added that the trustees had paid $300,000 to John Waihe'e's law firm to research the legal aspects of this possible move. Wong said he knew at the time it was "an explosive issue, political dynamite." Despite this, he had instructed the lawyers to "prepare all necessary papers for the transfer and put it on the shelf until we make a decision as to whether to go."

chapter 18

Trustees Surrounded

As the summer of 1998 drew to a close, it looked as if Ben Cayetano would not win re-election. The polls put him well behind his opponent—the mayor of Maui, Linda Lingle—and indicated that Hawai'i residents were ready for a change. An editor from the Washington-based *Cook Political Report* described Cayetano's job performance rating at that time as "among the very worst I've seen for any incumbent who wasn't under indictment."

Then things started popping on the Bishop Estate front: Colbert Matsumoto issued his final report; Margery Bronster announced that she would be asking the probate court to remove all five trustees and perhaps even put some of them in jail; "Broken Trust" co-author Gladys Brandt appeared on TV asking the public to support Cayetano because he had supported Hawaiians in their hour of need; another "Broken Trust" co-author, Walter Heen, publicly labeled Lingle's campaign position on Bishop Estate "pure *waha*" (empty words); and a Na Pua spokesperson questioned whether Lingle could be relied upon to pursue the investigation aggressively. The polls started to turn around, in Cayetano's favor.

Citing this as overwhelming proof, Peters, Wong, and Lindsey complained that they were being "lynched" to get Cayetano re-elected. Then they demanded that Judge Colleen Hirai replace Matsumoto as master because of a campaign letter that had included his name at the bottom, along with those of a half dozen other prominent lawyers. The letter listed the Bishop Estate investigation as reason to re-elect Cayetano. Arguing against the motion in front of Judge Hirai, Matsumoto's attorney, James Duffy, likened the majority trustees to "schoolyard bullies" who had chosen to beat up Matsumoto rather than respond meaningfully to the charges in Matsumoto's report. Hirai denied the trustees' motion.

Then Henry Peters formally asked the circuit court to remove Bronster for unwarranted and vicious attacks on the trustees. Bronster responded that Peters was just feeling the heat. In court documents, she called Peters' actions "feeble," "incoherent," "desperate." The court ruled against Peters.

When Colbert Matsumoto filed his preliminary report in November of 1997—the one he rushed in order to come in ahead of Patrick Yim and the IRS—he had known there was much more to be done. Completing his review would require more resources and involve some degree of personal risk. As Matsumoto later recalled, "I knew I would be out on a limb. I had to ask myself, 'Will the judge back me up?'"

Matsumoto met with Judge Hirai, told her why he thought the inquiry needed to be expanded, and asked if he could count on her support. There were reasons to wonder: Hirai's father, Seichi "Shadow" Hirai, had served for many years as clerk of the senate under Dickie Wong. *The Honolulu Advertiser* once described Shadow Hirai as "a man so politically connected that he sometimes was called 'The 26th Senator.'"

Judge Hirai had her own personal connection: before her appointment to the bench, she had been a partner in Chief Justice Moon's old law firm. But Hirai told Matsumoto, "Just do your job, and let the chips fall where they fall." Matsumoto took this as assurance that he would not be "left hanging."

When they responded initially to Matsumoto's preliminary report, Bishop Estate trustees and their lawyers had tried to make Steven Sakamaki, the accountant Matsumoto had relied on in putting together his first report, sound like a small-timer. To avoid any similar criticism, Matsumoto hired Arthur Andersen, a large international accounting firm, to help with the final report. In early 1998 the Andersen team, having quietly completed a full financial and management audit, reached some disturbing conclusions: under the regime of the five lead trustees, planning had been sporadic and piecemeal; investment decisions were sloppy and were often made without due diligence; and there were no benchmarks for measuring performance, especially in special situations where Bishop Estate was heavily invested. Andersen also identified issues the IRS was sure to question, including excessive trustee compensation and expenses, the small percentage of resources

Judge Colleen Hirai had personal connections to Dickie Wong and Chief Justice Ronald Moon that made some people wonder if she could be objective when deciding controversies involving Bishop Estate trustees.

devoted to the trust's tax-exempt mission, illegal involvement in political campaigns, questionable transactions between the tax-exempt trust and its wholly owned for-profit companies, and employment of high-priced lawyers for work that appeared to benefit individual trustees rather than the trust itself. Like Matsumoto and Yim in their earlier reports, the Andersen team disparaged the lead-trustee system, calling it a serious drag on productivity that gave rise to confusion, micromanagement, and staffers who were afraid to make decisions of any significance.

Colbert Matsumoto relied on these findings—which confirmed Sakamaki's—for his final report on August 7, 1998. In it he highlighted that the trustees had violated both Princess Pauahi's instructions and fundamental elements of trust law when they accumulated income rather than spending it, as directed, on the trust's charitable mission. He added that the accumulation had not been a misunderstanding, as suggested by the trustees, but was premeditated and systematic: "The fact that the trustees cloaked their decision . . . as being 'confidential' and 'privileged' spoke volumes regarding the forthrightness of their action."

Peters, Wong, Lindsey, and Jervis reacted immediately. They called Matsumoto's final report "the product of a flawed analysis, largely attributable to a failure of communications between the Estate staff and the master's accountant," and insinuated that they would have stopped accumulating income long ago if only the masters in prior years had pointed out the problem. Matsumoto could hardly believe that the trustees would have the gall to suggest this. He called it "outrageous" that trustees would "blame past masters for failing to discern the trustees' concealment."

Some of the trustees' other comments about Matsumoto's report were difficult to understand. For example, their stated reason for buying 30,500 acres of Big Island land when the trust already owned 262,000 acres on the same island was to "further diversify." Equally bizarre was their explanation for making it difficult to see that they were accumulating income: it was to make the financial statements "less confusing to persons unfamiliar with trust accounting." The trustees admitted that they had suffered almost $400 million in losses and loss reserves on investments from 1991 to 1996 but stressed that the trust had net income over that period of time. According to Matsumoto, "The trustees either miss the point or don't want to deal with it." The "point" was that the proceeds of involuntary land sales and income from leases entered into long before these trustees came to office should not be used to conceal the shockingly bad investments they had made. The normally restrained Matsumoto used uncharacteristically strong language in describing the trustees' responses to his report: "cavalier," "unsatisfactory," "flimsy," "troubling," "inconsistent," "misleading," "revisionist," "inadequate," "erroneous," "specious," "pathetic," "ludicrous," "egregious," and "alarming."

Matsumoto's report prompted the frustrated deputy attorney general, Kevin Wakayama, to make a move he knew his boss would not like. He had clashed with Bronster many times before. There were issues of turf, style, and loyalty. Bronster had been heard complaining to others that Wakayama sometimes acted as though he was working for Matsumoto, not her. Wakayama maintained that a deputy attorney general's primary duty was to the public.

Their relationship was at a breaking point. Wakayama believed that Matsumoto's findings provided all the evidence needed to remove the trustees immediately, but Bronster was saying that she did not want

Deputy Attorney General Kevin Wakayama did not see eye-to-eye with Attorney General Margery Bronster. She said Wakayama sometimes acted as if he was working for the master, Colbert Matsumoto, rather than for her. Wakayama said Bronster did not understand trust law and was more interested in headlines than results.

to ask the court to take action until her own investigation was complete. Convinced that Bronster's investigation would take years longer, Wakayama made a bold move, one that would almost cost him his job. Under the guise of preparing the office's response to the Matsumoto report, Wakayama drafted what amounted to a petition to remove all five trustees. He restated Matsumoto's factual findings and then applied specific provisions of trust law; the inescapable conclusion, according to Wakayama, was that the trustees had committed a shocking number of serious breaches of trust, any one of which warranted their immediate removal. Wakayama's draft also stated that, in extreme cases such as this one, the probate court had responsibility to act *sua sponte* (on its own initiative). Essentially, he was telling the court that there was no legal or logical reason to wait for Bronster to finish her investigation.

When Bronster saw what Wakayama had prepared, she reacted exactly as Wakayama had expected: "Kevin, you're pushing me off the edge of a cliff." Wakayama acknowledged that his approach could render her investigation meaningless. The whole idea was to get the job done, he said. Bronster told Wakayama that although she did not appreciate what he had done, she would not attempt to stop him from filing the document with the probate court. She did, however, order him to wait two weeks before doing so.

Over the next fourteen days Bronster and the other deputy attorneys general on her civil investigation team—Dorothy Sellers, Hugh Jones, and Daniel Morris—drafted and then filed a petition "on behalf of trust beneficiaries." The petition called for immediate replacement of all five trustees with a court-appointed receiver who would direct Bishop Estate operations until the court could decide which trustees should be removed permanently. The document also asked the court to fine all trustees

> for excessive compensation, for all benefits obtained from the trust for themselves and their family members and friends, for all trust monies expended on boodle and illegal payments for politicians, for all legal fees paid by the trust to benefit the trustees personally, for all advertising expenses paid by the trust to benefit the trustees personally, and for all other amounts necessary to make whole the trust and the beneficiaries.

These documents—one filed by Wakayama, the other by Bronster—changed everything. They were the first official calls for the removal of trustees. Wakayama's filing, technically no more than a response to the master's report, could only encourage Judge Hirai to remove trustees. But Bronster as *parens patriae* could theoretically force Hirai to make a decision one way or the other.

Na Pua quickly and effectively bolstered the official recommendations with a grassroots voice, publishing a list of "Key Steps to Be Taken." The first key step was "Remove 5 Trustees":

> *Pono* cannot be achieved if any of the present trustees are allowed to remain. . . . The beneficiaries of Bernice Pauahi Bishop will not accept a prolonged process that keeps these same trustees in power nor will we agree to legal tactics that threaten the integrity of the assets of the Estate. These trustees have mismanaged the legacy of Pauahi long enough! We see assets being wasted to protect the individual trustees at the expense of the Estate. This wanton squandering of Pauahi's gift to her people must stop.

The trustees were surrounded. Public opinion and the entire Kamehameha *'ohana* had united against them. The Supreme Court justices had abandoned them, and all but one of their friends in the legislature had actually voted to limit their compensation. Closing in from four different directions were Matsumoto and his team of accountants, Bronster and her civil and criminal teams of investigators and lawyers, investigators from the Campaign Spending Commission, and—scariest of all—the IRS.

Bishop Estate was everywhere on court calendars. There were three separate years of annual accountings being argued and processed in probate court; grand jury sessions and intermittent circuit-court arguments over Bronster's handling of the criminal investigations; seemingly endless hearings and appellate-court battles over subpoena enforcement; arguments over discovery in Stender's lawsuit to remove Lindsey; indictments, plea bargaining, and pretrial motions related to alleged campaign spending violations and related crimes; and a host of counteractions, including a trustees' threat to sue the Campaign Spending Commission and attempts to have the master and attorney general removed from the case. There also were former employees who were alleging wrongful discharge, and former business partners were claiming various kinds of harm owing to trustee misconduct.

The trustees' many lawyers needed to know where their respective client(s) stood on each issue. Sometimes a boardroom vote would be

"BOY, I'M BEGINNING TO SEE MORE OF THE FACULTY, THE TRUSTEES AND STUDENTS AROUND HERE THAN ON CAMPUS..."

Marshall Ige, Henry Peters' protégé, received illegal help from
Bishop Estate when his political campaign ran short of money.
In 2002 Ige pleaded guilty to unrelated crimes. Sentenced to six
months in jail, Ige said he finally understood how Americans of
Japanese ancestry must have felt during World War II when they
were forced into internment camps.

three to two, and separate legal positions would be argued by at least two sets of lawyers, one taking orders from the Wong-Peters-Lindsey majority, another speaking on behalf of the Stender-Jervis minority. Other times the vote would be four to one, with Stender the odd man out. There were also times when all five trustees found their interests aligned. Only in those rare cases did a single team of lawyers argue a single position on behalf of the trustees. The hordes of personal lawyers also were prominent fixtures during this time.

Stender and Bronster collided on one crucial issue: Bronster wanted Stender's lawsuit against Lindsey postponed indefinitely so it would not get in the way of Bronster's effort to remove all five trustees. Stender insisted that his lawsuit should come first. Both refused to budge.

As the legal wrangling continued, the trustees quietly gave themselves raises, increasing their own compensation to well beyond $1 million each.

Also during this time, the Campaign Spending Commission unanimously referred both Milton Holt and Marshall Ige for criminal prosecution in state court and sent letters to Namlyn Snow and Yukio Take-moto notifying them that they might face criminal charges too. The commission sent similar letters to five companies alleged to have been involved in the illegal payment of campaign debts for Holt and Ige. The U.S. Attorney's office also charged Holt separately, in federal court, for theft of campaign funds.

O_z Stender and his personal lawyers, Crystal Rose and Douglas Ing, likened the majority-trustees' control of Bishop Estate to a fragile house of cards: "Pull out one card and the rest will come tumbling down." But they and their client wanted to leave a card or two still standing. One Sunday afternoon in late September 1998, the three of them met with leaders from the Kamehameha 'ohana to ask for their kōkua (coopera-tion): Stender asked for support in his efforts to remove Lindsey and opposition to Bronster's petition for the removal of all five trustees. On previous occasions Stender had said he was willing to lose his trust-eeship if that was what it took to get the others out. Now he was say-ing that he wanted to stay. He was part of the solution, not part of the problem.

After making his plea, Stender left the room, but Rose and Ing stayed. Their arguments were passionate and personal. They said it would be wrong for the 'ohana to turn its back on Stender. He was not like the other trustees. He had graduated from Kamehameha, and that should mean something. The attorney general was well intentioned, but wrong; there was no need to remove Stender, and it would be shameful to do so.

Beadie Dawson responded that although everyone appreciated what Stender had done, a trial focusing exclusively on Lindsey would divert resources and give Judge Hirai an excuse not to rule on Bronster's peti-tion. Furthermore, in a trial to remove only Lindsey, Rose and Ing would naturally avoid raising issues that made their own client vulnerable.

One by one, the other thirty-five to forty people in attendance shared their mana'o (personal opinions). They did not want to turn their backs on Stender, but each of the represented organizations was already on re-cord as calling for the removal of five trustees. They felt great aloha for Stender, but they wanted to be steadfast, and, above all, they wanted to do what was best for the trust.

The meeting went on for nearly five hours. When a vote finally was taken, it went against Stender. The next day Stender's wife, Ku'ulei, and their daughter, Lee Anne, resigned from Na Pua, with a letter that was part sorrow, part anger. In a separate note to Gladys Brandt, Ku'ulei complained that the position attributed to the "Broken Trust" authors—a call for the removal of all five trustees—must have come from Randall Roth: "It smelled white."

Four days later, several hundred members of the Kamehameha 'ohana gathered on the lawn outside the circuit courthouse where Judge Hirai would soon be holding an important hearing. There was a joint statement, in writing, from various groups within the 'ohana: Na Pua, Na Kumu, the Kamehameha Schools Faculty Association, and the Kamehameha Schools Alumni Association Board of Presidents. It stated that the probate judge had the power to remove any trustee who knowingly failed to (1) follow the governing document, (2) obey court orders, (3) submit accurate accounts, (4) monitor the actions of a co-trustee, (5) work cooperatively with co-trustees, (6) invest prudently, (7) avoid conflicts of interest, or (8) pursue in good faith the trust's charitable mission. Then it listed findings from the Matsumoto and Yim reports indicating that the Bishop Estate trustees had failed on all eight of these points, and it called upon Judge Hirai to act expeditiously. It also showed that the Kamehameha 'ohana had not abandoned Stender:

> In many ways it does not seem fair that Oz Stender initially will be treated the same as the others, but this is the only way to get the court to remove the others now. The sorting out of individual levels of merit and culpability will take time. We love and admire trustee Stender and expect that he eventually will be reinstated as a trustee.

Following the customary *pule* and *mele* (prayer and song), Na Pua's Jan Dill decried the ongoing "political manipulation, greed and arrogance," and called upon fellow alumni to "act like 'good and industrious men and women'" and to insist that Judge Hirai remove the trustees immediately "so that *pono* (goodness and righteousness) can be restored."

Na Kumu's Charlene Hoe explained why the 'ohana had come to the courthouse steps wearing *ti*-leaf *lei:* "As the *lei* encircles us with its *mana* (power) and protection, we have come here today to encircle Pauahi's legacy. We are the *lei* of protection for her school, for her dream. We are those who must hold our leaders accountable to that dream. Judge Hirai, we urge you to act."

Na Pua a Ke Aliʻi Pauahi members formed prayer circles outside the courthouse where Judge Hirai had the opportunity to remove all five trustees immediately.

David Eyre, also of Na Kumu, was next: "Whatever happens tomorrow or in the days to come, our trust in the trustee majority is broken beyond repair, the faith is forever lost, the *mana* of their leadership is forever gone. What remains is the deep and lasting, the everlasting *hilahila,* the sense of shame." Like Hoe, Eyre ended with a direct appeal to Judge Hirai: "We have been held hostages long enough. Please place your arms around our campus and don't let them touch us any more!"

Off to the side about a hundred other Hawaiians held signs supporting the trustees. The counter-protestors had arrived on chartered buses from the Waiʻanae area, led by Henry Peters' mother, Hoaliku Drake. They lined the sidewalk and shouted as members of the Kamehameha *ʻohana* headed toward the parking garage: "How could you bite the hand that feeds you?" The worst of the taunts was *"Haole!"* The loaded meaning was that the Kamehameha Hawaiians had betrayed their own people.

That was too much for Na Kumu's Kēhau Abad to take. She had grown up in Waiʻanae. She had been a Hawaiian activist since she was a teenager, standing all-night vigils to protect burial sites threatened by development, and had worked with her father, Fred Cachola, who had

Hoaliku Drake, mother of Henry Peters and director of Hawaiian Homelands under Governor Waihe'e, led a group that viewed any attempt to remove a trustee as an attack on Pauahi's will.

been in charge of Bishop Estate's extension programs until Lindsey shut them down. Abad had resolved to maintain dignity as she passed the trustees' supporters and not even acknowledge the taunts. But she could not help herself. She found herself yelling back that they were ignorant, prostituting themselves, being used.

October 1998 was late in the day for anyone to hold onto the idea that the trustees and Princess Pauahi's trust were one and the same thing. Still, a few Hawaiians continued to assert that there could only be evil motives for criticizing the trustees, and that the force powering the evil was racial.

Lawyers for the majority trustees added fuel to these flames: Renee Yuen told reporters that the trustees' critics were pawns of non-Hawaiians who were attempting "the ultimate robbery of the Hawaiian people." Bruce Graham argued in court that the appointment of a temporary receiver to run the daily operations of the trust would effectively hand Pauahi's sacred legacy over to a Mainland *luna*—a word from plantation days that conjured up the image of a white-skinned foreman with a blacksnake whip. A trustee of the Office of Hawaiian Affairs (OHA), Frenchy De Soto, said that "they"—meaning *haole*—had broken the Lunalilo trust a hundred years ago and now they were going after Bishop Estate and the OHA. De Soto said Bronster ought to get on a plane and go back to the Mainland. Henry Peters called Bronster a New York Ivy Leaguer who was on a personal crusade against Pauahi's trust because the current trustees did not share Bronster's "missionary mentality." Peters was using the word "missionary" as a term of contempt, as shorthand for a grasping white oppressor.

All of this boiled down to a simple but powerful message that had been used effectively many times before: non-Hawaiians were now going after the little that had not already been stolen from Hawaiians.

The day after the *'ohana* rally, Judge Hirai gave the trustees four weeks to prepare legal arguments for why they should not be removed immediately. Then, on October 30, 1998, Bronster appeared in Judge Hirai's courtroom, ready to argue for exactly that. The courtroom was tense but orderly. Lawyers for all five trustees argued against being removed, stressing that they should be allowed to stay on the job at least until each had gotten the benefit of "due process." What they had in mind were five full-blown trials, each the kind that would take another year or more to prepare and then at least three or four months to conduct.

Na Pua submitted a friend of the court brief that addressed the trustees' position in terms anyone could understand.

> Imagine the Court having appointed a person legal Guardian of a minor. Then imagine that Guardian accused by the minor, the minor's parents, the minor's teachers, the Guardian's employees, a Master appointed by the Court to investigate the matter, an international accounting firm, the Attorney General, a sitting Federal Judge, a retired Appellate Judge and numerous experts and prominent members of the public, of stealing from the minor, depriving the minor of funds, jeopardizing the minor's assets, harming the minor psychologically and other sundry forms of malfeasance and mismanagement. Then throw in that the Guardian is indicted by the State for misappropriating the minor's money and under investigation by the IRS for overcompensating himself from the minor's assets and other IRS violations.

Under these circumstances, it would be reasonable to require the Guardian to relinquish control of the minor and his property, at least temporarily, until a full hearing could be held to determine the validity of the charges. It would not be reasonable to permit the accused Guardian to jeopardize the minor by retaining control of the care of the minor and his property. Cries of "due process," or consideration of the Guardian's supposed "rights" have no place in the consideration of interim removal.

The situation described above is the very one that has been before this Court for too long. The only difference is that the trustees are the guardians of thousands of children, not just one. Na Pua urgently asks this Court to invoke its equitable powers to immediately remove, on an interim basis, all five trustees before further harm occurs to the beneficiaries and the trust.

In an oral argument before Hirai, Bronster put it in legal terms. She stressed that the Yim and Matsumoto reports were presumed by law to be accurate, and that they described numerous serious breaches of trust, any one of which warranted immediate interim removal. Even if new evidence at a trial for permanent removal placed one or more of the trustees in a better light, the only question to be answered now was: what was best for the trust and its beneficiaries?

At the end of the hearing, Hirai could have made a decision then and there. Instead, she took the case "under advisement," meaning that she was not yet ready to make a decision. Because the basic facts and applicable law were clear, some legal observers were surprised by Hirai's indecision. Others had expected it. Hirai had the reputation of a judge who sometimes has trouble making up her mind, even when the stakes are not high. The decision she had been asked to make could have profound implications, not only for Bishop Estate and the judiciary, but also for a forty-five-year political dynasty. The stakes in the case facing her were higher than most judges would ever see in a lifetime.

Hirai gave no indication as to when she would be ready to make a decision. Publicly, Bronster's spokeswoman told reporters that Hirai's non-decision reflected "an abundance of caution." Privately, others in the attorney general's office were saying that Hirai looked like "a deer caught in headlights."

Meanwhile, there was a great deal of sparring and legal maneuvering in anticipation of Lindsey's removal trial, which was scheduled to begin the second week in November. Lindsey's lawyers intended to put

Patrick Yim on the stand, and to get the names of everyone who had spoken to him. Stender's lawyers also intended to call Yim as a witness, but they were against letting out the names of interviewees. Bronster sided with Lindsey's lawyers on this issue, saying the public should not be kept in the dark. Before Bronster could serve Yim with a subpoena, however, he announced that he had destroyed all his notes and records.

For the past year Jervis' name had appeared next to Stender's on the lawsuit to remove Lindsey. This provided some comfort to Stender after operating for years as a minority of one, but the partnership was not a happy one. Jervis was grumpy and quick-tempered, and he refused from the beginning to help pay for the Lindsey removal trial.

Most people viewed that trial as a showdown solely between Stender and Lindsey. Like the confrontations between Bronster and McCorriston, it got personal. Lindsey talked often about Stender's shortcomings as a trustee: he had poor attendance at board meetings and an inability to maintain a confidence. She insisted that Stender was masterminding a conspiracy against her. Stender, for his part, called Lindsey "paranoid," "crazy," and even "evil." He had a collection of Lindsey stories. He said when people called on her office phone, she had them call her back on her cell phone, as if that were more secure. She usually kept the drapes in her office closed, once commenting that there could be a man in the trees outside, spying, reading documents on someone's desk.

Stender said that Lindsey kept close track of him. Whenever he was on the Mainland on business, he liked to talk to alumni chapters. He would arrive in a city, make a phone call, and be told that Lindsey had already called the chapter and warned the alumni not to talk to him. According to Stender, Lindsey liked people to think she possessed more information about them than she did. One day she told Stender she had in her possession a damaging piece of evidence, a letter she said Stender had written to the justices. She said he might as well own up to it. Stender, knowing that no such letter existed, challenged Lindsey to produce it. She said she would not, because it was "confidential."

Lindsey had her own stories about Stender. One went back to a proposition put to the Bishop Estate board to acquire control of the Maui Land and Pineapple Company in 1995. After the trustees decided not to pursue the deal, Stender put together an investment *hui* (group) that seriously looked at the same deal. Lindsey hired a former FBI agent to find out what Stender had done, and then she asked Michael Hare of the Cades law firm to provide a confidential legal opinion. As written, Hare's letter left doubt in the reader's mind: "Whether or not trustee Oswald Stender engaged in any material breach of his fiduciary responsibilities as a trustee of Bishop Estate is inconclusive at this time." Lindsey leaked the story to a TV news reporter as a scandal.

There came a point when Stender told Lindsey he had enough to get her removed as a trustee. She replied that if that ever happened, she would "let slip" that the admissions process at Kamehameha had been bent in order to get Stender's granddaughter into the school. Knowing that to be untrue, and emotional almost beyond words, Stender told Lindsey that if she ever tried to drag his family into this mess, he would kill her.

End of the Line

At Bishop Estate during the 1990s senior staff members had impressive titles and generous salaries but not much authority. As they saw it, they had little to gain and much to lose by standing up to the trustees. One staff member told another while they were waiting to be called into the boardroom, "We go in there and all we're going to do is get blasted. They're not going to listen to us anyway. So give them what they want to hear."

As the trustees became increasingly preoccupied with their personal legal problems, decision making at Kawaiahaʻo Plaza slowed to a crawl. Relationships in the boardroom broke down completely. Abusive language, never unusual with this board, grew louder and coarser. One meeting nearly ended in a fistfight between Peters and Jervis. The tension and uncertainty had made itself felt at all levels of life at Kamehameha Schools—including the student body. Even the students feared reprisals.

In Cyd Gasper's sophomore year at Kamehameha, she and her friends could tell that Dr. Chun was going through a difficult time. They liked him, everybody did, and they could see how much he liked students. To show that they sympathized with him in whatever trouble he was having, they put together some little books for other students to write or draw in, and they gave the books to Chun one morning at chapel.

By the beginning of her junior year, Gasper was coming to a more measured evaluation of Chun. She still liked him, but at the time of the march on Kawaiahaʻo Plaza, Chun had told the students that they should not march. If they did, it would cost them a grade point in every class they missed. Something about this did not seem right. There were things badly wrong between Kamehameha and the trustees, and the march was supposed to set things right. She wondered why Chun did not support the march. Gasper had also been in *kumu* Eyre's Hawaiian language class the day he was threatened with being fired for insubordination. He and the other Na Kumu leaders had dared to speak up on behalf of a student, Kamani Kualā'au. Gasper could see strain and fatigue in Eyre's face and in the faces of many others. One of her favorite teachers already had quit in disgust and moved to the Mainland.

The problems at Kamehameha were discussed at family gatherings. Even in public, strangers would notice her Kamehameha uniform and ask about what was happening with the trustees. Bishop Estate and Kamehameha Schools had been front-page news for more than a year, and people had strong feelings about the issues. The question for Gasper and other students was whether to do something, or just to go about the business of being at school. The Kamehameha campus was big and scattered; the students were rarely all together. Even if students could get together to do something, what would it be, and would it have any influence? Besides, it could get them into trouble. They still remembered Kamani Kualā'au's being hauled out of class and taken to Lokelani Lindsey's office at Kawaiaha'o Plaza. Nobody wanted that, especially seniors with college-admission and financial-aid decisions pending.

Yet Gasper felt an urge to do something. If teachers were putting themselves on the line for students, it was right for students to offer support. Remembering how Karen Keawehawai'i Farias had buttonholed students in the parking lot three semesters ago, Gasper came up with the idea of a petition offering student support for teachers fighting for the removal of trustees. She talked about it with her teachers, and they helped her with the wording and made copies for her.

Gasper's friends were the first ones to sign. Then they took copies of the petition to other friends in their homerooms and classes. Some teachers gave them the go-ahead; others pretended not to see the petition circulating. No one told them to stop. Gasper and her friends took petitions with them to the library and to the dining hall at lunch. One friend, a student trainer in athletics, took petitions with her to the track.

There were concerns. What if the administration found out, and then parents found out that their children were risking a Kamehameha education, and not just their own, but their younger brothers' and sisters' chances for admission? The petition spread anyway. It was the Kamehameha grapevine—say something to someone, or do something interesting, and soon everyone knew. In just a few days, there were more than eight hundred signatures, half the enrollment in the high school. As a precaution, the girls spearheading the drive—and they were all girls—kept the signed petitions under lock and key.

The petitions later appeared at an *'ohana* rally outside the courthouse. The next morning, a photo of several petitions appeared in *The Honolulu Advertiser*. In legible letters at the bottom of each was the name Cyd Gasper. Seeing it in the newspaper took her breath away.

Later that day Gasper was to dance solo in a *hula* festival. She had worked hard on her *lei*; it was the best she had ever made. The *lei* judge, a woman Gasper had never seen before, looked at her name tag and said, "Oh, Cyd Gasper. I know you." Gasper's immediate thought was, "Oh no, I'm in trouble. This lady is going to be marking down my *lei*, all the way down. I'm not going to get any good scores on my *lei* just because of the stuff I did." But then the judge smiled and said, "You don't have to worry. I'm on your side." Back in the dressing room, Gasper could not stop crying.

In November 1998 Judge Hirai announced that she would not remove any trustee, even temporarily, without first giving him or her a full-evidentiary trial. Hirai added that these trials would have to wait until Stender's action against Lindsey had ended, which was likely to take four or five months. Two months earlier Bronster had asked for the immediate interim removal of all five trustees. Now that she knew Hirai was not going to do anything soon, Bronster amended her petition. She decided not to seek Stender's interim or permanent removal. That meant there would be an interim removal trial in Hirai's courtroom for four trustees—Peters, Wong, Lindsey, and Jervis—but it would not start for at least four months. It looked, for the time being, as if Stender would be spared.

Also in November, Ben Cayetano was re-elected by a five-thousand-vote margin. The following Monday morning, Judge Bambi Weil gaveled Lindsey's removal trial to order. It would be a non-jury trial, one that veteran trust lawyers later described as unlike any other trial they had ever seen. Legal issues took a back seat to emotional ones. Virtually none of the testimony related to the serious, ongoing breaches of trust Matsumoto had identified. Instead, witness after witness focused on Lindsey's arrogance and insensitivity. The *Star-Bulletin* called it "a modern day morality play."

Elisa Yadao, the trust's former director of communications, testified that she had been reduced to tears trying to deal with Lindsey, "more [times] than I'd like to count." Charlene Hoe, a leader of Na Kumu, described how Lindsey had "belittled an instructor" by saying that the student art hanging in that teacher's classroom "looked like laundry." Various teachers testified about Lindsey's dictate that only "traditional" Hawaiian words be used on campus. They were especially upset that Lindsey would do this when she did not even speak the language herself. Randie Fong, the director of Kamehameha's performing arts department who had threatened to resign in protest of Lindsey's heavy-handed management, testified that Lindsey's arbitrary directives made people feel "stupid and incompetent." When Fong added that Lindsey had once used the f-word in a conversation with him, the TV camera caught Lindsey mouthing a response to Fong: "You liar." That was the lead on all four TV news programs that night, and then replayed many times during the TV news coverage of the four-month trial.

Others testified that Lindsey had harmed students' self-esteem by releasing a report that unfairly cast doubt on the quality of education at Kamehameha. Crystal Rose, Stender's attorney, likened Lindsey's release of that report to "sending a guided missile into a schoolyard." Na Pua's Roy Benham testified that he and other alumni had gone to the campus the day after Lindsey launched that bombshell and held a sign that said to students, "You're OK, we support you."

The reason for this highly unusual courtroom strategy was obvious. Lawyers on both sides wanted to avoid the many issues in Matsumoto's report that would implicate their own clients. These included taking unreasonable compensation, using trust funds to fight the enactment of an intermediate sanctions law, accumulating income in violation of Pauahi's will, investing in ways that violated the Prudent Investor Act, misreporting financial results, intervening in political campaigns, and violating various court orders. Any one of these would be ample legal grounds for removing all five trustees.

Nearly a year before Lindsey's removal trial started, Stender had offered to pay Lindsey $1 million if she would resign. Lindsey's response at the time: "Absolutely not." Her lawyers seemed confident of a winning verdict, as did the psychic Lindsey had been seeing for years ("but not on Estate matters").

Shortly before the trial began, Judge Weil had ordered the parties to

Lokelani Lindsey provides advice to her lawyers during a trial that focused more on arrogance and insensitivity than on breaches of fiduciary duties.

try once more to reach an out-of-court settlement. A key session took place in the home of Michael Green, Lindsey's lead trial lawyer. Judge Marie Milks shuttled from Stender's lawyers in one room to Lindsey's lawyers in another. After hours of going back and forth, there was tentative agreement on the numbers: Lindsey would get $500,000 right away, plus $10,000 each month for the next five years. Her departure would be announced as a resignation, not a removal, and there would be a retirement party. One more thing: Lindsey wanted her portrait permanently displayed in a prominent place on campus.

Stender lined up the money. He had wealthy friends who would pay most of it, and Bishop Estate's liability insurance company had agreed to contribute.

Before the agreement could be finalized, however, Wong pleaded with Stender to allow Lindsey to stay. Wong said he would see to it that Lindsey stayed off campus and that he and Stender, working together, could make sure that Lindsey did not cause any more trouble. Stender replied that he did not want to play nursemaid to Lindsey; he wanted her off the board immediately, completely, and permanently. With that, Wong stood up, very upset, and said, "If you don't put an end to this, we're gonna fire Mike Chun." Stender decided to call what he believed to be Wong's bluff: "You want to fire Mike Chun over this, do it, just do it."

Soon after the meeting with Wong, Stender received word that Lindsey had changed her mind about stepping down. Presumably Wong and Peters had talked her out of it, fearful that any replacement for Lindsey would side with Stender and Jervis, putting Wong and Peters in the minority.

Well into her removal trial, Lindsey had second thoughts about having twice turned down the money offered her earlier. Judge Weil had just declined Lindsey's request to question Justices Klein and Levinson on the witness stand, and Lindsey presumably felt that this and other rulings weakened her case. So she asked her lawyers to find out whether Stender would be interested in resuming settlement discussions. Stender said he was, and negotiations began for the third time. It soon was clear, however, that the two sides were farther apart than ever. Lindsey was now demanding that Stender guarantee that the attorney general and IRS leave her alone if she resigned—which he did not have the power to do.

In their closing remarks, Lindsey's lawyers said she had been portrayed in the courtroom as "Attila the Hun." They called the trial "McCarthyism at its height," driven by "a public frenzy similar to that which fueled the Salem witch trials and the Spanish Inquisition."

On Stender's side, Douglas Ing's closing remarks focused on institutional esteem, spiritual loss, and a need for urgent action: "Kamehameha will not emerge from this poverty of character until trustee Lindsey has been permanently removed." Ing ended his closing argument with a prayer recited by Kamehameha students each year at Princess Pauahi's grave. As Ing prayed, Stender's supporters in the gallery could be seen mouthing the words, just as they had done when they were students at Kamehameha.

Then Lindsey nudged one of her lawyers and whispered, "Look, she's crying." The lawyer looked over, saw that Crystal Rose was crying, and said, "Don't worry about it, Crystal cries a lot." Lindsey replied, "No, I'm not talking about Crystal; I'm talking about the judge. Look at the judge." Judge Weil was wiping tears from her eyes.

The courtroom was not the only place where dramatic events were unfolding. Gerard Jervis' presence in Judge Weil's court was not required,

Judge Bambi Weil ruled in 1997 that Bobby Harmon had breached the confidentiality clause in his employment contract. In 1999 she presided over Lokelani Lindsey's removal trial.

but he had been there most days anyway, sometimes with his wife, Avis. Jervis often talked to reporters in the halls during breaks in the trial.

In the early days of March, however, with the trial nearing an end, Jervis was nowhere to be seen. Then, on March 12, the media reported that Jervis had attempted suicide. That was not all. Jervis' attempt was connected to the apparent suicide, nine days earlier, of thirty-nine-year-old Rene Ojiri Kitaoka, a lawyer for Kamehameha Investment Corporation, Bishop Estate's real estate development arm. Kitaoka's husband had found her body in her car with the engine running in the closed garage of their home. Investigators discovered a credit card receipt in her purse, signed by Jervis, for a $200 dinner at the Hawaiʻi Prince Hotel in Waikīkī the night before. When investigators checked with the manager of that hotel, he told them something they could hardly believe: after having dinner in the hotel's posh restaurant, Jervis and Kitaoka were found by a hotel security guard in a stall of a public restroom, engaged in a sex act.

Several days after Kitaoka's funeral, a TV news reporter, acting on a tip, had asked Jervis about the evening at the Prince Hotel. Rather than answer, Jervis got into his car, drove to his home in Kailua, and swallowed some sleeping pills—no one knows how many. His wife found him on the bathroom floor and had him taken by ambulance to Castle Medical Center, where he recovered fully.

This all happened at the very end of Kamehameha's quarter term. Examination results were coming, and Song Contest was just weeks away. Yet the only thing students, teachers, and administrators talked about was Jervis.

Oz Stender was dumbstruck. He had had no idea about the relationship between Jervis and Kitaoka. The secretaries knew; one said it had been going on for about two years. Kitaoka had come to Bishop Estate from the Cades law firm. Jervis personally chose her for the top legal job with Kamehameha Investment, where he chaired the board of directors. They traveled together on business. One of the staffers at Kamehameha Investment recalled Kitaoka coming to take away Jervis' credit card statements—the originals, not photocopies—saying Jervis had sent her. Letting someone take the originals was not standard office procedure, but what a trustee wanted, a trustee got.

As a trustee of a charitable trust founded on Christian ideals, with a mission of educating children, Jervis had disgraced himself—and in the opinion of some, he had also brought shame to the trust. Jervis reportedly saw it differently. Asked by a fellow trustee if he would be resigning, Jervis replied, "Why would I resign? Things like this happen all the time."

Shortly after Jervis' suicide attempt, Michael Chun spoke to the campus community on closed-circuit TV about the need to remember that Kamehameha was a family, the need to feel for people as a family, to have sympathy, forgiveness. He asked everyone to pray.

Jervis made his suicide attempt only eighteen days before the scheduled start of his own interim removal trial. Now his lawyer was asking for a postponement, saying Jervis was in no condition to defend his personal interests effectively. This was ironic: In resisting his own interim removal as a trustee, Jervis was asserting that he was presently capable of protecting the interests of others. But now his lawyer was seeking a postponement on the grounds that Jervis was not able to protect even his own interests.

Deputy Attorney General Dorothy Sellers argued that Jervis' self-destructive behavior was reason enough for removal. Judge Kevin

At a time when the Bishop Estate controversy looked like it could spin wildly in just about any direction, Chief Justice Ronald Moon assigned Kevin Chang to the probate court. Chang made decisions that led to a quick end to the various investigations.

Chang, recently reassigned by Chief Justice Moon to probate court, disagreed with Sellers and granted the requested postponement.

The list of related trials had grown: There was Lindsey's, which was about to end in Judge Weil's courtroom; Peters' and Wong's upcoming trials in Judge Hirai's courtroom; and Jervis' trial, which would be presided over by either Chang or Hirai once Jervis recovered. There would also be one or more permanent removal trials for as many as four trustees sometime in the future, perhaps a year or two from now, and the trustees surely would appeal if they lost. At this rate, it would be at least several more years before things could be sorted out.

But then, on the last day of 1998, something big happened. Like a guillotine blade released in slow motion, the IRS issued notices of proposed adjustment, known as Form 5701. These documents could not have been more sharply worded. Essentially, the IRS officials had concluded that the level of abuse at Bishop Estate was unprecedented, leaving them no real choice but to revoke the trust's tax-exempt status.

Normally the IRS would be willing to discuss the 5701s with the trustees, but this time was different. The trustees had irreconcilable conflicts of interest and could not be trusted to adhere to any agreement that might be reached: they had "a history of ignoring probate court orders, master report recommendations, probate court stipulations, and the advice of independent experts." The IRS flatly refused to communicate with the trustees or their agents.

The trustees' personal interests directly conflicted with the trust's interests because the IRS was demanding that each trustee reimburse the trust for millions in excessive compensation. The IRS was also troubled by the trustees' use of trust funds to defend their jobs, level of compensation, and other personal interests.

Judge Chang agreed with the IRS. In early February 1999 he ruled that the trustees had "actual, adverse, and material conflicts of interest in matters involving the IRS audit." Chang then appointed five "special-purpose" trustees to deal with the IRS on behalf of the trust estate. Chang's way of handling the trustees' conflict of interests was "startling" and "unprecedented," according to several national authorities who were quoted in the media. They said it was unworkable. How could two sets of trustees function independently of each other, simultaneously?

The new special-purpose trustees—Ronald Libkuman, a former law partner of Chief Justice Moon; Constance Lau, a savings bank executive; David Coon, the retired headmaster of 'Iolani School; Francis Keala, a former Honolulu police chief; and Robert Kihune, a retired U.S. Navy admiral—immediately gathered in a conference room at Arthur Andersen's suite of offices. Their first task was to review the 5701s and its 2,500 pages of attachments. The contents were sobering. The IRS was proposing tax deficiencies, based on "creative" transactions between the trust and its wholly owned subsidiaries, totaling hundreds of millions of dollars. And that was not the worst of it. The real shocker was the IRS' decision to revoke the trust's tax-exempt status retroactive to July 1, 1989. An Arthur Andersen tax accountant estimated that this would cost the trust nearly $1 billion up front, and much more over time.

Soon, however, there was reason for hope. The IRS extended a highly unusual offer: officials from the national, regional, and district offices were willing to gather in Los Angeles with the special-purpose trustees and their advisers to discuss a way of resolving the matter without hurting Kamehameha Schools. When that meeting began on April 19, 1999, there were no pleasantries. One of the special-purpose trustees later described it as "something out of a movie"—ten to twelve very serious people on one side of a long table, facing a similar number of equally serious people on the other side. Marcus Owens, who headed the IRS' Exempt Organization Division at the time, began the meeting by saying he would be doing the talking; the special-purpose trustees were there to listen.

Owens said nobody liked the idea of revoking Bishop Estate's exemption, but the scope and magnitude of abuse were unparalleled. The IRS was willing to negotiate anyway, but only if it was assured of fundamental change at Bishop Estate. He had a list of specific steps that needed to be taken, and the first item on his list was that all five current trustees must resign or be removed. These conditions, Owens said, were absolutely "non-negotiable."

The special-purpose trustees reported all this to Judge Chang, who gave Stender, Wong, Peters, Lindsey, and Jervis one week to resign or "show cause" why he should not remove them. Chang also ordered the trustees to stop paying compensation to themselves. This was five weeks after the end of Lindsey's removal trial in front of Judge Weil and two days after closing arguments in Peters' and Wong's removal trials in front of Judge Hirai. Weil's and Hirai's decisions were still pending, and neither had given any indication as to when a decision would be forthcoming.

Four days later Goldman Sachs stock began trading on the New York stock exchange. Bishop Estate sold nine million shares at $53 per share as part of the initial offering. The $477 million it received was nearly as much as the trustees had invested in the first place, and the Estate had another twenty-two million shares that it expected to sell sometime soon.

Henry Peters told reporters it was ironic that his compensation had just been stopped and another grand jury had just been convened: "Anywhere else they would have a parade for me. Here they kick you in the butt and indict you."

In the 5701s the IRS stated that Bishop Estate had ceased to function primarily as a charity. To the IRS it looked more like "a personal investment club," one that paid grossly excessive fees, gave preferential treatment to insiders, engaged in excessive lobbying, and involved itself, illegally, in state and federal political campaigns. The 5701s pointed out that when the trust began to receive large cash infusions from forced sales of leasehold land, "school expenditures dropped from the greater part of total expenditures to a fraction well below half." In addition to accumulating income in violation of Pauahi's will, the trustees had made improper payments to friends, relatives, business associates, and elected officials, and had failed to collect millions of dollars of debts owed to the trust "without any apparent justification." The 570s also provided numerous examples of misleading financial information and the adverse consequences it had on the trust. For example, by not following generally accepted accounting principles, the trustees artificially inflated their fees by more than $5 million over a two-and-a-half-year period during the early 1990s.

From every angle, the IRS viewed the fees that the trustees had taken for themselves as "grossly excessive." The trustees' compensation studies had been a "complete waste of trust funds," and their argument that compensation should be high because of unlimited personal liability was "totally without merit." As viewed by the IRS, competent trustees had more than adequate protection against personal liability: "The trustees have a right to indemnification from the trust. . . . The vast assets of the Estate would appear more than ample to protect the trustees from any conceivable liability. Also, the trustees benefit from liability insurance policies purchased by the Estate."

The IRS all but ridiculed the trustees' claim to superior investment results. In the 570s the IRS noted that Bishop Estate had experienced "a spectacular rise in income in the last decade" but attributed it to forced sales of land. Once those gains were factored out, the trustees' investment performance was poor. The IRS also took aim at the Supreme Court justices who had selected these trustees: "The process of selection of trustees apparently has not been conducted in any kind of systematic manner designed to discover and evaluate the most qualified individuals."

While the special-purpose trustees were discussing the 570s with IRS officials, the Hawai'i legislature was in session, and a battle royal was shaping up. Shortly after Cayetano's re-election, he had asked Bronster to continue in office. For this to happen, however, a majority of the senators had to agree.

Some political observers thought that Bronster would be a shoo-in: she had just been re-appointed by a governor who was a Democrat, and twenty-three of the twenty-five senators were Democrats. From the public's point of view, the case for a yes-vote could be summed up in two words: Bishop Estate.

Peters and Wong still had friends in the legislature, however, and Larry Mehau had gotten involved, meeting privately with four first-term senators who wanted more say in the senate. They were all working against Bronster's re-appointment. Members of the governor's cabinet would normally lobby aggressively on behalf of a fellow department head, but that was not happening. Several cabinet members said privately that it might be time for a new attorney general. There was a sense that the office had not functioned well, and some resented what they described as Bronster's tendency to grandstand. Cayetano said he wanted Bronster to stay on as his attorney general but acknowledged that he, too, had not always seen eye to eye with her. One of the no-voters would certainly be Marshall Ige. He was a primary target of Bronster's ongoing investigation, and he made no secret about wanting Bronster out.

There were others with a personal interest in the vote: Whitney Anderson, whose wife was part of Lindsey's entourage, and Joe Tanaka, who had received a $42,000 fee from Bishop Estate on a recent real estate transaction.

As the confirmation vote neared, crowds for and against Bronster rallied at the Capitol. Hoaliku Drake—Henry Peters' mother—and her friends from Wai'anae were there with signs: "'A'Ole Bronster" (No Bronster). They were outnumbered by Bronster supporters who had signs of their own.

Every senator voted, and the count went against Bronster, fourteen to eleven. When the tally was announced, the packed gallery erupted in booing. The trustees' lawyers, however, were giving each other high fives, and one soon was on his cell phone telling Dickie Wong, "She's out!" Another was heard saying of Bronster, "Ding dong, the witch is gone." When reporters called Henry Peters to ask what he thought about Bronster's fate, he said, "That's what you get for being arrogant."

Because of the senate vote, Bronster was out of office before her investigation really got going. But she had stood up to Bishop Estate trustees. That inspired hope when hope was needed, and people would remember that. The outpouring of public adulation for Bronster continued for weeks after the senate vote. Letters to the editor were filled with *aloha* for her and indignation that she had not been reconfirmed. People sent gifts to her office and her home; shoppers hugged her in the supermarket; motorists honked when they saw her. While she was having lunch at the Kahala Mandarin Hotel, the food servers gave Bronster a standing ovation and paid for her meal. At a Rotary meeting attended by hun-

Under different circumstances, Margery Bronster might have been a shoo-in to continue as attorney general: she enjoyed public support and had just been re-appointed by a Democratic governor, and twenty-three of the twenty-five senators were Democrats.

dreds, she was compared to Joan of Arc. "Remember Bronster" bumper stickers appeared. Na Pua handed out T-shirts with the names of the fourteen no-voters on the back. The front said, "Remember Bronster."

Bronster's memory was long; she later campaigned personally against the senators who had voted against her. In a state where incumbents almost never lose, seven of the fourteen were defeated. Another three chose not to run. She also did not forget the pushback from within her own office. Her last official act as attorney general was to demote Kevin Wakayama.

On cMay 6, 1999, Judge Weil announced her decision. Stender's strategy had worked: Lindsey was out, permanently. Weil did not explain the curious timing of her announcement; the trial had ended more than a month earlier, and it would be another six weeks before she would be ready to issue findings of fact and conclusions of law.

The next day Judge Chang's courtroom was packed, as were the halls and lobby. This was the trustees' last chance to show cause why they should be allowed to keep their jobs, even if it meant the trust would lose its tax-exempt status. McCorriston implored Judge Chang not to "cave in" to the IRS or get caught up in the current "mob mentality" that wanted "a mass execution of the entire board of trustees." He added that his clients had satisfied the court's direction to hire a CEO by retaining Gilbert Tam, the former Bishop Estate employee who had been on Lindsey's short list for vice president of Kamehameha Schools.

Crystal Rose said her client, Oz Stender, was ready to step aside, but only if the others also resigned or were removed. She added that Stender was embarrassed by Tam's hiring, which he considered a sham. The agreed-upon deadline for installing the CEO-based management system had passed long ago, and Tam's name had come up only within the last twenty-four hours—practically pulled out of a hat, with no discussion of duties, no written communication, no notice of the opening, no interview, no résumé, no nothing. "The other trustees are growing more dysfunctional by the day," said Rose.

The lead counsel for Dickie Wong stressed the trustees' "enormous personal exposure" and claimed that every day they were "betting their entire net worth, putting it on the line." For that and other reasons, he argued, these trustees earned every penny of their compensation. Unlike the special-purpose trustees, who let themselves be intimidated by the IRS, the majority trustees were "warriors" willing to defend the trust estate from an IRS and state tax department "money grab."

Deputy Attorney General Sellers suggested that the trustees' refusal to step aside was because of their "exalted compensation." She said the trustees' legal arguments boiled down to "me, me, me." She called the last-minute hiring of Gilbert Tam "a farce." Then Colbert Matsumoto told the court clearly and directly that these trustees had to go. He was "flabbergasted" by their behavior.

After listening patiently for more than five hours, Chang accepted Stender's temporary resignation and removed the others on an interim basis. He said with so much at stake, all but Stender had committed serious breaches of trust by not offering to step aside voluntarily, and also by not implementing a CEO-based system of governance, as they had agreed to do. He also "unhired" Gilbert Tam. Chang then appointed the special-purpose trustees to serve as "interim" trustees, and invited them or the attorney general to file a petition within ninety days seeking the permanent removal of all five trustees.

Henry Peters "went ballistic." He accused the IRS of "extortion" and said he was going to sue it. As for Chang's decision, "It was so bad they could smell it in Russia." Stender praised the decision, saying that it paved the way for "a new era for Kamehameha Schools and a new era for the management of the trust." Lindsey drew a parallel to the end of the monarchy in 1893, describing Chang's decision as "the second overthrow." Jervis was not available for comment. And Wong was outraged. "I don't know what I'm guilty of and why I am being removed. I am not going to walk away."

In the end, though, that was exactly what they all had to do—Jervis and Peters, Wong and Lindsey, even Stender. Unlike the adulation that had been showered upon Bronster when she was banished from the attorney general's office, the five fallen trustees were the subjects of ridicule and scorn.

$\mathcal{P}$rior to the protest march on May 15, 1997, public opinion of Bishop Estate trustees had been mixed, but a high percentage of native Hawaiians still believed the trustees were doing an excellent job overall. By May 1999, however, that had changed. In a poll the *Star-Bulletin* commissioned shortly after Judge Chang's decision on May 7, 1999, island residents were asked whether their opinion of each trustee was favorable, unfavorable, or neutral. The unfavorable-to-favorable ratio was twenty-two to one for Jervis, thirty-one to one for Wong, seventy-one to one for Peters, and eighty-three to one for Lindsey. The public was even down on Stender: he had three times as many unfavorables as favorables.

The former trustees were facing more than just a hostile public. Deputy attorneys general were seeking a new round of criminal indictments and were planning to ask the probate court to impose fines, called surcharges, in excess of $200 million. Under these circumstances, most people expected the trustees to resign. For them to do otherwise would add to the already long list of transgressions.

Jervis was the first to submit a resignation letter, on August 20, 1999. He said if he had done anything wrong, which he was not admitting to in any event, it must have been due to bad advice from people who should have known better. Besides having relied on these unnamed others, Jervis stressed that he had not even been a trustee when the illegal activity started:

All of the factual predicates of the IRS' threats to revoke the tax exemption are based on decisions and practices adopted by the Estate well before I became a trustee in December of 1994, virtually all of which, in turn, were based on the advice of well experienced professional employees and outside consultants; all of which received repeated judicial approval; and some of which— relating to compensation—were based on legislation.

Jervis made no mention of moral misconduct in his resignation letter. Peters mentioned it for him. He said Jervis should have resigned for "inappropriate behavior."

About a month later, on September 27, Stender was the second trustee to resign permanently. He said he would have preferred to serve out his term, but at least he could resign knowing that he had done his best and had always put the beneficiaries' interests first.

Wong was looking tired and stressed. He and his wife, Mari, had just divorced, and deputy attorneys general were still pursuing his crimi-

Dickie and Mari Wong were indicted for a number of crimes. Dickie Wong could hardly believe what was happening; he told reporters that even Al Capone had never had his wife indicted.

nal prosecution. Asked about the possible surcharges hanging over his head, Wong said those kinds of numbers would "scare the hell out of anyone I know." Wong had said many times that he never would go willingly, but by mid-November it was obvious that he was thinking seriously of resigning. On December 3, he did. Speaking for him, his lawyer said Wong needed to move on with his life. Wong's letter of resignation was characteristically short, just one paragraph.

Henry Peters had always been the most combative. He, too, had said repeatedly he would never resign, insisting it was the interim trustees who should step down, for caving in to the IRS, an evil force that wanted to end the admissions preference for Hawaiians at Kamehameha. Peters told reporters he was thinking about suing the interim trustees, along with the IRS. "I wish to advise you," he said in an unsolicited four-page letter to the interim trustees, "of my intention to return as the rightful trustee of Kamehameha Schools Bishop Estate."

But on December 13, 1999, the day his permanent-removal trial was to begin, Peters resigned permanently. In his resignation letter, Peters said that he was proud of his fifteen years of service, and that the prosperity of the trust and the future of the schools had been and always would be his primary concern:

> But for more than two years, various highly vocal special interests and individuals have allowed federal and state bureaucrats to transform the trust into a political entity and to judge the trustees on the basis of politics and popularity, and not because of the trustees' work and accomplishments for Kamehameha Schools Bishop Estate. When this occurs it becomes impossible for any trustee to fulfill the princess's wishes on a long-term basis.

Peters stressed that he was not admitting any wrongdoing; what had happened to him was the equivalent of "an old-time lynching."

Peters was no longer a trustee, but his income did not stop completely. After resigning, he became entitled to approximately $600,000 a year under a deferred-compensation contractual arrangement that he had arranged while a trustee. Deputy attorneys general believed these payments would continue for the rest of Peters' life. A 2001 *Advertiser* article said Peters was contemplating a run for public office and described him reminiscing about his years at Bishop Estate:

> [Peters] smiles as he remembers those thrilling days of buying low and selling high. . . . He still talks to his former financial peers at Goldman Sachs. The former president of that money dynamo, Jon Corzine, is now a senator from New Jersey. They had talked about the heavy-handed ways of the IRS that morning, and the misconduct of Hawai'i courts.

Asked on the TV program *60 Minutes* in 2000 whether he had any regrets, Peters said he wished he had purchased the *Honolulu Star-Bulletin* when it was for sale prior to the publication of "Broken Trust."

The moral victory of Oz Stender, one of the individuals most responsible for bringing change to Bishop Estate, came at great personal cost. For more than a year the IRS insisted that he pay about $5 million in intermediate sanctions, and the attorney general's office sought considerably more than that in surcharges. Stender also had personal legal bills from Crystal Rose and Douglas Ing that totaled nearly $2 million.

In 2000 Stender sued the attorney general's office, arguing that his personal interests had been harmed when that office failed to take action against the other trustees in 1992 and 1995 when he had requested it. Then Stender hired high-powered Washington, D.C., lawyers to negotiate a settlement with the IRS and asked the probate court to order the interim trustees to pay his legal fees, arguing that the trust had benefited from his efforts to remove Lindsey.

Judge Chang decided it was appropriate to use trust money to pay Stender's legal fees, but only to the extent those fees were "reasonable," which Chang determined to be a few hundred thousand dollars less than the amount claimed. Stender personally paid some of the excess, and Rose and Ing wrote off the rest.

After extensive negotiations, the IRS agreed to settle with Stender for $120,000. Stender's differences with the attorney general's office—its action against him for surcharges and his claim against it for dereliction of duty—were resolved privately, with no cash exchanging hands.

Stender gave serious thought to suing the justices, whom he considered ultimately responsible for all the trust's problems. He said he decided not to sue them only because he "ran out of money." In 2000 he ran for a seat on the board of trustees for the Office of Hawaiian Affairs and won easily.

Judge Weil had removed Lindsey permanently on May 6, 1999, one day before Judge Chang removed her temporarily. Lindsey appealed Weil's decision to the state Supreme Court and vowed to fight Chang's ruling, too. Some lawyers believed that Weil's ruling was flawed legally.

Lindsey never stopped wanting to reclaim her trusteeship, but she, too, lacked the money to continue fighting. It had been more than seven months since her last Bishop Estate paycheck. She was delinquent on her personal taxes, and the IRS had put liens on all her properties. Standing in front of reporters on December 16, 1999, Lindsey said, teary-eyed, that she had come to the end of her resources and the end of her fight. In a resignation letter submitted to the court, Lindsey denied any wrongdoing and said that she knew in her own heart she had never done anything to damage or hurt the trust or its beneficiaries. She had fought, she said, to preserve Pauahi's will and to preserve Hawaiian wealth for Hawaiians. She said this was not about her; it was about non-Hawaiians wanting Pauahi's estate: "It is a sad day for the princess, and I only wish I can go to her grave site and place black ribbons on her grave."

In 2004 Lokelani Lindsey served six months in a federal prison for bankruptcy fraud. U.S. District Judge David Ezra had delayed her incarceration three times, for a total of eleven months, so Lindsey could care for her husband, who reportedly was terminally ill. Ezra changed his mind, however, when informed that Lokelani had been seen on several different occasions in a Las Vegas casino.

chapter 20

"Healing" and "Closure"

The day after the last of the trustees resigned, the interim trustees announced a name change. Looking forward, the historic trust would be called "Kamehameha Schools." This was not the first time trustees had changed the trust's official name, but the Bishop name had always been prominent. Now it was gone. The stated reason was to provide a sense of "closure" on the turmoil of the past few years and to promote "healing."

The former trustees were gone, permanently, but the story was not over. Surely there would be serious consequences for the many individuals who had participated in the abuse of Princess Pauahi's trust, or who had witnessed it and done nothing to stop it. Trust law requires new trustees to hold former trustees (and their lawyers) accountable for harm done to a trust. Also, the new trustees had promised IRS officials a thorough "housecleaning." The only question was, just how thorough would it be?

In a 1998 court filing Bronster had asked the probate judge to appoint a single full-time, highly qualified administrator to run the Bishop Estate organization until all the legal issues could be sorted out in court. Judge Chang declined to take that approach in May 1999 when he emptied the boardroom at the IRS' behest. He chose instead to upgrade the five special-purpose trustees to "interim trustee" status, and left it to them to figure out how to run Bishop Estate. The management and accounting systems were virtually dysfunctional. It was essential that the interim trustees hire the right kind of people to deal effectively with the many educational, business, and legal issues that had accumulated during the years of abuse, controversy, and turmoil.

Saying that this required "a good law firm," the interim trustees retained Watanabe, Ing and Kawashima, a politically *akamai* (smart) firm —Douglas Ing was one of its senior partners. The interim trustees also retained Bruce Graham and Michael Hare and their firms—lawyers who had served the former trustees for more than a decade. That was the legal team.

To run the organization the interim trustees chose Nathan Aipa, explaining that "he knew where things were." Because Aipa had been the trust's chief in-house lawyer since 1986, he probably did have a lot of inside information. Under the circumstances, however, that hardly seemed like a good reason to promote him to the top executive position in the organization. The former trustees had literally set a world record for trust abuse on Aipa's watch. He may have been actively involved. In the 5701s, the IRS likened him to "a sixth trustee." Now, rather than being forced to resign like the five actual trustees, the "sixth trustee" was at the helm of the multi-billion-dollar Bishop Estate. That gave him control over the flow of information to and from this brand-new board of part-time trustees.

To fill Aipa's old position, the interim trustees chose Colleen Wong, who had been Aipa's right-hand person for the last ten years. There had been no housecleaning; instead, the old guard had been put in charge and handed the keys.

All this shocked Dorothy Sellers, Hugh Jones, and Daniel Morris, deputy attorneys general who had worked for the past two years on cleaning up the mess at Bishop Estate. They immediately contacted the interim trustees and explained that lawyers who served the former trustees had either provided flawed legal advice or stood by silently— and illegally—as the trustees ignored good advice. The deputies also explained that the former trustees were sure to defend any legal action against them by arguing that they had just followed their lawyers' advice. This meant that those lawyers—the ones the interim trustees had just re-hired and put in charge of the entire organization—had a very strong personal incentive to prevent any finding of serious misconduct by the former trustees. They added that a lawyer such as Ing, who had recently represented a now-former trustee, should not be advising the

Deputy Attorneys General Daniel Morris, Dorothy Sellers, and Hugh Jones (left to right) were shocked when the interim trustees put Nathan Aipa in control of trust operations and sought legal advice from lawyers who had served the former trustees for many years.

interim trustees on their duty to pursue claims against former trustees, which included Ing's former client, Stender. The deputies explained that Ing had a classic conflict of interest, which might tempt him to try to protect his former client, even at the expense of the trust. The interim trustees listened and then essentially told the deputies to mind their own business.

Several months later Ing filed a petition in the probate court on behalf of the interim trustees that sought the permanent removal of four trustees—not Stender. Deputy Attorney General Dorothy Sellers immediately reminded Ing and his clients, the interim trustees, that the IRS had demanded the replacement of five trustees, not four. She explained that it would jeopardize the trust's tax-exempt status to reinstate Stender, and added that Stender had committed many serious breaches of trust during his eight and a half years as a Bishop Estate trustee. The issue became moot only when Stender resigned.

It was ironic, said the deputy attorneys general, that dealing with the interim trustees did not feel different from what they had experienced before: The former trustees had received legal guidance from Bruce Graham, Michael Hare, Nathan Aipa, and Colleen Wong, and now, despite years of trust abuse, legal wrangling, emotional turmoil, and the complete change of trustees, the interim trustees were relying on these same four lawyers, plus Douglas Ing.

Legal tactics that the deputies described as "stonewalling" went on unabated. One typical exchange began when a deputy accidentally discovered that Bruce Graham's and Michael Hare's firms had each responded to a former trustee's discovery request without telling the attorney general's office about it. This would be difficult to justify under the applicable rules, yet when the deputy attorney general requested copies of the firms' responses, Colleen Wong instructed the two firms not to provide them. In a strongly worded letter, Deputy Attorney General Sellers called these "deliberate obstructionist tactics."

On another occasion, a letter signed by Colleen Wong refused Deputy Attorney General Hugh Jones' request to review legal opinions that Graham, Hare, and other lawyers had provided to the former trustees prior to the controversy that began in 1997. Wong contended that she had not looked to Graham for help in making this decision, but the word-processing code in the bottom corner of her letter contained Graham's initials—which, according to Jones, meant that the letter "apparently had been drafted by Graham but signed by Wong."

The issue of the attorney general's right to review old legal opinions eventually wound up in court. Jones argued before Judge Chang that the attorney general's office needed to know what the ousted trustees had been told by their lawyers regarding any number of questionable actions, such as investing personally in trust investments, spending trust money to fight enactment of the intermediate sanctions law, and accumulating trust income in violation of Pauahi's will. When it was Ing's turn to address the court, rather than make a legal argument, he pointed at Jones and others sitting at that table, all of whom were *haole,* and suggested the existence of a hidden agenda: "They claim to come here on behalf of the beneficiaries, but look at them, Judge. Do you see in them compassion for Princess Pauahi Bishop's will? Do you understand what Kamehameha means to the people of Hawaiian ancestry?" Ing contended that people from the attorney general's office cared little about Hawaiians; people from that office served politicians who coveted Bishop Estate's wealth. The primary threat, according to Ing, was not the former trustees, but those who were seeking to "wrest control of Pauahi Bishop's legacy from Hawaiians."

Judge Chang—who happened to have been Ing's law partner at the Watanabe firm before his appointment to the bench—ruled in Ing's favor.

Not long after taking control of Bishop Estate, the interim trustees announced their intention not to assist in efforts to surcharge the former trustees, a decision that appalled the deputy attorneys general. Lawyers for the interim trustees had advised their clients that any form of cooperation with the attorney general's office on this matter would jeopardize $75 million of insurance coverage: Insurance policies purchased by the former trustees essentially said that the companies did not have to pay any claim in which one policyholder sued, or assisted in a lawsuit against, another policyholder. This arguably included a present trustee suing, or assisting in a lawsuit against, a former trustee.

Such a contract provision, however, violated public policy, making it unenforceable. Trust law does not allow former trustees to tie the hands of their successor trustees like that. If asked, the court would have declared invalid that provision of the contract—but the interim trustees did not ask any court to do that. Instead, they treated this convenient but illegal contract provision as clearly enforceable. Reminded of their fiduciary duty to hold their predecessors accountable for harm done to the trust, the interim trustees responded that they had no interest in "seeking retribution." They said it was time to "look forward, not backward."

When Judge Chang picked the special-purpose trustees, he told them it wouldn't require a major time commitment: a few meetings with the trust's tax counsel and then a few negotiating sessions with the IRS. Two of them were retired, so they had some time to give; the other three had demanding jobs, but Chang saw no reason for them to resign or even to seek a reduced workload.

When the special-purpose trustees became interim trustees, the question of compensation arose. They asked for $15,000 a month, each. In light of the former levels of trustee compensation, this figure perhaps did not seem all that large, even for part-time work by people with full-time jobs elsewhere. Deputy Attorney General Jones pointed out that

members of charitable organizations usually serve because they love the institution, not the compensation, and asked, "Why should Bishop Estate trustees be any different from board members of other schools and charities?" According to Jones, the closest comparison to Kamehameha was the Milton Hershey School in Pennsylvania. Members of its board served without compensation.

Judge Chang approved the $15,000 per month amount as a temporary arrangement, and then appointed a compensation committee to determine what the pay, if any, should be in future years. He specifically instructed this committee to retain a compensation expert to guide its work. The committee did so but then rejected the expert's recommendation that trustee fees be capped at $50,000, recommending instead that each trustee be paid a base amount plus additional amounts per meeting. It all added up to $120,000 for the chairman and $97,500 for each of the other trustees. The understanding among committee members at the time was that once the CEO-based system matured, there would be fewer trustee meetings, and trustee compensation would decrease significantly. Four years later, though, another court-appointed trustee compensation committee recommended that compensation be *increased*—to $180,000 per trustee, plus an extra $27,000 for the board chair. This recommendation was met with harsh criticism in the media and from the attorney general's office, which submitted information indicating that this would make the trustees of Kamehameha Schools the most highly compensated for any charitable organization in the nation. Judge Hirai approved the proposed increase anyway, but then, bowing to public pressure, the trustees agreed not to take the proposed raise. According to Douglas Ing, doing so in the current climate would not be "politically appropriate."

Why was it, critics asked, that Hawai'i's judges continued to insist upon maintaining tight control over the trustee-selection process for this particular trust? And why did they think Kamehameha Schools trustees, most of whom were holding down full-time jobs elsewhere, should receive financial compensation that was dramatically higher than that at any other public charity in the nation?

In May 2000 a new master, Robert Richards, reported on legal fees that the former trustees paid out of trust funds during their last eight months on the job. Richards concluded that the former trustees should be required to repay $5 million of the total amount to Kamehameha Schools, and that some of the law firms that had received trust funds should be required to return all or part of the money to Kamehameha Schools.

Richards, a no-nonsense litigator who had played professional football before going to law school, did not spare the feelings of his fellow lawyers. He questioned the retention of Atlanta-based Sutherland Asbil and Brennan, and concluded the work done by that firm served the personal interests of the majority trustees rather than those of the trust: "If, in fact, the final invoice has not been paid, it should remain unpaid." He also singled out Seattle-based Davis Wright Tremaine, a firm that had "researched the issue of payment of attorneys' fees out of trust estate for legal services rendered to trustees (yet never petitioned the court pursuant to the statute for the right to do that)." Richards criticized Bruce Graham's firm, Ashford and Wriston, for not seeing that there were "hopeless conflicts related to trustee misconduct." Regarding the work done by Bill McCorriston's firm, McCorriston Miho Miller and Mukai, Richards reached what he called "certain inescapable conclusions":

> The most critical is that this was a defense of the trustees, not of the trust. There were monumental efforts made to keep trustee conduct from coming to light or, if it did come to light, to rationalize it. Second, there was an effort, despite clear realization of problems with conflict, to explain away any conflict. That is best exemplified by reliance upon the so-called "enterprise" theory of representation. . . . There was the adoption by the Trustees of a strategy of obstruction and delay. The apparent thought was to make every inquiry so difficult that the opposition would either become confused or give up. . . . Finally there was also apparently the adoption of a "destroy the opposition" strategy.

Richards was equally critical of Cades Schutte Fleming and Wright, which Richards described as lurking in the "shadows":

> In many ways the most "troubling" of all legal expenditures were those incurred by Cades Schutte Fleming & Wright, under the direction of its lead counsel Michael Hare. . . . [A]s time progressed it appears that its purpose and goal more than any other law firm involved in this review was to represent the interests of the majority of the split board, namely the interests of Trustees Peters, Wong and Lindsey. Except in very limited instances . . . the work of this firm was not only duplicative and wasteful, but also cannot be described in any fashion as benefiting the trust.

Richards criticized the work of other firms, too, including Verner Liipfert Bernard McPherson and Hand, the firm of the former governor, John Waiheʻe. It was the one that had looked into moving Bishop Estate to a Sioux Indian reservation, and it had led the lobbying effort against enactment of the intermediate sanctions law. According to Richards, it was "inconceivable that a lawyer would hold that this type of work . . . was appropriate to be paid from trust assets."

Instead of following Richards' recommendations, the interim trustees listened to their own lawyers' advice, which was to hire two large Mainland firms, Philadelphia-based Morgan Lewis and Bockius and Washington, D.C.-based Miller and Chevalier, plus law professors John

Langbein from Yale and John Leubsdorf from Rutgers. For fees totaling $1 million, this team prepared a follow-up report that—unlike the Richards report—was somewhat sympathetic to the former trustees' lawyers, essentially concluding that most of them were skilled advocates who had just followed their clients' instructions. This follow-up report included practical advice:

> In considering whether to file a claim, the Trustees will want to consider both the cost of prosecuting such an action as well as the length of time such a proceeding might take. The Trustees will also want to consider the impact on Kamehameha Schools of negative publicity and controversy that would accompany prolonged litigation—precisely the type of controversy that Kamehameha Schools has worked so hard over the last 18 months to put behind it.

Deputy Attorney General Sellers could hardly believe what was happening. She pointed out that Miller and Chevalier as well as Professor Langbein had themselves rendered significant legal services for the former trustees, so the study was "not independent." It was also "self-serving," according to Sellers, because the interim trustees were currently paying the Cades firm to do what the former trustees had previously paid that firm to do: "hinder the attorney general."

The interim trustees did not respond to Sellers' accusations. Instead, they announced that they would not be suing any of the former trustees' lawyers or seeking a refund of trust money paid to them for work that, according to the Richards report, did not benefit the trust.

Before copies of the $1 million follow-up report could be made and distributed, lawyers for the trust asked Judge Chang to place it under seal, which he did. Even lawyers from the attorney general's office, whose job it was to monitor all charitable trusts, were denied further access, for the sake of "closure."

One of the many problems with the old trustees' way of doing things had been the hiring and contracting process, or lack of one. The interim trustees had an opportunity to change this, starting with their search for a permanent CEO. They began by telling an executive search firm that it would be good if candidates were Hawaiian, and even better if they were Kamehameha alumni, but neither was essential. They had total confidence in the president of Kamehameha Schools, Michael Chun, so the new CEO, they said, did not have to be an educator. Candidates should, instead, have a proven track record in the areas of business and finance, with the demonstrated ability to lead a multi-billion-dollar organization.

Less than six weeks later, the search firm produced a list of ten candidates, all strong in business and finance. One rose above the rest, but the kind of money he was used to making was considerably more than what the new trustees were willing to pay. Also, he wasn't Hawaiian—there were concerns about his ability to relate well to the Kamehameha ʻohana.

Then Hamilton McCubbin, a professor of school psychology and child welfare from the University of Wisconsin, stopped by Kawaiahaʻo Plaza. He was in town doing scholarly research on the lottery admissions program that had been used by Kamehameha Schools during the 1980s. Three of the interim trustees met with him as a courtesy and were impressed with his intelligence and ideas. The other two trustees met with him over the next few days, and they, too, liked what they saw. They later learned that McCubbin had been a finalist for the presidency of Kamehameha Schools ten years earlier, when the job had gone to Michael Chun.

McCubbin was Hawaiian and a Kamehameha alumnus, and his professor's salary was barely a third of the $325,000 that the interim trustees were prepared to pay for a CEO. That made him an attractive candidate in their eyes. But McCubbin lacked any background whatsoever in areas of special need to the trust at that time: real estate, finance, law, and the management of complex organizations. The interim trustees hired him anyway. Then, rather than trusting his judgment to assemble a qualified management team, the interim trustees appointed Nathan Aipa to the position of chief operating officer and made permanent Colleen Wong's temporary appointment as the trust's top legal officer. At the same time, the interim trustees hired Wendell Brooks, a local real estate expert, to serve as the trust's chief investment officer. Normally a new CEO would at least be given an opportunity to provide input into the making of such decisions.

When word of all this reached IRS officials in Washington, D.C., they said they wanted to see McCubbin immediately, even before he reported for duty at Kawaiahaʻo Plaza. At that meeting, six IRS officials stressed to McCubbin and the lawyers he took with him that the last thing the IRS wanted to do was take away Kamehameha Schools' tax-exempt status. Then they laid out what was troubling them so much:

the interim trustees' failure to "clean house." They wanted everyone in Hawai'i to understand that the IRS was serious about the need for real reform. The trustees were skating on thin ice. The IRS officials reminded McCubbin that the trust was officially on probation, and when it came to the trust's all-important tax-exempt status, nothing should be taken for granted.

As time passed, it became clear that McCubbin was no more inclined to "clean house" than were the new trustees. There also was grumbling about McCubbin's management style, especially when he put himself in charge of investments and asset management and got personally involved in running the school. He and Chun clashed regularly, and most staff members sided with Chun. One staff member at Kawaiaha'o Plaza said working for McCubbin—whom she and her co-workers called a "coconut," brown on the outside, white on the inside—made her nostalgic for "the Hawaiianness of a Henry Peters." Oz Stender also was critical of McCubbin. He said publicly that hiring McCubbin had been a huge mistake, that he lacked the business background to serve as CEO, and that when it came to dealing with the Hawaiian community, McCubbin "didn't have a clue."

In May 2003 McCubbin abruptly resigned, following allegations by several employees that he was having an improper relationship with a female co-worker. The *Star-Bulletin* then reported that one month before the Kamehameha Schools trustees had hired McCubbin to serve as the trust's first CEO, McCubbin's former employer, the University of Wisconsin, had paid $85,813 to settle charges that he sexually harassed a female professor.

Whether the Kamehameha Schools trustees knew about McCubbin's legal situation was unclear. Saying it was "time to move on," the trustees agreed to a confidential severance package reportedly worth $400,000 and declined to comment further on the matter.

The IRS had accused Bishop Estate of breaking just about every applicable rule in the Internal Revenue Code. Tax lawyers from Washington told the interim trustees that the trust and its wholly owned businesses would almost certainly have to pay tens of millions of dollars in tax assessments because of overly aggressive tax maneuvers during the 1990s. However, it turned out that the IRS wanted more than just money. In order for the trust to keep its tax-exempt status there had to be a fundamental transformation. Bishop Estate would need to institute:

- a coherent screening and selection process that would yield qualified trustees in the future;
- a governance system in which trustees would limit themselves to setting policy and providing oversight to a well-trained staff;
- the explicit agreement of each new trustee to seek the removal of any co-trustee who might fail to fulfill a basic fiduciary duty;
- an independent internal auditor whose reports would be sent directly to the IRS as well as to the attorney general and probate court during a five-year probationary period;
- a thorough review of all existing employment and consulting contracts to ensure that services were necessary and the level of compensation was reasonable;
- adoption and rigid enforcement of a policy on conflicts of interest;
- development and implementation of a strategic plan, including investment and spending policies that would ensure prudent investing and proper funding of the trust's charitable mission;
- the use of generally accepted accounting principles;
- a way for the public to access meaningful financial information;
- procurement practices that would replace cronyism and patronage with merit selection; and
- adoption of a policy against employing, reimbursing, or otherwise compensating any member of the legislative, judicial, or executive branch of government.

Non-financial demands such as these would normally have been left exclusively to the probate court to make. For the IRS to be making them was an unprecedented signal that it, the IRS, did not think any of these changes would be made without outside pressure.

The interim trustees eventually settled IRS claims for back taxes, interest, and penalties: the trust itself paid $13 million because of unrelated business income that the former trustees had not reported, and the trust's wholly owned companies paid another $72 million to settle a host of transgressions, including the way the Goldman Sachs investment had been reported. Judge Chang approved the settlement, but only after noting that the IRS' insistence on fundamental reform had intruded on the probate court's turf, though he added that it was not altogether unexpected, "in light of the trust's recent history." Chang said the agreement would allow all the parties to achieve "closure" and begin "the healing process."

The deputy attorneys general asked Judge Chang to surcharge the former trustees more than $200 million and to support a thorough investigation of the justices, politicians, lawyers, and others whose behavior might have violated a civil or criminal law. Instead, Chang engineered a "global settlement" that included the interim trustees, the former trustees, Attorney General Earl Anzai, the trust's wholly owned insurance company, and dozens of lawyers. At Chang's request, James Duffy and David Fairbanks mediated this settlement. Duffy had been Bishop Estate master twice in the early 1990s, and Fairbanks, whose father had served as the probate judge many years earlier, was currently serving as chair of the Judicial Selection Commission.

Liability insurance played a key role. There appeared to be two policies, one for $50 million and another for $25 million, but coverage on the larger policy had been lost when in-house lawyers for the trust failed to inform the carrier in a timely fashion of the potential claims. The smaller policy was still enforceable, but it had a "cannibalizing" feature, so the amount of coverage got smaller and smaller as the insurance company paid lawyers who were defending the trustees. By the time of the settlement, the carrier had already paid $5 million to the trustees' lawyers, so only $20 million of coverage remained. The insurance carrier agreed to pay the remaining $20 million as part of the global settlement. The attorney general's office received $1.3 million of this for out-of-pocket costs, and the trustees' lawyers took another $5 million. That left about $14 million for the trust. Under the terms of this agreement, the former trustees did not have to pay any surcharges, damages, or restitution. Nor did they have to admit they had done anything wrong. The agreement described all of this as "another important step bringing the painful, litigious, and expensive controversy surrounding the former trustees to a conclusion, and allowing the new trustees and executive management team to focus all their time, energy, and talents on the sole purpose of the trust—educating Hawaiian children."

Judge Chang ordered the entire file sealed, again citing a need for "closure and healing."

In 2002 a panel of substitute Supreme Court justices—selected by Chief Justice Moon—threw out the criminal indictments against Peters, Wong, and Stone on procedural grounds. Without deciding whether crimes had or had not been committed, the substitute justices sharply

criticized the attorney general's office for being overzealous in its efforts to secure indictments: "The State's interest in prosecuting these crimes is, at this point, clearly outweighed by the lack of fundamental fairness that would ensue were we to allow these prosecutions to continue." The justices did more than just throw out indictments. They unanimously declared the entire matter *pau* (completely done): no new round of indictments could be sought.

The various civil investigations were also ended abruptly. A team of investigators that had been hired by Margery Bronster to look into Bishop

Estate's political activities asked her successor, Earl Anzai, for authority to interview various politicians regarding possible bribery and campaign spending violations. Saying that it was unlikely the individuals in question would admit to anything and that any violations were probably of minor significance, Anzai refused; he had decided that further investigation would be too expensive and was beyond what the public wanted. Anzai did not make the investigators' report public, nor did he share it with the deputy attorneys general who had worked on Bishop Estate matters exclusively for the past three years. In each case, the reason given for the decisions to seal information and to let investigations lapse was to provide "closure" and "healing."

$\mathcal{B}ack$ in $late$ 1997, when the turmoil over Bishop Estate was approaching its height, Henry Peters, Dickie Wong, and Lokelani Lindsey had sent out official invitations to celebrate the one-hundredth anniversary of the Bishop Memorial Chapel at Kamehameha Schools. They described the service as one of "healing."

Monsignor Kekumano, one of the authors of "Broken Trust," was among the invited. He had been keeping a low profile, battling a cancer that was spreading. Kekumano was so annoyed by the trustees' use of

the chapel for what he perceived to be their self-interest that he wrote a letter to the editor of the *Star-Bulletin*, in which he cautioned that true healing could only come when an open dialogue and free flow of information had been achieved, and when consciences were clean—not before. Saying that "there are no honest answers coming from their koa-paneled boardroom," Kekumano questioned the true intentions of the trustees' invitation to a healing prayer session in a house of God:

> They surely need God. But before they kneel and try to talk to God, they ought first to be sure that absolutely no influence of the devil is involved in any of their actions. When they can in good conscience open their books and records, then would be a good time to pray for "healing."

As the former trustees had done in 1997, their replacements were stonewalling the attorney general's office, having records sealed, and asking the Kamehameha *'ohana* to join them in prayers for "healing." People wondered about it all. Why wouldn't the new trustees want an open dialogue and free flow of information?

chapter 21

Eternal Vigilance

When four of the Supreme Court justices announced that they would no longer select trustees, they did not say how they thought future Bishop Estate trustees should be chosen. After considering several proposals, Judge Chang announced criteria for new trustees and a process in which the probate judge would appoint members of a screening committee and then select each new trustee from a list of three names provided by the committee. In 2000 Chang, following the new procedures, asked two of the interim trustees, Robert Kihune and Constance Lau, to continue serving. He also named three new trustees: Diane Plotts, Nainoa Thompson, and Douglas Ing.

Plotts had been a general partner with Hemmeter Investment, which developed five-star resorts in Hawai'i during the 1980s. Thompson was the son of a former trustee, Myron Thompson. He had spent his entire adult life leading a revival of traditional arts associated with long-distance ocean voyaging in Hawai'i. Ing and his firm had at various times served as legal counsel to the former trustees, to Michael Chun, to Oz Stender, and to the interim trustees.

The new trustees faced many ongoing challenges and questions. Some of these received a great deal of publicity, but others were rarely, if ever, discussed in public. Most of these issues concern cultural, political, and legal developments Pauahi could not have foreseen.

Over the course of a little more than three generations, Hawai'i had gone from kingdom to republic to territory to state. What it means to live in Hawai'i and to be Hawaiian has changed dramatically since that time. And yet Pauahi's will remains exactly as she wrote it. As time passes, tension inevitably grows between the good reasons for honoring

The trustees and their CEO came under heavy fire in 2002 following the admission of a haole to Kamehameha Schools. Left to right: Nainoa Thompson, Robert Kihune, Constance Lau, Douglas Ing, Hamilton McCubbin, and Diane Plotts.

a trust's charitable mission and the likelihood that any specific charitable mission will come to be seen as outdated. Such pressures in Pauahi's trust have involved religion, race, and Hawaiian culture.

Although religion permeates Pauahi's will, its position faded, over time, into the background. For example, Judge Chang's announced criteria for future trustees does not even mention religion, and the screening committees that he and Judge Hirai appointed declined to say to what extent they took religion into account. This led many people to believe that religion plays little, if any, role in selection decisions.

The marginalization of Pauahi's religion was not an overnight change. The justices had stopped asking candidates about religious affiliation years before their own involvement in selecting trustees finally ceased. Some of the individuals the justices had selected were raised Catholic or Mormon, not Protestant. Either the justices believed that these candidates had had last-minute conversions to Protestantism, or they ignored both the spirit and the letter of Pauahi's requirement that trustees always be "persons of the Protestant religion."

Pauahi's will also required that Kamehameha teachers "forever be persons of the Protestant religion," and for many years anyone wanting to teach at Kamehameha had to present a baptismal record or letter of membership in a Protestant church. A local trial court in the 1960s held this to be unlawful discrimination, but the Hawai'i Supreme Court reversed that decision. Because Kamehameha was considered a religious school, it could legally discriminate on the basis of religion.

The issue arose again in the early 1990s, when a Jewish woman applied for a teaching position at Kamehameha. Told that non-Protestants were ineligible, she sued. Federal District Court Judge Alan Kay decided against her for reasons similar to those expressed in the earlier state Supreme Court opinion, but the Ninth Circuit Court of Appeals overruled Kay. Unlike the usual situation, in which a school is owned by a church, said the court, the chapel on the Kamehameha campus had become a church owned by Bishop Estate, "a large and overwhelmingly secular business."

More than just the business side of the trust had become secular. Although school materials from the early 1900s stressed the importance of religion, reverence, worship, and Protestantism, by the latter part of

"NOW EVERYBODY HAS A SAY ON THE SELECTION PROCESS BUT ME..."

the century the school catalog said only that students were expected to develop to the best of their ability "a system of values which reflects positive feelings about self and others and awareness of the rights and responsibilities of the individual within society." Today Kamehameha Schools is widely viewed as a secular institution, where both teachers and trustees can be non-Protestants, despite clear wording in Pauahi's will to the contrary.

The criteria for trustee and teacher selection have changed completely over the years, but these issues have not been nearly as public and contentious as the criteria for student admission. From the very beginnings of the trust, there have been questions about the kind of children Kamehameha Schools should be serving. The answer has always involved that longest-running of American social issues: race.

It only makes sense that Princess Pauahi had Hawaiian children primarily in mind when she wrote her will, particularly the many children who had lost one or both parents and who were indigent. Even before the boys' school opened in 1887, however, the trustees approved a "prospectus" that said the boys' and girls' schools "will not be exclusively Hawaiian." According to the trustees at that time, "The noble minded Hawaiian chiefess who endowed the Kamehameha Schools put no limitations of race or condition upon her general bequest." A few years later Charles Bishop explained that "the schools were intended to be perpetual," and that given the rapid decline in the number of Hawaiians, "it was impossible to tell how many boys and girls of aboriginal blood would in the beginning and thereafter qualify and apply for admission." Bishop later noted that while "there is nothing in the will of Mrs. Bishop excluding white boys or girls from the schools, . . . only those having native blood are to be admitted, at present."

In 1924 the Bishop Estate master, Charles S. Davis, wrote that Kamehameha Schools "must be maintained not as Hawaiian schools, but as schools to which all children of all races in the territory may be admitted." But the attorney general and probate judge at that time saw things differently. They concluded that Davis had "underestimated the provision of the will which [authorized the trustees] . . . to regulate the admission of pupils."

The master in 1957, Louis LeBaron, had been a territorial Supreme Court justice. He perceived a legal problem with Kamehameha's admissions policy because of *Brown v. Board of Education,* the 1954 U.S. Supreme Court case that had ordered an end to racial segregation in public schools nationally. LeBaron concluded that Kamehameha was engaging in racial discrimination that amounted to unlawful segregation. The trustees responded with a statement that focused on Pauahi's will and applicable trust law:

> Mrs. Bishop's will does not require that only students of Hawaiian blood may attend Kamehameha Schools but neither does it forbid such a policy. The will gives the trustees "full power to make all such rules and regulations as they may deem necessary for the government of said schools and to regulate the admission of pupils." Others—such as Mr. LeBaron—might differ from the trustees in the wisdom of restricting admissions but this is not a judicial question. So long as the trustees do not act beyond the bounds of reason, neither the master, the attorney general nor any court may substitute their judgment and discretion for the judgment and discretion of the trustees.

The attorney general who had appointed LeBaron, Herbert Y. C. Choy, and the presiding probate judge, William Z. Fairbanks, agreed that the question should be put to the territorial Supreme Court. That court ruled that the holding in *Brown v. Board of Education* only applied when there was state action: as a private school, Kamehameha was free to admit or exclude students on the basis of race.

In a 1972 concurring opinion, Hawai'i Supreme Court Justice Kazuhisa Abe addressed the admissions question from a purely legal point of view:

> As a matter of the interpretation of the will, it seems unquestionably clear that Mrs. Bishop did not intend to establish a school which would completely exclude all persons who lack Hawaiian ancestry. Indeed, the language seems so clear in its intention that it is rather startling that it was ever interpreted otherwise.

In fact, there have been non-Hawaiian students at Kamehameha, but not many. A Samoan or two. A Micronesian. A Portuguese. *Hānai* children who had no Hawaiian blood themselves. A handful of exchange students from the Mainland. And, by special dispensation, *haole* children of faculty. How many non-Hawaiians attended Kamehameha over the years, the largest number at any one time, the quality of their experience, the reaction of Hawaiian children to their presence—and the benefit, if there was any—no one knows. A historical record of non-Hawaiians at Kamehameha was not maintained.

At no time did the legal debates or the presence of a few non-Hawaiians affect the general understanding in the community that Kamehameha was for Hawaiians. Each time the possibility was raised that non-Hawaiians might be admitted—meaning in significant numbers and as a policy—Hawaiians in significant numbers said no, and loudly so.

Pauahi's will did not make Kamehameha sacrosanct to Hawaiians. In truth, neither did Bishop Estate trustees, Supreme Court justices, state attorneys general, or court-appointed masters. It was Hawaiians who preserved Kamehameha Schools for Hawaiians.

As it became increasingly clear that Kamehameha was to be only for Hawaiians, another question grew increasingly difficult to answer: "Who is Hawaiian?"

From the earliest contacts between Hawaiians and *haole*, Hawaiian women *ali'i* married *haole* ship captains, businessmen, and entrepreneurs. The descendants of these marriages formed a *hapa* (part) *haole* class, with its own place among Hawai'i's elite. Hawaiian women also married immigrant men who came to work on the plantations. There were Hawaiian Chinese (Hakka and Punti), Hawaiian Japanese (including Okinawans), Hawaiian Portuguese (from Madeira and the Azores), Hawaiian Puerto Ricans, Hawaiian Koreans, and Hawaiian Filipinos (Tagalog, Ilocano, Visayan, and Pangasinan).

Prior to the Hawaiian Renaissance, many Hawaiian parents encouraged their children to marry non-Hawaiians, and many of the children did so. Generation by generation, there were ever more combinations, bloodlines with four, six, eight ethnic strains. Hawaiian blood was more and more widespread, and the wider it was spread, the smaller the actual quantum of Hawaiian blood in any one child was likely to be. According to government censuses, there were about 50,000 "pure-blooded" Hawaiians and 2,500 part-Hawaiians in 1870—a twenty-to-one ratio. Within two generations, the ratio was approximately one to one. In slightly more than another generation, the ratio was one to ten. Today, it is believed to be about one to one thousand.

The trustees never set a minimum quantum of Hawaiian blood for admission to Kamehameha, nor did they give preference to applicants with a relatively high blood quantum. At the start of the 1950s only one in thirty Kamehameha students was full-blooded Hawaiian. In 1975 the ratio was one in three hundred. In 1985 there was a small but growing number of students who were no more than 1/64th Hawaiian. The number of pure-blooded Hawaiian students at Kamehameha that year was zero.

In 1998 the IRS' district office concluded that the trustees had to start admitting non-Hawaiians to Kamehameha Schools if they wanted to maintain tax-exempt status. That position was eventually reversed by the IRS' national office, based in part on a Ninth Circuit case then being reviewed by the U.S. Supreme Court.

Then in 2000 the U.S. Supreme Court reversed the Ninth Circuit, declaring unconstitutional a law that permitted only Hawaiians to vote in elections of the state Office of Hawaiian Affairs. A narrow reading of this, the *Rice v. Cayetano* decision, suggested that it affected only discrimination in state elections. A more expansive reading, however, suggested that it could pose a risk to either Kamehameha's Hawaiians-only admissions policy or its tax-exempt status.

Lawyers for the trust explained to the trustees that the risk of losing tax-exempt status could be lessened by severing Kamehameha's ties to all government programs, such as ROTC, anti-drug initiatives, and subsidized lunches for low-income students, and also by forgoing plans to get actively involved in running public charter schools in Hawaiian neighborhoods. After much internal debate, the trustees decided to make all of these adjustments. Meanwhile they considered other ways to assemble a Hawaiian student body. According to the trustees' lawyers, an admissions committee could safely take into account an applicant's "demonstrated interest in Hawaiian culture, language, music, dance, art and history . . . and family history of involvement in Hawaiian cultural and community affairs." That approach might work just as well as did the requirement that every student have some quantum of Hawaiian blood, according to the lawyers.

Not many Hawaiians realized that the trustees were reconsidering the Hawaiians-only policy, or their reasons for doing so. That changed abruptly and dramatically in July 2002, when Kamehameha Schools let it be known that a non-Hawaiian applicant had been admitted to attend at the new Maui campus. Hawaiians on all islands reacted to the news immediately, and in the loudest and strongest of negative terms. Many demanded that the CEO and all five trustees resign, and they meant it.

On short notice, the trustees held an open meeting on the main campus to explain the situation. More than six hundred people packed the auditorium. Virtually everyone there was Hawaiian, except for reporters and camera crews from all the TV stations and the daily newspapers. A University of Hawaiʻi professor, Haunani-Kay Trask, who had graduated from Kamehameha in 1967, said, "You could almost smell people's anger."

The meeting began with the blowing of a conch shell, a *pule,* and a chant. Then the first of the trustees to speak, Constance Lau, told the crowd that the admissions policy had not changed, that no board of trustees had ever provided more than just a preference for Hawaiians. The audience looked stunned. Then Lau added, "We had no idea this would cause such an uproar." At that, the crowd erupted with loud booing and hissing. Visibly shaken, Lau sat down.

Hamilton McCubbin, the trust's CEO at the time, followed with a slide presentation that included a detailed description of the admission process, complete with numbers and charts and technical jargon. His bottom-line message was that every qualified Hawaiian applicant had been accepted: "We exhausted the list." This was met with more jeering and angry shouts demanding McCubbin's resignation.

Then Nainoa Thompson approached the microphone slowly, with crossed arms and a pained look on his face. His speech, when it came, was filled with long pauses.

> I am here to respond to a community I am supposed to be serving. I come with no excuses or alibis, but to speak honestly and in truth. I just want to say how sorry I am for hurting so many Hawaiians. Our duty is to protect this trust. Our tax-exempt status is at great risk. It's not "if," but "when" people will attack this institution. If we lose our tax-exempt status, the cost is a billion dollars.

Thompson asked the crowd to understand that there were things he wanted to say but could not; there were boundaries beyond which he could not go. With that, he sat down.

Last, Douglas Ing talked to the audience about "a huge chess game being played across the country." He described players on the other side of the table as people "determined to eliminate and erode the rights of indigenous and native people." Presumably in reference to the single non-Hawaiian recently admitted to Kamehameha, Ing told the gathering, "It may be necessary for us to give up a pawn here and a pawn there."

In the days following the public explanation of how a non-Hawaiian had gotten into Kamehameha, Oz Stender expressed bitter disappointment in McCubbin and the new trustees, and especially in his former lawyer, Douglas Ing. Stender insisted that not every qualified Hawaiian had been admitted. His own grandnieces had recently been turned down for admission to Kamehameha on Maui. His point was bigger than individual admissions decisions. Stender wanted people to understand the destructiveness of this new policy: "What they're telling Hawaiian children is, they are not good enough. . . . If not enough Hawaiians qualify for admission, it's time to lower the standards." Stender added, "I've always disagreed with the policy of taking the brightest. What we should be doing is helping the kids who need it the most." Then Stender said something that everyone already knew but that needed to be said anyway: "There are thousands of Hawaiian families that would give their right arms to get their child into Kamehameha."

Two weeks after announcing the decision to admit a non-Hawaiian student to the Maui campus, the trustees issued a public statement:

> We have felt the overwhelming hurt and the anger from those who fear the trust will fall. The reaction has been resounding and powerful, and we are listening attentively. If we have learned nothing else from this, it is that Hawaiians want us to educate more of Ke Aliʻi Pauahi's children. We couldn't agree more. Ke Aliʻi Pauahi intended the Kamehameha Schools to serve a broad range of students. However, for the last decade the admissions process has been heavily weighted toward academic performance, which is only one measure of talent and potential. We have pledged to work with the Hawaiian community to carefully review our admissions process so we can align our campuses and programs with the needs of the specific communities they serve.

The debate over the admission of a single non-Hawaiian student to the Maui campus had evolved into a new question: which Hawaiian children should benefit from a preference?

This debate had nothing to do with blood quantum. Instead, it focused on Hawaiian "haves" versus Hawaiian "have-nots." Should Kamehameha Schools be available only to academically gifted children, the ones who might be expected to succeed at any school, or should it focus primarily on the Hawaiian children who are most at risk? It was a twenty-first-century version of the debate sparked by Senators Trask and Heen in 1943.

The trustees even considered reviving the controversial lottery admission system that had been terminated abruptly after Michael Chun was hired in 1989. They listened as McCubbin explained that while many people on the campus wanted to teach only the "best and the brightest," Kamehameha should be more than just that. Speaking of high-risk children from difficult circumstances, McCubbin said, "Give these kids the right opportunities, the right challenges, the right environment, and you can give them lives they never thought they'd have."

The trustees talked specifically about a group of elementary-school students who had not been accepted for admission at Kamehameha Schools. They were from Waimanalo, a predominantly Hawaiian area of the island of O'ahu, and were visiting Kawaiaha'o Plaza as part of an extension program outing. These children sang songs and completely charmed the interim trustees. As they were getting ready to head back to their bus, one little boy walked over and, for no apparent reason, hugged one of the trustees. That trustee commented later that these students "actually looked Hawaiian" and that they were the kind of children that Pauahi probably had foremost in mind when she wrote her will.

Lokelani Lindsey had advocated comprehensive schools with a vocational track, but the campus community strenuously opposed them, contending that such a track would inevitably lower the school's academic standards and reputation. That sentiment had been voiced at various times and at various volumes throughout the twentieth century.

Several years after Lindsey's departure, a majority of Kamehameha Schools trustees embraced the comprehensive-school concept for the outer islands, voting to make the new campuses "dual tracked," as the new trustees called it. The Kamehameha administration and teachers resisted again, including those on the outer islands, but it was the trustees' decision to make.

Meanwhile, the legal status of the race-based admissions policy remained unsettled. In August 2003 the *haole* mother of a seventh-grader from the island of Kaua'i sued Kamehameha Schools in federal court on behalf of her *haole* son, accusing Kamehameha of discriminating against the boy because of his race. He had already been accepted to Kamehameha as a boarding student and assigned a dorm room. He was just two days away from getting on an airplane for the island of O'ahu when school officials told him not to come.

Kamehameha officials contended that the admission decision had been based on misleading and inaccurate documentation regarding the student's Hawaiian ancestry. The boy's mother responded that she had not meant to mislead Kamehameha; she always thought of herself and her son as Hawaiians. Her stepfather—the only father she had known—had Hawaiian blood. She believed that as his *hānai* daughter, she, and therefore her son, should qualify as Hawaiian.

Kamehameha's lawyers defended the Hawaiians-only admissions policy as one designed to remedy past injustices, to produce racially diverse leadership, and to help preserve Hawaiian culture and identity: "What Kamehameha Schools tries to do is bring redress and hope." However, Federal Judge David Ezra suggested at a preliminary hearing that the plaintiff might prevail in this action: "There is a legitimate question as to whether or not the boy in this case, for the purposes of [Pauahi's] will, is Hawaiian." Nona Beamer, a mother to a *hānai* son and a *hānai* daughter, had similar thoughts: "If we are going to honor the *hānai* system, shouldn't we disregard the Hawaiian blood issue?"

Before Ezra issued a final decision, the parties agreed to a settlement. The boy was allowed to attend Kamehameha in exchange for dropping the lawsuit.

Another lawsuit was brought that same year, this one on behalf of an admittedly non-Hawaiian child who had been denied admission. His lawyers—the same lawyers who represented the plaintiffs in the earlier case and in *Rice v. Cayetano*—said their latest client's civil rights had been violated. The Kamehameha *'ohana*, led by Na Pua, gathered 83,950 signatures on petitions supporting the Hawaiians-only admissions policy. They also sought statements from community leaders. Linda Lingle, who was elected governor in 2002, said programs that favored Hawaiians were in response to historical injustices done to Hawaiians: "I believe, both as governor and in my own heart, that what is right and just for the native Hawaiian people is really what is right for the state, and if native Hawaiians gain, we all gain," said Lingle, a Republican. George Ariyoshi, a Democrat who served as governor from 1974 to 1986, echoed Lingle's comments, saying the high incidence of poverty and social and health problems among Hawaiians was "a black mark" on the local community: "With its fine educational programs, Kamehameha Schools must be allowed to continue to develop native Hawaiian leaders, role models that other Hawaiians can look up to and follow."

U.S. District Court Judge Alan Kay upheld the school's admissions policy in this case, stressing that the situation was "exceptionally unique." He noted that Bishop Estate was established before Hawai'i was a state, and that Kamehameha was intended to benefit the indigenous people of Hawai'i, even if the will did not state that explicitly. Kay

In 2005 Hawaiians staged large protest marches on all islands when the U.S. Ninth Circuit Court of Appeals ruled that Kamehameha Schools' Hawaiians-only admissions policy had violated the civil rights of a non-Hawaiian applicant.
© *Melvin Ah Ching Productions*

also considered it relevant that Kamehameha Schools had stopped taking government funds and that Congress had formally acknowledged "the United States' wrongful participation in the demise of the Hawaiian Monarchy."

In August 2005 the Ninth Circuit Court of Appeals reversed Judge Kay in a two-to-one split decision, ruling that the existing "preference" for Hawaiians was in reality an absolute bar to non-Hawaiians. Tens of thousands of Hawaiians marched in protest on all the major islands, and the trustees vowed to fight the ruling to the very end.

Walter Heen reviewed this decision from a Hawaiian point of view on behalf of Na 'A'ahuhiwa (the Black Robes), a group of retired Native Hawaiian judges. In an op-ed piece that appeared in the *Advertiser* on August 30, 2005, Heen noted "how ridiculous and alarming it is that a civil rights statute, enacted to help oppressed minorities and slaves, is being used to strike down Kamehameha Schools' admissions policy, which helps to strengthen the Native Hawaiian population." He noted what the dissenting judge had written and what the two-judge majority had misunderstood.

Kamehameha Schools argued in the district court, and the court agreed, that the policy "serves a legitimate remedial purpose by addressing the socioeconomic and educational disadvantages facing Native Hawaiians, producing Native Hawaiian leadership for community involvement, and revitalizing Native Hawaiian culture."

Heen took issue with the majority statement that the admissions policy was "exclusively racial." That was something Kamehameha Schools had never conceded.

To the contrary, the school has vigorously asserted throughout the litigation that Native Hawaiians have a special trust relationship with the United States akin (though not identical) to that of Native Americans and Alaska natives that must be taken into account in construing the application of the statute upon which the lawsuit is based. . . .

From the beginning, Kamehameha Schools' position has been that its admissions policy must be viewed in the unique context of remedying extreme educational and socioeconomic deficiencies faced by a population that (a) descended from people whose sovereignty and culture were upended and nearly destroyed, in part by the actions of the United States, and (b) consequently enjoys a special trust relationship with the United States government that parallels that between the federal government and Native Americans.

Who counted as Hawaiian and to what extent Hawaiians could legally be "preferred" were not the only questions for the new century. The trustees also debated at great length the trust's responsibility to preserve and promote Hawaiian culture. In the trust's early years, specific prohibitions having to do with Hawaiian language and dance had been enforced. There also were informal restrictions on the hiring of Hawaiian teachers and an overriding goal of turning Hawaiians into Americans. This eventually changed, but the trustees never articulated whether Kamehameha was to be a school for Hawaiians or a Hawaiian school. The two were not mutually exclusive, but to move forward together, Hawaiians needed to agree on what a "Hawaiian" school was. Hawaiian history, language, and culture were being taught at most schools in

Hawaiian groups complained for years about Bishop Estate efforts to divert stream water to Waiahole Ditch for development purposes. The new trustees' decision to discontinue these efforts was well received by most Hawaiians, even though it arguably reduced the value of the trust estate.

the state. Some people wanted to know how Kamehameha should be different, if at all.

In 2002 the trustees withdrew from a long legal battle involving their attempt to divert mountain stream water for land-development purposes. Although this decision may have reduced the value of Bishop Estate land, an *Advertiser* editorial praised the trustees:

> Trustees of Kamehameha Schools, now painfully aware of how sensitive their role can be, made a wise decision last week to drop efforts to use Waiahole water for a Leeward subdivision project. The withdrawal of the request for a 4.2 million-gallon diversion avoids a fight with Hawaiians and others who believe Waiahole water belongs in Windward streams.
>
> The move should help heal wounds left open when trustees

decided to admit a non-Hawaiian student to their Maui campus without fully consulting beneficiaries, including parents, faculty and Hawaiian organizations. In that sense, the withdrawal could be seen as a "strategic" or political move by trustees eager to re-establish their credibility with their beneficiaries.

The new trustees hired Yale law professor John Langbein to help them understand and adhere to their fiduciary duties. When the professor learned that the trustees were holding more than 350,000 acres of unde-veloped land, he reportedly called it "a disaster in the making."

Trust law generally requires trustees to make the entire trust estate productive by using each asset either to carry out the trust's charitable mission or to generate income to spend in pursuit of that mission. The 350,000 acres in question were not being used for either purpose. The trustees explained to Langbein that this was a sensitive issue. Many in the Hawaiian community viewed the land in question—Pauahi's *'āina*— as the last vestiges of the royal past. Hawaiians would rise up in anger if the trustees were to try to sell or develop significant amounts of this land.

Langbein reportedly responded that the trustees had a duty not only to make trust property productive, but also to diversify trust invest-ments. Even if the land in question were producing income, 350,000 acres of very valuable real estate might be considered "too many eggs" to keep in just "one basket." Unless the trustees had a plan for eventu-ally selling these huge tracts of land or making them productive, the legal risk would be great. The prudent course, according to Langbein, would be to sell this land and invest the proceeds in marketable securi-ties. That would diversify trust holdings and increase significantly the amount of money available to educate Hawaiian children—a move that Pauahi would arguably have approved of, since her will specifies that her trustees may sell land when it is in the best interests of the trust to do so.

The trustees listened intently and then made a change, but not the one Langbein recommended. They designated the 350,000 acres as "pro-gram assets," to be held in trust indefinitely "for educational purposes." They also decided not to include the market value of this land on the trust's financial statements.

Like the water decision, this one was both popular and not easy to justify under trust law. In both cases, the Hawaiian community appeared to approve of what the trustees did, and so the attorney general, master, and probate judge neither said nor did anything about it.

The events surrounding the *pilikia* (distress) at Princess Pauahi's trust lingered in the minds of the people who lived them. During the writing of this book, Margery Bronster expressed disappointment that fourteen senators prevented her from completing her investigation and that the probate court sealed so many records. Colbert Matsumoto hoped that a retelling of the story would stimulate a public discussion of what could be learned from the controversy. He said that the most important and inspiring lesson, for him, was the power and importance of grassroots democracy.

Gladys Brandt half-seriously proposed that a statue of Lokelani Lindsey be erected in a prominent place on the Kamehameha campus. In her words, "Had it not been for Lokelani Lindsey, nothing would have changed at Bishop Estate." Roy Benham had a similar thought: "You know, we Hawaiians are kind of funny. You can waste or even steal our money; that's one thing. But when you hurt our children, that's something altogether different."

Brandt, whose life was so intimately connected with Kamehameha Schools, died on January 15, 2003, at the age of ninety-six, having remained actively involved in ongoing reform efforts until the final few weeks of her life. She once explained why she had agreed to serve as principal at the Kamehameha School for Girls:

> I thought having a Hawaiian woman as principal could make a further statement to these young ladies. I wanted them to witness a Hawaiian in a leadership position, so that they would know that as a group we were not all born to be followers. I wanted them to see a Hawaiian take on weighty responsibilities, so that they might become more confident in assuming such challenges for themselves. I wanted them to share in another Hawaiian's success, so that they would realize that is our right and our potential.

I mua Kamehameha.

Afterword *Jan Hanohano Dill*

I find myself struggling with two powerful emotions. On one hand, the recounting of the long history of Hawaiians marginalized in their own land triggers a feeling of *kaumaha*, a sense of heaviness and grief.

Kaumaha is what happens when a people are stripped of the social, cultural, and ethical anchors that have given them worth and stability. King and Roth paint a vivid and compelling picture of how Hawaiians at the Kamehameha Schools were systematically disconnected from the rich culture of the Hawaiian people by a school and a society that held them in no esteem. The goal of being "good and industrious men and women" that Princess Pauahi set for her people was translated by the *haole* leadership of Kamehameha into the goal of producing compliant and submissive laborers for the powers then controlling the fate of these islands.

This account of the recent battle to bring *pono* to the legacy of Princess Bernice Pauahi Bishop also stirs within me powerful feelings of pride and hope. It is a story of great courage, vision, and perseverance in the face of overwhelming odds. Despite enormous political and economic power on the part of Bishop Estate trustees and their political supporters in 1997, Hawaiian men and women and others from our community made the decision to stand and proclaim, "Enough!" People without much money or power decided that the abuses of authority at the Bishop Estate and Kamehameha Schools were so egregious, so contrary to Hawaiian values, and so destructive to the ideals of Princess Bernice Pauahi Bishop and the children her legacy served that they chose to leave the comfort of their routines, put on their sneakers, and march and speak out for what is right. One of the early T-shirts of Na Pua a Ke Ali'i Pauahi had a simple message that said it all: "Do The Right Thing."

The conflicts of Bishop Estate and Kamehameha Schools chronicled here have led to a dawn of hope and a strengthening sense of self-worth in more and more Hawaiians. There is a growing recognition that Hawaiians as a people must set goals for our community that transcend individual and small-group interests; and there is a growing belief that one day the *kaumaha* of over a century will lift.

In traditional Hawaiian culture, the relationship of the *ali'i* with the commoners was that of an unstated compact of common benefit. The chiefs enjoyed power because they committed themselves to caring for the larger community in a form of servant leadership. Part of the outrage in the Hawaiian community in the Bishop Estate battle was the violation of this relationship by Bishop Estate trustees, the *ali'i* of contemporary Hawai'i. All of Hawai'i has learned from this remarkable series of events that the Hawaiian people, like their forefathers, are prepared to hold their leaders to this traditional standard. It is a wonderful source of encouragement, hope, and pride for all Hawaiians, and it is a responsibility we need to keep before us as a community.

Pauahi deeply loved her people and desired to nurture, educate, and enable them through her legacy. Hawaiians are beginning to understand how great a privilege, and how awesome a responsibility, this represents to each of us.

This is not merely a story for Hawaiians or for people living in Hawai'i; it is a human story. It demands from all of us a commitment to engage in the issues of our community, to be vigilant against the abuse of power, and to be willing to stand for what is *pono*, what is right, despite intimidation and threats. And to act wisely, we must stay informed. We may not always agree, but we need to keep talking—to discuss and debate the issues and insights this story provides for our lives.

E ola mau ka makana a Pauahi! Long live Pauahi's legacy!

 Appendix *The Charitable Trust Provisions of*
Princess Pauahi's Will and Two Codicils

I give, devise and bequeath all of the rest, residue and remainder of my estate real and personal, wherever situated unto the trustees below named, their heirs and assigns forever, to hold upon the following trusts, namely: to erect and maintain in the Hawaiian Islands two schools, each for boarding and day scholars, one for boys and one for girls, to be known as, and called the Kamehameha Schools.

I direct my trustees to expend such amount as they may deem best, not to exceed however one-half of the fund which may come into their hands, in the purchase of suitable premises, the erection of school buildings, and in furnishing the same with the necessary and appropriate fixtures furniture and apparatus.

I direct my trustees to invest the remainder of my estate in such manner as they may think best, and to expend the annual income in the maintenance of said schools; meaning thereby the salaries of teachers, the repairing buildings and other incidental expenses; and to devote a portion of each year's income to the support and education of orphans, and others in indigent circumstances, giving the preference to Hawaiians of pure or part aboriginal blood; the proportion in which said annual income is to be divided among the various objects above mentioned to be determined solely by my said trustees they to have full discretion.

I desire my trustees to provide first and chiefly a good education in the common English branches, and also instruction in morals and in such useful knowledge as may tend to make good and industrious men and women; and I desire instruction in the higher branches to be subsidiary to the foregoing objects.

I give unto the trustees . . . the most ample power to sell and dispose of any lands or other portion of my estate, and to exchange lands and otherwise dispose of the same; and to purchase land, and to take leases of land whenever they think it expedient, and generally to make such investments as they consider best; but I direct that my said trustees shall not purchase land for said schools if any lands come into their possession under my will which in their opinion may be suitable for such purpose; and I further direct that my said trustees shall not sell any real estate, cattle ranches, or other property, but to continue and manage the same, unless in their opinion a sale may be necessary for the establishment or maintenance of said schools, or for the best interest of my estate.

I also give unto my said trustees full power to make all such rules and regulations as they may deem necessary for the government of said schools and to regulate the admission of pupils, and the same to alter, amend and publish upon a vote of a majority of said trustees.

I also direct that my said trustees shall annually make a full and complete report of all receipts and expenditures, and of the condition of said schools to the Chief Justice of the Supreme Court, or other highest judicial officer in this country; and shall also file before him annually an inventory of the property in their hands and how invested, and to publish the same in some Newspaper published in said Honolulu; I also direct my said trustees to keep said school buildings insured in good Companies, and in case of loss to expend the amounts recovered in replacing or repairing said buildings.

I also direct that the teachers of said schools shall forever be persons of the Protestant religion, but I do not intend that the choice should be restricted to persons of any particular sect of Protestants.

I direct the school for boys shall be well established and in efficient operation before any money is expended or anything is undertaken on account of the new school for girls.

It is my desire that my trustees should do thorough work in regard to said schools as far as they go; and I authorize them to defer action in regard to the establishment of said school for girls, if in their opinion from the condition of my estate it may be expedient, until the life estates created by my said will have expired, and the lands so given shall have fallen into the general fund.

I also direct that my said trustees shall have power to determine to what extent said school shall be industrial, mechanical, or agricultural; and also to determine if tuition shall be charged in any case.

I appoint my husband Charles R. Bishop, Samuel M. Damon, Charles M. Hyde, Charles M. Cooke, and William O. Smith, all of Honolulu, to be my trustees to carry into effect the trusts above specified.

I direct that a majority of my said trustees may act in all cases and may convey real estate and perform all of the duties and powers hereby conferred; but three of them at least must join in all acts.

I further direct that the number of my said trustees shall be kept at five; and that vacancies shall be filled by the choice of a majority of the Justices of the Supreme Court, the selection to be made from persons of the Protestant religion.

Credits for Photographs and Editorial Cartoons

PHOTOGRAPHS

Bernice Pauahi Bishop Museum: 20, 85

Melvin Ah Ching Productions: 294

Bobby Harmon: 205

Hawai'i State Archives: 10, 27, 33a, 33b, 34, 36, 39, 49, 66, 120b

Gary Hofheimer Photography: 161

Honolulu Star-Bulletin: 44, 56, 57, 59, 61, 63a, 63b, 68, 70, 72, 74, 86, 87, 90, 92, 94, 98, 103, 106, 108, 112, 120a, 122, 126, 129, 130, 138, 140, 142, 145, 157, 159a, 159b, 168, 172a, 172b, 189, 202, 216, 220, 226, 236, 239, 240, 249, 251, 253, 258, 262, 284, 296

Hugh Jones: 269

KHON TV-2 News: 214, 231

Kevin Wakayama: 233

EDITORIAL CARTOONS

Dick Adair, *The Honolulu Advertiser:* 82, 136, 144, 152, 180, 182, 201, 221, 223

Daryl Cagle, *Midweek:* 165, 260, 272, 280

Clay Jones, *Honolulu Star-Bulletin:* 99, 101, 117, 154, 162, 163, 178, 215, 281

Corky Trinidad, *Honolulu Star-Bulletin:* 191, 235, 285

Index

dictment, 217–218, 279–280; interim-removal trial, 247, 252–253, 259–260; on investment losses, 199; IRS demand for removal of trustees, 255; lead trustee for asset management, 85–86, 97, 180, 198, 204–205; Lindsey's removal trial, 250; Lindsey's report, 177; on lobbying activities, 206–208, 221; management of Milton Holt, 220–221; May 1997 protest march, 141–142; memorandum from Namlyn Snow, 94–96; political aspirations, 263; public opinion, 261; resignation, 262–263; response to "Broken Trust" essay, 164; response to community activism of 1997, 138–139; response to Matsumoto's report, 232; response to Yim's report, 179–180; Robert Trent Jones Golf Club, 84–85; slur against Bronster, 241; Van Dyke collection, 114

Peterson Consulting Group, 187–188
Pfeiffer, Robert, 91, 96
Plotts, Diane, 283, *284*
politics, 7, 104; activist and establishment Hawaiians, 67; campaign contributions, 203, 208; Case's reform initiatives, 222–227; failed re-appointment of Bronster, 256–258; fund-raising tickets, 208; gubernatorial election of 1998, 229–230; Hawaiian cultural renewal, 77–79; investigation of Holt, 221–222, 236–237; lobbying activities, 94–95, 152, 206–208, 210, 221–222; overthrow of Hawaiian monarchy, 77–79; party domination, 65; retainers for allies, 201–202, 225–226, 257; trustee appointments, 65–79, *86–87*, 89–92,

94–96, 151–152, 183. *See also* community activism
Pope, Ida May, 37–40
Porteus, Stephen, 50
The Price of Paradise radio show, 155
probate court, 6–7; Ad Hoc Committee for a Hawaiian Trustee lawsuit and appeal, 67–68; appointment of interim trustees, 260, 267–268; appointment of special-purpose trustees, 255–256; appointment of trustees, 183–184; appointment of Yim as fact-finder, 137–139, 147; approval of annual accounts, 46–47; approval of IRS settlement, 278; CEO-based management, 6, 86, 259–260, 275–277; Ching's suit against Takabuki, 69; compensation-committee recommendations, 7, 272–273; court-appointed receivership, 234; extension programs, 117; global settlement, 279; interim trustees' legal team, 270–271; IRS revocation of tax-exempt status, 253–256, 259; master-review system, 101–103; Matsumoto's report, 168–169, 170, 174–175, 178–180, 229, 230–233; oversight responsibilities, 1, 84–85, 101–102, 167, 170, 183–184; payment of Stender's legal fees, 263–264; removal of trustees, 233–237, 241–244, 247, 259–260; Richards' report, 273–275; rules on investigations of charitable trusts, 169, 170; sealing of records, 275, 279, 282, 298; September 1998 courthouse rally, 238–240, 247; Stender's lawsuit against Lindsey, 235–236, 242–244, 247–251, 259; trustee-appointment role, 7, 46–47, 283–284

programs at Kamehameha Schools:
center-based preschool, 116; college scholarships, 127; distance
learning, 115–116; extension division, 7, 54, 116–117, 123–124, 201,
292; military training and ROTC,
36–37, 48, 54–55, 107; satellite
schools, 116–118; Song Contest,
119–122, 134; student activities,
107; trade-school origins, 33, 36,
38–42. *See also* curriculum
Punahou School, 32, 47, 49, 100,
146, 175, 177, 190, 192, 200

Queen Liliʻuokalani Trust, 2, 91,
153

racial issues: Bishop Estate trustees' defense, 225, 239–241; discrimination lawsuits, 292–295;
Hawaiians-only admissions
policy, 45, 49–50, 286–296; Ing's
courtroom argument, 270–271;
Ninth Circuit Court of Appeals
ruling, 294–295; Peters' confrontation with Midkiff, 164, *Rice v.
Cayetano*, 289, 293
Ramil, Mario, 161, 183. *See also*
Supreme Court of Hawaiʻi
Ramos, Tony, 71, 113, 121; administrative staff problems, 189–190;
interrogation of Kamani Kualāʻau, 128–129, 147; WASC accreditation report, 192–193
real estate. *See* land management
reasonable-compensation bill,
224–227
Reed, Rick, 72
religion requirements: of teachers,
35, 285–286, 302; of trustees, 35,
108–109, 284, 303
resignations of trustees, 261–262,
269
Rice v. Cayetano, 289, 293

Richards, Atherton, *56, 57, 68*
Richards, Robert, 273–275
Richardson, William S., 65–67, 68,
69, 91–92, 96
Robert Trent Jones Golf Club,
84–85
Rodrigues, Gary, 8, 91–92, 151
Rose, Crystal, 237, 248, 250, 259–
260, 264
ROTC programs, 54–55, 107
Roth, Randall, *157*; "Broken Trust"
essay, 1–3, 153–164
Royal School, 15–16, 19, 21, 34
Rubin, Robert, 198–199
Rubin, Winona K. D., 175
Ruth Keʻelikōlani, princess of
Hawaiʻi, 21, 22–23, 26–28, *27,*
29
Ryan's Graphics, 203

Sakamaki, Steven, 168, 175, 179–180,
195, 230
Santos, George, 62, 64
satellite schools, 116–118
Say, Calvin, 221–222, 227
Sellers, Dorothy, 234, 252–253, 259,
268–270, *269,* 275
Senior Home Management Cottage,
38–40, 55
September 1998 courthouse rally,
238–240, 247
Shapiro, David, 1, 104, 158–160
Shim, Alvin, 91, 96, 102–103, 151
Smith, William O., 31, 34–35
Snow, Namlyn, 94–96, 206–208,
225–226, 237
SoCal Holding, 196
Song Contest, 119–122, 134
Souki, Joseph, 221, 223, 226–227
special-purpose trustees, 254–255
staff of Bishop Estate: CEO position,
6, 259–260, 275–277; employee
handbook, 99, 135; Harmon's
whistle-blowing attempts,

Supreme Court of Hawai'i *(continued):* dismissal of criminal indictments, 279–280; *ex parte* communications, 212–213; failed appointment of Mehau, 70–73; fiduciary duties, 96, 211–213; Hawaiians-only admissions policy, 287–289; IRS critique of, 256; judicial appointments, 89, 139; Judicial Selection Commission, 4, 5, 88–95, 154, 279; letter from student leaders, 127–128; May 1998 protest march, 227; oversight responsibilities, 84–85, 101–102; petitions to remove trustees, 234; politicization of trustee appointments, 65, 67–68, 96, 101, 211; response to community activism, 135; "rigged" selection process, 75; "smoking gun" memorandum, 94–96; trustee-appointment role, 1, 4–6, 46–47, 65–68, 96, 101, 153–154, 182–184, 211, 224, 256, 283. *See also* conflicts of interest; fiduciary duties of Supreme Court

Sutherland Asbil and Brennan, 273

Takabuki, Matsuo, 65–70, *68*; on admissions policies, 106–107; Ching's lawsuit against, 69; Goldman Sachs, 197–198; lead-trustee role, 69, 83–85, 97; response to Stender's memo on fiduciary duties, 75; trustee-selection panel, 91, 96; *An Unlikely Revolutionary*, 106–107

Takemoto, Yukio, 97, *98*, 152, 203, 237

talk story, 5, 107, 132

Tam, Gilbert, 111, 115, 259–260

Tanaka, Joe, 221–222, 257

tax-exempt status, 6, 200–201, 204, 209–210; effort to spare Stender, 269; Hawaiians-only admissions policy, 289; instructions to "clean house," 267–271, 276–277; lobbying activities, 222; reform requirements, 277–278; revocation, 253–256, 259

teachers. *See* faculty; Na Kumu o Kamehameha (the Teachers of Kamehameha)

Thompson, Myron "Pinky," 5, 69, 89–90, 283

Thompson, Nainoa, 283, *284*, 290

Thompson, Uldrick, 35–36

Toguchi, Charles, 109

Tokuhara, Rochelle "Rocky," 131–132

Tom, Terrance, 221–222, 225–226

Town, Michael, 216–218

Trask, David, 49–51, 54, 291

Trask, Haunani-Kay, 79, 290

Trask, James, 69–70

Trask, Mililani, 79

Travis, Joe, 138, 145

trustee concerns, 2–8, 45; access to information, 97; accountability, 4–7, 100–104, 267; attorney-client privilege, 84, 98–99, 177, 209, 217, 270–271; decision-making process, 69, 74–75; independent assessment of schools, 187–188; IRS reform requirements, 277–278; liability insurance, 279; Matsumoto's recommendations, 179–180; minutes and record-keeping, 96–98; organizational structure, 85–88, 180; outside consultants, 201–202; personal liability, 256; plan to move trust situs, 228, 274; private business deals, 82–88; rethinking the mission, 53–54; secrecy, 174–175, 177, 205; "smoking gun" memorandum, 94–96; strategic planning, 75, 278; union organizing,

190; Yim's report, 179–181. *See also* breaches of trust; conflicts of interest; fiduciary duties of trustees; interim trustees; land management

United States, 24–25, 78–79
United States Supreme Court: *Brown v. Board of Education*, 288; Hawai'i's leasehold conversion law *(Hawai'i Housing Authority v. Midkiff)*, 81, 100; *Rice v. Cayetano*, 289, 293
An Unlikely Revolutionary (Takabuki), 106–107

Valley Isle article, 71–72
Van Dyke, Robert, 113–115, 173, 202
Verner Liipfert Bernard McPherson and Hand, 274

Waihe'e, John, 70–71, 88–89, 90, 110; "Broken Trust" essay, 151, 163; failed appointment to Bishop Estate board, 89, 92–93; judicial appointments, 89; plan to move trust situs, 228, 274; Washington lobbying activities, 94–95, 152, 228, 274
Wakayama, Kevin, 146–147, 170–171, 232–237, *233*, 258
Walker, Henry, Jr., 91, 92
Wall Street Journal article, 1, 83, 169
Watanabe, Ing and Kawashima, 268–271
Weil, Bambi, 205–206, 247–251, 259, 264
Western Association of Schools and Colleges (WASC), 190–193
Wilcox, Johanna, 42
Wise, John, 35
Wong, Colleen, 208, 268, 270, 276

Wong, Mari Stone, 217, 261–262
Wong, Richard "Dickie," 5, 86–88, 202; "Broken Trust" essay, 151, 160–161, 164; Bronster's failed reappointment, 256; cancellation of talk story, 132; Cayetano reelection, 229–230; criminal investigation and indictment, 217–218, 279–280; Goldman Sachs, 198; hiring of Yukio Takemoto, 97–98, 152; interim-removal trial, 247, 252–253, 259–260; IRS demand for removal of trustees, 255; KDP Technologies, 196; on lead-trustee system, 100; lead trustee for government relations, 97; Lindsey's removal trial, 249–250; Lindsey's report, 177; May 1997 protest march, 141–142; May 1998 protest march, 228; meeting with Na Pua, 145–146; on photographs of protest marchers, 164; plan to move trust situs, 228, 274; public opinion, 261; resignation, 261–262; response to community activism, 137–139; response to Matsumoto's report, 232; response to Yim's investigation, 175; response to Yim's report, 179–180; Song Contest of 1997, 121–122; strategic planning, 118; threats to fire Chun, 148–149, 249–250

Yadao, Elisa, 146, 147, 160, 164, 206, 248
Yim, Patrick, *138*; investigation of problems at Kamehameha Schools, 137–139, 147, 167–168, 174–179, 242; Stender's lawsuit against Lindsey, 242–243

About the Authors

Samuel P. King received his undergraduate and law degrees from Yale University. After serving in the U.S. Navy as an intelligence officer during World War II, he returned to Hawai'i to practice law. In 1972, after having served as president of the Hawai'i State Bar Association and as a Hawai'i Circuit Court judge and co-founder of the state's family court system, King was appointed a U.S. District Court judge. His father, Samuel W. King, was a Bishop Estate trustee from 1957 until his death in 1959.

Randall W. Roth has taught at the University of Hawai'i William S. Richardson School of Law since 1982. In 1997 he was a visiting professor at the University of Chicago Law School, and in 2003 he served as Hawai'i Governor Linda Lingle's senior policy adviser during her first year in office. He also has served as president of the Hawai'i State Bar Association, Hawai'i Justice Foundation, Hawai'i Institute for Continuing Legal Education, and Hawai'i Estate Planning Council.